APOSTOLIC AND PROPHETIC

Apostolic & Prophetic
Ecclesiological Perspectives

GESA ELSBETH THIESSEN

CASCADE Books • Eugene, Oregon

APOSTOLIC AND PROPHETIC
Ecclesiological Perspectives

Copyright © 2011 Gesa Elsbeth Thiessen. All rights reserved. Except for brief quotations in critical publications or reviews, no part of this book may be reproduced in any manner without prior written permission from the publisher. Write: Permissions, Wipf and Stock Publishers, 199 W. 8th Ave., Suite 3, Eugene, OR 97401.

Permission has been granted to republish the following material, partly in revised form:

Parts of Chapter 3 appeared as "Seeking Unity: Reflecting on Methods in Contemporary Ecumenical Dialogue" in Ecumenical Ecclesiology: Unity, Diversity and Otherness in a Fragmented World. Edited by Gesa E. Thiessen. New York: Continuum, 2009. An earlier version of Chapter 4 is published in Denomination: Assessing an Ecclesial Category. Edited by Barry Ensign-George and Paul Collins. New York: Continuum, 2011. An earlier version of Chapter 5 was published as "The Week of Prayer for Christian Unity." Irish Theological Quarterly 72:1 (2007). An earlier version of Chapter 6 appeared as "Dorothee Sölle: A Radical Theologian." Milltown Studies 46 (2000).

New Revised Standard Version Bible, copyright 1989, Division of Christian Education of the National Council of the Churches of Christ in the United States of America. Used by permission. All rights reserved.

Cascade Books
An Imprint of Wipf and Stock Publishers
199 W. 8th Ave., Suite 3
Eugene, OR 97401

www.wipfandstock.com

ISBN 13: 978-1-60899-813-5

Cataloging-in-Publication data:

Thiessen, Gesa Elsbeth.

Apostolic and prophetic : ecclesiological perspectives / Gesa Elsbeth Thiessen.

xiv + 192 p. ; 23 cm. —Includes bibliographical references and index.

ISBN 13: 978-1-60899-813-5

1. Church. 2. Sölle, Dorothee. 3. Eagleton, Terry, 1943– I. Title.

BV600.2 .T44 2011

Manufactured in the U.S.A.

Eva Maria Thiessen und Gerold Donker,
Jonah und Mila,
Hans Holger Thiessen und Nicola Hüesker,
Nele und Lina
gewidmet

The kingdom of God is not coming with things that can be observed; nor will they say, "Look, here it is!" or "There it is!" For, in fact, the kingdom of God is among you.

Luke 17:20–21

In the last days it will be, God declares,
that I will pour out my Spirit upon all flesh,
   and your sons and your daughters shall prophesy,
and your young men shall see visions,
   and your old men shall dream dreams.

Awe came upon everyone, because many wonders and signs were being done by the apostles. All who believed were together and had all things in common; they would sell their possessions and goods and distribute the proceeds to all, as any had need. Day by day, as they spent much time together in the temple, they broke bread at home and ate their food with glad and generous hearts, praising God and having the goodwill of all the people.

Acts 2:17, 43–47

Contents

Acknowledgments ix

Introduction xi

PART I *Apostolicity: Past, Present, Future*
1. *Ad fontes*: Apostolicity in the Early Church 3
2. Apostolicity in Select Ecumenical Documents of the Anglican, Lutheran, and Roman Catholic Churches 19
3. Looking Ahead: Possibilities and Challenges in Ecclesiology and Ecumenical Dialogue 40

PART II *Unity, Diversity, and Ecumenical Praxis*
4. Denominations: Churches in (Post)modernity— The Lutheran Church (A Case Study) 67
5. Ecumenism in Praxis: Critical Observations on the Week of Prayer for Christian Unity 89

PART III *Towards a Radical Church*
6. A Theology of Liberation: Dorothee Sölle 109
7. A New Left Church? Terry Eagleton 127

Conclusion: Towards an Apostolic, Ecumenical, Radical and Prophetic Church 166

Bibliography 177

Index 185

Acknowledgments

MY SINCERE THANKS TO friend and colleague Professor Peter de Mey, Department of Theology, Katholieke Universiteit, Leuven, for the invitation to contribute to an ecumenical research project and who kindly afforded me five months accommodation in the Begijnhof in Leuven in 2006. I also thank the KU Department of Theology and its library for the opportunity to conduct part of my research there and for their kind hospitality.

I would like to thank Peter de Mey for reading chapters 1–3 and 5, and Dr. Geraldine Smyth and Martin Sauter for reading an earlier version of chapter 5.

Further thanks to my colleagues and friends at Milltown Institute of Theology and Philosophy and to the Institute's library staff. I am indebted to Professor Gerard Mannion and members of the steering group of the Ecclesiological Investigations Research Network for their friendship and encouragement, including Dr. Paul Collins and Dr. Barry Ensign-George for inviting me to write an article on "denomination" from a Lutheran perspective.

Herzlichen Dank to my parents and family for their always loyal support and encouragement.

Mein herzlicher Dank also to Dr. Declan Marmion who read all chapters, providing encouragement, support, humour and advice. *Go raibh maith agat.*

Introduction

How do we perceive the church today? Must it always be the case that churches as institutions are prone to sin and failure? What can churches offer in an age that has seen so many abuses of power in the church? This book does not claim to provide comprehensive answers to these complicated and age-old problems. Rather I intend to do something more modest, namely to reflect on some diverse, yet topical, themes in contemporary ecclesiology and ecumenical dialogue.

Glancing through the table of contents, the reader may be struck by the somewhat diverse range of topics. This points to the genesis of this book. The seven chapters contained here were not originally planned to make up a book. Rather, in the last few years I had the opportunity to write separate articles, partly invited, partly chosen by myself, which I have included here. The idea of a book emerged in 2009 when it became clear that the ecclesiological and ecumenical themes I had worked on largely embraced three marks, or attributes, of envisioning the church: the church as apostolic, ecumenical, and radical. Thinking about it further, I then decided to assemble, revise, and add new material in order to present a coherent volume. Considering the intrinsic connections between these three marks, i.e., the fact that they are linked and how they are linked, I thus want to formulate my central thesis: The church, if it is truly apostolic, is radical, and the church, if it is truly radical, is apostolic; both marks shape the vision of an ecumenical and prophetic church. This is the book's basic thesis which underlies its critical engagement with several distinct, yet related, themes pertinent to my argument.

Perceiving the church as apostolic, ecumenical, radical, and prophetic essentially means a church that is aware and proud of its origin

Introduction

and roots. It is a church that appreciates its tradition but always also critically questions it and is ready to learn, and willing to change. Further, it is aware of its political and social dimension. It means that Christians who embrace such a vision will not content themselves with personal piety, as important as this may be, but are strongly committed to the church as community. Such is the church that Jesus intended for the people of God. We read in Acts that the earliest community had all things in common. This is a far cry from what separates Christians today—not only their different denominational affiliations and a wide variety of theological convictions, but also scandalous discrepancies between rich and poor, north and south, "first" and "third" world. The vision of a radical church, a church that respects its roots and the otherness of the kingdom of God, as Jesus taught it, thus includes a political, at times countercultural and subversive dimension. The body of Christ, if it is true to its roots and its faith in the kingdom of God, can therefore never content itself with socio-political establishments and economic systems which display little or no interest in seriously promoting social responsibility and tackling the ever-increasing divide between rich and poor.

The first part of the book, then, examines apostolicity from different angles. Apostolicity, including ministerial offices in the church, remains at the heart of ecumenical concerns. Over the last forty years remarkable progress has been made in a common understanding of apostolicity, in particular, in issues of church ministry. Yet despite such advances, the slow progress in the reception of bi- and multilateral ecumenical statements in the churches is felt amongst those who have dedicated themselves to ecumenical dialogue.

In the first chapter we will consider the role of the apostle, apostolicity, and ministry in the early church. Changes in perceptions of apostolate/apostolicity occurred in the first few centuries, which have had lasting consequences to this day. Naturally within the scope of this book, we can only briefly focus on some of the most important aspects. Yet this is essential as the biblical witnesses and the beginnings of the church are still relevant to any contemporary ecumenical agreement on what remains the most difficult obstacle in church unity, namely ministry.

Chapter 2 will give an account of and analyze how the notion of apostolicity has been developed in some recent ecumenical statements

Introduction

of the Roman Catholic, Lutheran, and Anglican churches. As a member of the Lutheran Church residing in Ireland, and as one who has worked for many years in an institute of Catholic theology, my ecumenical interest has centred especially on Roman Catholic–Lutheran relations. Further, given the close theological and ecclesiological connections between Anglicans and Lutherans that have been affirmed and expanded through the Meissen and Porvoo agreements, these dialogues are also taken into the discussion. We will see how the Porvoo agreement is especially groundbreaking and encouraging in enabling Lutheran and Anglican Churches in setting out on genuinely new steps towards visible unity.

Over the last three decades, ecumenism in itself has become divergent, multifaceted, lacking in cohesion, and above all a unified vision. The third chapter thus focuses on current unresolved issues in ecumenism, including reflections on method in ecumenical dialogue. In particular, albeit briefly, I will consider the process of reception, and the notion of "differentiated consensus" statements, as well as pneumatological freedom in shaping the church of Christ. I also will take up an idea, first noted by Karl Rahner, about the relevance of the "factual" faith of the people of God and their ecclesiological understanding vis à vis church teaching, which, if further developed, could have a bearing on perceptions of the four marks of the church, as well as on a more radical vision of what is essential to being church, and on our search for unity.

The second part of the book examines two specific ecclesiological and ecumenical issues: the church's concrete modern manifestation as denominations and the worldwide annual celebration of the Week of Prayer for Christian Unity. Chapter 4 looks at the concept of "denomination." What is a denomination and what does it mean for the churches to understand themselves as such and in relation to other denominations? My focus here concentrates specifically on my own Lutheran denomination, especially as it emerged and developed in the United States. Of course, denominations will be with us into the future, yet, while peaceful denominational co-existence grants Christians diversity, one wonders whether it is or can be sufficient for visible unity among the churches. Hence the tension between unity and diversity, as well as specific ecclesial histories need to be addressed when discussing the church as "denomination."

Introduction

The fifth chapter follows with a critical reflection on the Week of Prayer for Christian Unity. The Octave, once a driving force in the ecumenical quest, seems to lack the potency it once possessed. It has become something of an "institution," *reminding* us of the unity we already have and the unity for which we hope(d), rather than functioning as an inspiring, exciting instrument towards new stages of unity. The chapter outlines the history and theology of the Week and concludes with some critical observations and suggestions for its future.

In the final section, the second "mark" of the book's title comes especially to the fore: envisioning the church as radical and prophetic, i.e., radical and prophetic in its commitment to justice, freedom, and love, radical in its commitment to the four marks of the church, and ultimately to the kingdom of God, which, as Jesus tells us is—and should be—among us. Today this includes a preferential option for the economically poor, for outcasts and the marginal groups in society. Here I will discuss the work of theologian Dorothee Sölle and of literary critic and (unofficial) theologian Terry Eagleton. Working in twentieth-century German and British contexts respectively, the concerns of these two seminal thinkers, one Lutheran, the other Roman Catholic, correspond in their (left-wing) theological-political engagement. Sölle proposes a vision of Christianity that must always seek first the kingdom of God and embrace the cross of Christ. This centrally includes a siding with those on the margins as well as reflections on ecological matters. Her emphasis on a theology that must start and end in praxis is akin to liberation theologians in Latin America who significantly inspired her own work and thought. Eagleton has critically examined (Catholic) church structures and advocated the idea of a Christian society in his early writings. Latterly, he has written again on religious matters, e.g., a critical defense of Christian faith in the context of recent atheistic attacks on the *raison d'être* of religion itself.

Finally, in an engagement with the work of some contemporary ecclesiologists, such as Nicholas Healy and Richard Gaillardetz and others, the book concludes with a reflection on, and advocacy of, a church committed to being apostolic, ecumenical, radical, and prophetic in our age and into the future.

PART I

Apostolicity: Past, Present, Future

1

Ad fontes: Apostolicity in the Early Church

WHAT DOES APOSTOLICITY MEAN in a modern context? Certainly it would be tempting to delve immediately into this subject. But concepts about the marks of the church—unity, holiness, catholicity, and apostolicity—lead us right back into the roots of the church. An assessment of what apostolicity connotes today cannot be properly discussed without an inquiry into what it meant for the early followers of Christ and theologians, i.e., for those who founded the church and whose ideas about the *notae ecclesiae* therefore must be considered if one wants to be faithful to theology's task of reinterpreting the Christian message in one's own age and contexts.

The Gospels, Acts, and Paul

"Apostolos," "someone who has been sent," occurs eighty times in the New Testament. It can be translated as "messenger" of the Good News or "delegate" of Jesus.[1] "Saliach," the corresponding term in Hebrew, appears to have been used by the early Christian community, connoting someone who has been given full authority.[2] The apostle has such authority that he or she can fully represent the one for whom they are a delegate. Further a "saliach" was understood as a prophet in the sense of

---

1. Betz, "Apostle," in *Oxford Companion to the Bible*, 41.
2. Ibid.

Part I: Apostolicity: Past, Present, Future

the Hebrew Scriptures' understanding of prophet since they spoke with the authority of God's word, but which came to include the message of the crucified and risen Jesus.[3] However, Jürgen Roloff and other New Testament scholars have shown that we cannot presuppose a unified concept of "apostle" in the early Christian communities.[4] Rather there are already tensions between the concepts of Paul, on the one hand, and Luke, on the other. Roloff points out that it is the Pauline notion that is crucial as Paul is the only apostle from whom we have an authentic interpretation concerning his office.[5] Paul often spoke about and defended his office.[6] As he was not one of the original Twelve, he seems to have needed to do so in order to clarify his role, even though he regarded himself as the least of the apostles (1 Cor 15:9). While Paul takes up previous ideas on the role of the apostle, he also contradicts such notions; thus his interpretation "provides a key" also for pre-Pauline and other notions of apostolate of that period.[7]

In 1 Cor 15:1–11 Paul mentions those in Jerusalem who had been there before him to whom the risen Christ had revealed himself: Cephas (Peter), the Twelve, "five hundred brothers and sisters," James (Jesus' brother), "then to all the apostles. Last of all . . . he appeared also to me."[8] Although he sees himself as "unfit" to be called an apostle because he persecuted the Christians, he is deeply aware that it is God's grace that has made him what he is and that he has "worked harder than any of them" (1 Cor 15:9-11). The Twelve "almost certainly" must be counted among the apostles, since Paul makes special mention of

---

3. Burkhard, *Apostolicity Then and Now*, 11–12. Burkhard's book is an excellent study on apostolicity, both in its analysis of this mark of the church through history and in the relevance of apostolicity in a postmodern context for an ecumenical church.

4. See the comprehensive entry on "Apostel, Apostolat, Apostolizität" by Roloff in *Theologische Realenzyklopädie (TRE)* 3, 430–45, at 432.

5. "So ist *erstens* deutlich geworden, dass ein einheitliches urchristliches Verständnis des Apostolats nicht ohne weiteres vorausgesetzt werden darf; vielmehr ist mit der Möglichkeit zu rechnen, dass bereits in früher Zeit verschiedene Ausprägungen nebeneinander existiert und dass Entwicklungs- und Interpretationsprozesse stattgefunden haben. *Zweitens* ist man sich darin einig, dass das paulinische Apostolatsverständnis den entscheidenden Fixpunkt jeder Untersuchung dieses Themas zu bilden hat. Denn Paulus ist der einzige Apostel, von dem wir eine authentische Interpretation seines Amtes haben" (ibid., 432).

6. See Betz, "Apostle," in *Oxford Companion to the Bible*, 42.

7. Roloff, "Apostel, Apostolat, Apostolizität," 432.

8. Biblical references are taken from the NRSV.

Peter as their leader.⁹ A significant difference between Paul's and Luke's understanding is the fact that the former has a much broader understanding of "apostle" than the latter who only regards the Twelve as apostles (Acts 1:21–26).

The apostles' calling was a kerygmatic symbol of the twelve tribes of Israel in the eschaton, of Israel's restoration and redemption. The choosing of the Twelve therefore involves a profound eschatological dimension; the entire concept of the church's apostolicity and catholicity is underlined by this eschatological aspect born of resurrection faith.[10] In Jesus' life, death, and resurrection, the kingdom had already been revealed. It was Jesus' appearance after his resurrection that therefore "implied not only the confirmation of his own mission but also its revival for the disciples."[11] Luke makes clear that it is not just Jesus who institutes the apostles but that it is God who gives them their status; their choice is divine (Luke 6:12ff).[12] In Acts 1:2, moreover, we read that Jesus chose his apostles through the Holy Spirit. In this way one might speak of the triune God who chose the apostles, even if the dogma of the Trinity was, of course, not to be formulated for some centuries.

Wolfhart Pannenberg observes that "the apostolic" (*das Apostolische*) does not just entail "the *conservation*" of apostolic teaching, but, above all, the "presentation of the finality, i.e., the truth of that which occurred in the person of Jesus and was proclaimed by the apostles . . . the future truth . . . which is bringing this incomplete world to its completion."[13] The Twelve therefore are the symbol of God's covenant with God's people "now entering into its final, eschatological

---

9. Roloff, "Apostel, Apostolat, Apostolizität," 433.

10. See Pannenberg, "Significance of Eschatology," 410–29.

11. Ibid., 415–16. "The apostles' activity does not only result from God's eschatological action in Jesus Christ, but itself aims at realizing the content of the eschatological promise and itself becomes an instrument of God's activity, opening up the way to God's kingdom. The present power of God's reign in Jesus' teaching and work finds its apostolic counterpart in the universal mission to all nations" (416).

12. Jervell, *Luke and the People of God*, 86.

13. Pannenberg, "Significance of Eschatology," 417.

realization."[14] For Luke their "primary task lies in the future."[15] Roloff notes that while there is no reason to doubt the pre-Easter Twelve as being historical, one should not over-emphasize their importance. Although they were central in building the original community in Jerusalem, they were soon pushed aside from their leading functions. Already in ca. 35/37 AD, on his first visit to Jerusalem, Paul did not find the Twelve but the "apostles" whose leaders were Cephas and James. James did not belong to the circle of the Twelve. Further, it is quite certain that Andronikus and Junias also belonged to the apostles in Jerusalem. Thus in a very short time the concept of the Twelve lost its importance in the emergent communities.[16]

For Paul, then, the criterion of being an apostle is the calling and sending out by the risen Christ (1 Cor 15). This calling happens through God's grace. In this way he can see himself as an apostle as he knows he has been chosen by Christ. Luke, on the other hand, limits the notion of apostle to those who are witnesses to the earthly Jesus and to his resurrection (Acts 1:21-22). He therefore did not regard Paul as an apostle. It appears that both Mark (6:30) and Matthew (10:2) shared this view.[17]

While in Jerusalem the apostolate was constituted by having been called and sent by the resurrected Christ, some rather different criteria developed in Antioch, its Syrian hinterland and in Gentile mission areas. Here we find an apostolate that was *pneumatic* and *charismatic* with a clear aim of mission.[18] In Acts 13:1-4 Paul and Barnabas are sent out through the Holy Spirit to mission (Cyprus). In Acts 14:4,14, Paul and Barnabas, on mission (in Iconium), are referred to as apostles. This, in fact, is the only time that Luke acknowledges Paul as an apostle. Thus both were regarded as apostles in Antioch since the Holy Spirit had sent them to bring the Good News to the Gentiles. Hence in addition to the calling and sending, and the apostles' eschatological motivation, there is another dimension, the pneumatological one. It is for this rea-

---

14. Burkhard, *Apostolicity Then and Now*, 3. See also Roloff, "Apostel, Apostolat, Apostolizität, " 438: "Der Apostel als Träger und Bote der abschliessenden eschatologischen Selbstkundgabe Gottes, des Evangeliums, das durch die Propheten lediglich vorherverheissen worden war (Röm 1,1f)."

15. Jervell, *Luke and the People of God*, 67.

16. Roloff, "Apostel, Apostolat, Apostolizität," 434.

17. Ibid., 430, 433–34. Betz, "Apostle," in *Oxford Companion to the Bible*, 42.

18. Roloff, "Apostel, Apostolat, Apostolizität, " 435.

son that the wandering apostles were at times regarded as prophets.[19] These apostles, who included both women and men, were delegates or charismatic preachers sent out by churches, like Antioch.[20]

Paul incorporated in himself both the Jerusalem "type" of appearance-calling apostolate and the Antioch type of pneumatic-charismatic apostolate. The Christophany he had experienced on his way to Damascus probably led the community in Jerusalem to accept his apostolate as authentic. Moreover, he added a further significant dimension to the meaning of apostolate in that he considered it within a fundamental theological context: the community in Jerusalem accepted that the content of his apostolic mission was the proclamation of the Gospel, free of the law, to the Gentiles.[21] It was the apostles' goal to give concrete shape to the Gospel and bring about the historical realization of the Good News in the church made up of Jews and Gentiles.[22] In his or her own very being and way of life the apostle had to explicate the Gospel.

Let us take another look at Luke. His idea of the twelve apostles was crucial to the concept of apostolic succession, a topic that continues to be a major point of controversy in the ecumenical quest. Roloff notes that for Luke the apostles were the "guarantors" of the Jesus tradition as being foundational to the church, and they were "prototypes" of eccle-

---

19. Ibid. "Neben die *eschatologische* tritt hier eine starke *pneumatische Motivation*: Die wandernden Apostel sind Geistträger; sie werden darum vielfach in dieser Traditionslinie nicht klar von den Propheten unterschieden (Matt 7,15. 21ff; Did 11, 3–12)." See also Jervell, *Luke and the People of God*, 93.

20. Betz, "Apostle," in *Oxford Companion to the Bible*, 42.

21. Roloff, "Apostel, Apostolat, Apostolizität," 437. "Das paulinische Apostolatsverständnis ist jedoch mehr als bloss eine Synthese ursprünglich differenzierter Konzeptionen. Paulus hat vielmehr das vorgegebene Faktum des Apostolats dadurch auf eine neue Ebene gehoben, daß er es als Bestandteil eines fundamentalen theologischen Zusammenhangs begriff. Dabei ist die *christologische Begründung* durch den Auftrag des Auferstandenen nur eine Komponente, zu der als weitere die *Zuordnung zum Evangelium* und die *Ausrichtung auf die Kirche* treten. Apostolat ist für Paulus bevollmächtigter Dienst im Namen und Auftrag Christi, dessen *Ursprung* in einem geschichtlich einmaligen Akt der Sendung durch den Auferstandenen liegt, dessen *Inhalt* das in der Auferstehung Christi gründende, auf Wort und Weg des Menschgewordenen zurückverweisende, in Lehre und Leben des Apostels zu verkündigende Evangelium ist, und dessen *Ziel* im Bau der Kirche als des auf dieses einmalige geschichtliche Zeugnis gegründeten endzeitlichen Gottesvolkes besteht."

22. Ibid., 439.

sial office holders.[23] However, it is now widely acknowledged among Scripture scholars and systematic theologians of various denominations that Luke did not intend to establish "the normative model of an ecclesial central office."[24] To begin with, from Acts 16 onwards the Council in Jerusalem vanishes from sight, and nothing is said about its possible future role. As Jervell insists, the Twelve "are not the first ecclesiastical officials," a college that will lead the church in the future.[25] In fact, Luke hardly had any interest in church institutions. Consequently it is impossible to ascertain what kind of church Luke envisaged. For Luke "the church is the continuation of Israel's history"; the Twelve are not at the origin of any ecclesiastical office, nor is their position an "office."[26] Appointments are not one of their tasks; it is Jesus who appoints, as, for example, in Luke 10:1–11, when "the Lord appointed seventy others." The deacons, mentioned in Acts 6, are chosen by the congregation, not by the Twelve. Upon their election, the apostles "prayed and laid their hands on them." A few times Acts also mentions elders, together with the apostles or as authorities in the congregations (e.g., 15:4, 6, 22f.; 16:4), but it is never said that the apostles were responsible in establishing the elders as an institution. It appears that Luke may not have known how the elders had emerged as an institution in the Jewish faith and culture.[27] Prophets and teachers are also mentioned in Acts but again there are no links made with the Twelve as those who might have appointed them. Thus, as Jervell concludes, we have "no basis for claiming that Luke traces the ecclesiastical offices back to the Twelve."[28]

While the Twelve did not hold an "office" in the early church, the apostles represent an incipient office.[29] They had authority, as did the elders, deacons, teachers, and prophets, some of whom were female. The early Christian communities appear to have adopted the model of

---

23. Ibid., 442.

24. Ibid., 443. "Nichts allerdings deutet darauf hin, dass Lukas das normative Modell einer kirchlichen Zentralbehörde hätte schaffen wollen, denn das Jerusalemer Gremium verschwindet von Act 16 an aus dem Blickfeld, ohne das die geringsten Andeutungen über die Weitergabe seiner Konsquenzen gemacht würden."

25. Jervell, *Luke and the People of God*, 94.

26. Ibid., 95. See also Hall, "Early Idea of the Church," 42–43.

27. Jervell, *Luke and the People of God*, 95–96.

28. Ibid., 96.

29. Burkhard, *Apostolicity Then and Now*, 21.

the synagogue for governance, "where elders, president, and assistant provide a pattern for what became the universal church," i.e., presbyters, bishops and deacons.[30] The apostles were respected in the community, they prayed for the community and they laid hands on those who had been chosen by the community, such as the deacons. They also had concern for one another and appear to have aimed always at unity among themselves and in and between the communities.

Yet, in *Lumen Gentium*, article 19, we read: "These apostles he [Jesus] established as a college or permanent group over which he placed Peter, chosen from among them."[31] I agree with Burkhard's conclusion that one can hardly see the "strictly collegial character" in the first-century apostles. The twelve apostles, headed by Peter, are not the first existing college of bishops with Peter as Pope.[32] Communion amongst them was a concern (Gal 2:1–14), no doubt. This, naturally, would have been vital in building up the church. But there was also room for diversity and Rome as the central place of exercising power had not yet been established.

Why did apostolicity come to be of such importance in the church? The mark "apostolic" was, in fact, the last of the notes to be included in the creed.[33] Unlike unity and holiness, which can be clearly traced back to Scripture, catholicity and apostolicity are not scriptural. Yet, the latter two *notae* were to become increasingly significant in the face of heresies, notably Gnosticism in the second half of the second century, and in quarrels within the early church communities. As the church grew into an institution, the early theologians concerned themselves with unified teaching, church identity and leadership. Several of the early theologians are relevant in this context, especially in view of apostolicity and apostolic succession.[34] The aim here cannot be a detailed exploration of these but rather we will briefly note what recent scholarship has established about their writings on this issue.

---

30. Hall, "Early Idea of the Church," 43.
31. Tanner, *Decrees of the Ecumenical Councils*, 2:863.
32. Burkhard, *Apostolicity Then and Now*, 21.
33. Ibid., 25.
34. These include Clement, the Didache, Ignatius of Antioch, Irenaeus, Clement of Alexandria, Origen, Tertullian, Cyprian of Carthage and the collection *Traditio Apostolica*, probably written by Hippolytus, a presbyter in Rome. See Burkhard, *Apostolicity Then and Now*, chapter 3. See also Hall, "Early Idea of the Church," 42–54.

Part I: Apostolicity: Past, Present, Future

The Early Theologians

In the second century a comprehensive understanding of apostolicity emerged.[35] The transition from a more collegial type of presbyter-bishop to monarchical episcopacy was to be one of the most significant developments during this time. The letter of Clement I (ca. 95 CE)[36] was concerned with the legitimate powers of office in the church. Clement writes:

> The apostles have preached the Gospel to us from the Lord Jesus Christ; Jesus Christ [has done so] from God. Christ therefore was sent forth by God, and the apostles by Christ. Both these appointments, then, were made in an orderly way, according to the will of God. Having therefore received their orders, and being fully assured by the resurrection of our Lord Jesus Christ, and established in the word of God, with full assurance of the Holy Ghost, they went forth proclaiming that the kingdom of God was at hand. (42) . . . Our apostles also knew, through our Lord Jesus Christ, that there would be strife on account of the office of the episcopate. For this reason, therefore, inasmuch as they had obtained a perfect fore-knowledge of this, they appointed those [ministers] already mentioned, and afterwards gave instructions, that when these should fall asleep, other approved men should succeed them in their ministry. (44)

While Clement is concerned with a "divinely willed orderliness in the church," one can, however, only speak in a very limited way about apostolic succession, as all he does is mention a general legitimacy of church office as having been instituted by the apostles. He says nothing about their teaching or their personal individual authority. Moreover, he was addressing a specific church in a specific situation.[37] Walter J. Burghardt asserts that Clement in his instructions about approved men does not

---

35. Blum, "Apostel, Apostolat, Apostolizität II. Alte Kirche," 445.

36. Some scholars suggest that this letter may have been written at a later date, either 118–125 CE or 125–138 CE. It is not clear whether Clement was an "anonymous presbyter writing on behalf of the governing body of Roman presbyters" or "the presiding bishop of the church of Rome." Obviously the answer to this question would have implications for apostolic succession. Burkhard, *Apostolicity Then and Now*, 43.

37. Ibid., 48. Blum, "Apostel, Apostolat, Apostolizität II. Alte Kirche," 445. Hall, "Early Idea of the Church," 45: "The church order presupposed for Rome and Corinth by Clement appears to involve government by a number of presbyter-bishops who have (although we have little detail) deacons to assist them."

refer to a "succession to apostleship" but to a "succession to *episcope* which the apostles had exercised."[38]

Ignatius of Antioch, writing between 100 and 118 CE, was the first to use the word "apostolic," which meant to him the model of the apostle. He was concerned with the unity of the churches in Asia Minor and Rome. Ignatius regarded the bishop as a symbol of Christ and of the universal church. Contrary to Clement, Hermas, and the *Didache*, he insists that there is only one bishop "whose singularity symbolizes the unity of God" and with his congregation he also symbolizes Christ and the universal catholic church.[39] With Ignatius the idea of a monarchical episcopate arose. Yet, while he exhorts the Christians to do everything in harmony with their presbyters, deacons, and bishops (e.g., in his *Epistle to the Magnesians*), he does not supply an apostolic legitimization of a monarchical episcopal office.[40]

It was Irenaeus of Lyons who was central in developing a comprehensive idea of apostolicity and apostolic succession.[41] Writing against various gnostic unorthodox beliefs, which emphasized a notion of a pre-existent, heavenly, and spiritual church, Irenaeus concentrates on the unity of doctrine. For him apostolicity is not a speculative but concrete issue.[42] *Traditio* encompasses the whole life in the church and it is markedly apostolic. Apostolicity with him gained a more authoritative dimension.[43] As Christ had given full authority to the apostles, it

---

38. Burghardt, "Apostolic Succession," 174.

39. Hall, "Early Idea of the Church," 46. Ignatius, *Letter to the Smyrnaeans*, 8:1: "[But] shun divisions, as the beginning of evils. Do ye all follow your bishop, as Jesus Christ followed the Father, and the presbytery as the Apostles; and to the deacons pay respect, as to God's commandment. Let no man do aught of things pertaining to the Church apart from the bishop. Let that be held a valid eucharist which is under the bishop or one to whom he shall have committed it." 8:2: "Wheresoever the bishop shall appear, there let the people be; even as where Jesus may be, there is the universal Church. It is not lawful apart from the bishop either to baptize or to hold a love-feast; but whatsoever he shall approve, this is well-pleasing also to God; that everything which ye do may be sure and valid."

40. Blum, "Apostel, Apostolat, Apostolizität II. Alte Kirche," 445. Hall, "Early Idea of the Church," 46.

41. Burkhard, *Apostolicity Then and Now*, 49.

42. Ibid., 50. Hall, "Early Idea of the Church," 47.

43. Burkhard, *Apostolicity Then and Now*, 52. Blum, "Apostel, Apostolat, Apostolizität II. Alte Kirche," 450: "Für Irenaeus ist die apostolische Tradition die umfassendste Konzeption für die Quelle, die Norm und die Aktualität der christlichen

is through them alone that we can ascertain truth. In the face of conflicting views of faith and church, Irenaeus saw the need for doctrine, which, although no substitute for the faith, would be instrumental in safeguarding it against false interpretations. Irenaeus developed the concept of the succession of presbyters (*episkopoi*). The bishop is the master teacher who teaches his community about Christ. Thus succession here does not mean sacramental ordination of those who had succeeded to the sacramental role of the original apostles, rather the bishops are now regarded as those who, like the apostles, guarantee the proper *paradosis* of the faith and are the charismatic leaders.[44] Irenaeus mentions both the succession of presbyters and of bishops that reflects the fact that bishop and presbyter had been used interchangeably in the early communities: "Wherefore it is incumbent to obey the presbyters who are in the Church—those who, as I have shown, possess the succession from the apostles; those who, together with the succession of the episcopate, have received the certain gift of truth, according to the good pleasure of the Father."[45]

Burkhard argues that the "reason for two forms of succession had to do with the tradition itself" as, in fact, the presbyter-bishops had been involved in teaching the faith.[46]

Irenaeus' ideas were of far-reaching significance for the role of the Roman church. In *Adversus Haereses* 3.2 apostolicity and catholicity become deeply intertwined. Irenaeus refers to Rome as the place where the universal church had been founded by the *gloriosissimis* apostles Peter and Paul and he insists that all churches must be in agreement with Rome due to its "pre-eminent authority."[47]

Wahrheit."

44. Burkhard, *Apostolicity Then and Now*, 55. Blum, "Apostel, Apostolat, Apostolizität II. Alte Kirche," 451.

45. Irenaeus, *Adversus Heraeses*, 4.26.

46. Burkhard, *Apostolicity Then and Now*, 56.

47. Irenaeus, *Adversus Heraeses*, 3.2: "Since, however, it would be very tedious, in such a volume as this, to reckon up the successions of all the Churches, we do put to confusion all those who, in whatever manner, whether by an evil self-pleasing, by vainglory, or by blindness and perverse opinion, assemble in unauthorized meetings; [we do this, I say,] by indicating that tradition derived from the apostles, of the very great, the very ancient, and universally known Church founded and organized at Rome by the two most glorious apostles, Peter and Paul; as also [by pointing out] the faith preached to men, which comes down to our time by means of the successions of

Tertullian of Carthage, the first Latin theologian, employed a historical-empirical and functional understanding of apostolicity.[48] For him the notion of apostolicity is the key that establishes the conditions for the truth of revelation to be handed on and kept in the church.[49] He emphasizes apostolicity mainly with regard to the norm churches, Corinth, Thessalonika, Philippi, Ephesus, and Rome; a church is apostolic if it has been founded by a norm church, and if the churches stayed in communion with one another.[50] Like Irenaeus, he writes in the context of current heresies, but he does not employ one single criterion for judging the apostolicity of a church. He acknowledges the office of the bishop and speaks of their succession, yet he seems to limit the idea of apostolic succession as, for him, in the full sense it operates only in the normative churches. For Tertullian, the "office is not at the origin of the truth, only the apostles themselves are."[51] For our own current ecumenical and ecclesiological contexts, John J. Burkhard's comment is noteworthy: "Although Tertullian's teaching regarding apostolicity lacks rigorous consistency, the abundance of theological perspectives more than makes up for this lack. It might be well for Christians today to remember this in their ecumenical discussions."[52]

---

the bishops. For it is a matter of necessity that every Church should agree with this Church, on account of its pre-eminent authority, that is, the faithful everywhere, inasmuch as the apostolical tradition has been preserved continuously by those [faithful men] who exist everywhere."

48. Blum, "Apostel, Apostolat, Apostolizität II. Alte Kirche," 452.

49. Ibid., "In *De Praescriptione Haereticorum* ist für Tertullian das Apostolische der Inbegriff dafür, unter welchen Voraussetzungen und Bedingungen die Offenbarungswahrheit in die Gegenwart hinein tradiert und von der Kirche bewahrt werden kann."

50. Burkhard, *Apostolicity Then and Now*, 57–58. Tertullian, *De Praescriptione Haereticorum*, 20: "They (the apostles) then in like manner founded churches in every city, from which all the other churches, one after another, derived the tradition of the faith, and the seeds of doctrine, and are every day deriving them, that they may become churches. Indeed, it is on this account only that they will be able to deem themselves apostolic, as being the offspring of apostolic churches. Every sort of thing must necessarily revert to its original for its classification. Therefore the churches, although they are so many and so great, comprise but the one primitive church, (founded) by the apostles, from which they all (spring). In this way all are primitive, and all are apostolic, whilst they are all proved to be one, in (unbroken) unity, by their peaceful communion . . ."

51. Burkhard, *Apostolicity Then and Now*, 59.

52. Ibid., 58.

A collection known as the *Traditio Apostolica* is one of the most important texts of the third century, and it is of central importance concerning apostolicity. Its authorship is disputed, but traditionally it has been ascribed to Hippolytus. In fact, the text has been used in conciliar and postconciliar writings of Vatican II.[53] Blum has demonstrated that the author built on Irenaeus' ideas. He develops a predominantly pneumatological idea, which he relates to the *paradosis* of doctrine and to the whole life of the church.[54] In the face of heresies within the church he does not focus on apostolic succession; rather a totally new perspective emerges, as he sees the ordination of bishops as a creative act, whereby the Spirit is bestowed. The church is seen primarily as the creation of the Spirit, who continues the work of Christ in salvation history.[55]

Cyprian of Carthage similarly wrote in a situation of internal dissent. Apostolic-evangelical teaching, according to him, manifests itself in the Scriptures. He was convinced that the life of the church is dependent on its bishops, which in the face of schism does not surprise. For him the church is one and so is episcopacy:[56]

> And this unity we ought firmly to hold and assert, especially those of us that are bishops who preside in the Church, that we may also prove the episcopate itself to be one and undivided. Let no one deceive the brotherhood by a falsehood: let no one corrupt the truth of the faith . . . The episcopate is one, each part of which is held by each one for the whole. God is one, and Christ is one, and His Church is one, and the faith is one, and the people is joined into a substantial unity of body by the cement of concord.[57]

However, Cyprian considered the pope as *primus inter pares*. The bishop of Rome is only attributed an honorary primacy, "the true apostolic tradition is always entrusted to the whole church and not to one community."[58]

---

53. Ibid., 61–62. He was definitely not Hippolytus of Rome.

54. Blum, "Apostel, Apostolat, Apostolizität II. Alte Kirche," 453.

55. Burkhard, *Apostolicity Then and Now*, 53–64. See also Blum, "Apostel, Apostolat, Apostolizität II. Alte Kirche," 453.

56. Blum, "Apostel, Apostolat, Apostolizität II. Alte Kirche," 454. Hall, "Early Idea of the Church," 52.

57. Cyprian of Carthage, "On the Unity of the Church."

58. Blum, "Apostel, Apostolat, Apostolizität II. Alte Kirche," 454. See also Cyprian,

Ad fontes: *Apostolicity in the Early Church*

In the school of Alexandria, Clement and Origen wrote primarily in pneumatological terms on apostolicity. Gnosis/the gnostic is the key concept in Clement's writings. In the *Stromata* he continuously refers to the true gnostic: "On every hand, then, the Gnostic alone testifies to the truth in deed and word. For he always does rightly in all things, both in word and action, and in thought itself" (*Strom.* 7.9). He speaks about apostolic truth, the unity of doctrine and the supernatural status of the church. For him the pneumatic *paradosis* is not given through church officials but rather by a chain of teachers.[59]

In *De Principiis*, Origen notes that the ecclesial kerygma coheres with the apostles' message of salvation.[60] As with Clement, his ideal is the spiritual-intellectual Gnostic, but he has a greater regard for the institutional, outward church.[61] His is a mystical and speculative theology. "What matters to him is that his spiritual-intellectual explication of Christian faith does not require any legitimation through a chain of teachers or office holders." He thought that Christ himself had shared his spiritual understanding with a small group of apostles and with the initiated.[62] The bishop's power is dependent in how far he shares the faith of Peter. Yet Origen points out that the church is not built on, and the keys are not given to, Peter alone but also to the other apostles: "But if you suppose that upon that one Peter only the whole church is built by God, what would you say about John . . . or each one of the Apostles? Shall we otherwise dare to say, that against Peter in particular the gates of Hades shall not prevail, but that they shall prevail against the other Apostles and the perfect? . . . For all bear the surname of rock who are the imitators of Christ."[63]

Origen goes so far as to say that the spiritual layperson can be superior to the bishops "who disgrace their profession."[64] Indeed bishops

---

"On the Unity of the Church": "Assuredly the rest of the apostles were also the same as was Peter, endowed with a like partnership both of honour and power; but the beginning proceeds from unity."

59. Blum, "Apostel, Apostolat, Apostolizität II. Alte Kirche," 454–55. Hall, "Early Idea of the Church," 49.

60. Blum, "Apostel, Apostolat, Apostolizität II. Alte Kirche," 455.

61. Hall, "Early Idea of the Church," 50.

62. Blum, "Apostel, Apostolat, Apostolizität II. Alte Kirche," 455.

63. Origen, *Commentary on the Gospel of Matthew*, 12.11.

64. Hall, "Early Idea of the Church," 50. Cf. Origen, *Commentary on the Gospel of Matthew*, 12.14.

and clergy are obliged to seek personal holiness so that their way of life reflects their teaching.[65]

Augustine, finally, regards the apostles as the fathers of the church. They are the foundation on which the church is built. Like Cyprian, he held that the bishops are the apostles' successors. For him, however, "the guarantee of the true tradition (*Überlieferung*) is neither the unity of the episcopate founded by Peter nor the primacy of the bishop of Rome, but rather the lifelong connection of the invisible pneumatic church to Christ, her head."[66] However, Peter's primacy is sign and symbol of the universal church, as he has received the keys. Hence apostolicity and catholicity are closely connected. It was Augustine's spiritual concept of the invisible, hidden church that would feature a millennium later in Luther's writings amongst others.

Conclusion

What has emerged in our brief analysis is the fact that there is no clear and unified understanding of apostolicity in the early church. Rather, we find a diversity of emphases, from empirical, functional, and authoritarian notions to pronounced pneumatological and charismatic ideas of apostolicity. These ideas would have been influenced by the religious, theological, cultural, social, and political environment in which the early theologians and communities found themselves, as well as by these theologians' own interpretations of how the *ecclesia Christi* ought to develop and be shaped in the future. The early church had to defend herself against persecutions in the Gentile and Jewish world and had to discern orthodox teaching in the face of heresies from without and within. This played no small role in the development of ideas of a unified, holy, catholic, and apostolic church. The dominant emphasis on the need for unity does not come as a surprise, since minority survival was a primary issue for Christians in the first few centuries until the Christian faith finally emerged as the state religion in the Roman Empire in the late fourth century.

It is clear that the apostles—not only the Twelve—were seen as essential to the handing on of faith, as they were the ones who had been

---

65. Hall, "Early Idea of the Church," 50.
66. Blum, "Apostel, Apostolat, Apostolizität II. Alte Kirche," 457.

entrusted with the definitive truth of Christ. They had been given full authority; they were teachers and prophets. While the early theologians evidently laid stress on apostolic succession, the somewhat simplistic notion of an historic apostolic succession in a seamless "clinical" chain of a laying on of hands from the apostles to the bishops into our own time certainly cannot be defended. In fact, most scholars no longer adhere to this understanding, even though apostolic succession and the role of the episcopate has been re-appraised in recent ecumenical dialogues, notably in the Porvoo agreement and in the agreements between the Lutheran and Episcopal Churches in the United States.

Bishops were appointed but not in a physical "pipeline" succession. Also, as we saw, Irenaeus refers to the succession of both bishops and presbyters. What is relevant in our contemporary context of ecumenical discourse between episcopal and non-episcopal churches is the fact that *both* bishops and presbyters were entrusted with "the certain gift of truth" (Irenaeus). Primary was the handing on and guarding of the Christian truth.

For Tertullian, apostolicity is the condition to establishing that the revealed truth may be properly handed on. Reading the church fathers, one is struck again and again by their focus on truth. Having to defend the Christian faith in the context of Greek philosophy, such emphasis on the notion and defense of truth is not surprising. In the various writings, apostolic succession seems to be taken for granted and is not so much under discussion, while the *content of the message* which is to be made known in the gentile world is what occupied the early theologians. This is particularly apparent in Clement of Alexandria, Origen, and the *Traditio Apostolica* (Hippolytus) who proposed ostensibly pneumatological ideas concerning apostolicity: Hippolytus (*Traditio Apostolica*) with his idea of the bishop's ordination as a Spirit-filled act, the church as a creation of the spirit, and his concern with Christian teaching to be imparted to the whole church; Clement and Origen for whom it is the "true Gnostic" who testifies to the truth. A chain of teachers (Clement) hands on the truth, and the teaching of the faith requires no legitimation through a succession of office holders.

The apostles and apostolicity are of central concern in the early writers, but, as we have seen, there are various emphases, tensions, and inconsistencies, not least in understanding the role of the bishop and of apostolic succession. Of course, bishops were to safeguard unity in doctrine and unity in and among the churches. Yet, evidently, the church fathers do not all attribute the same significance to the bishops' apostolic role. What is definite is that offices in the earliest years of the church were not completely new but rather developed from the model of the synagogue communities. Offices in the church arose earlier than a unified understanding of these, i.e., there was no cohesive development of offices in the early church communities. The most significant example is the fact, as Otto Hermann Pesch points out, that while far into the second century the Roman community was still led by a collegiate of presbyters, the "monarchic" episcopate had already been established in Palestine.[67]

---

67. Pesch, "Hermeneutik des Ämterwandels?," 424–25.

2

Apostolicity in Select Ecumenical Documents of the Anglican, Lutheran, and Roman Catholic Churches

IN THIS CHAPTER WE will make a leap and land in the ecumenical age of the twentieth and twenty-first centuries. For a contemporary understanding of apostolicity and an apostolic church, an analysis of what some recent ecumenical documents say about these issues is relevant. As noted earlier, my interest has been particularly in the Lutheran–Roman Catholic dialogue. Further, recent developments and significant progress between Lutherans and Anglicans are of interest, not only in themselves, but also with regard to the Roman Catholic Church, i.e., notably the insights gained in the Porvoo agreement and their possible relevance for future agreements between Catholics and Lutherans and Catholics and Anglicans. We will consider what can be gleaned from these documents for ideas for a growing consensus on apostolicity among these churches.[1]

In this context the work by two ecumenical scholars, John J. Burkhard and Margaret O'Gara, must be mentioned. Both have analyzed recent bilateral and multilateral documents regarding apostolicity. O'Gara, who focuses on the Lutheran–Roman Catholic dialogue, rightly compares ecumenical statements to a jigsaw puzzle that still

---

1. See Burkhard, *Apostolicity Then and Now*, 165–99. O'Gara, "Apostolicity in Ecumenical Dialogue," 175–212.

awaits completion. In relation to apostolicity she points out that the central themes in the ecumenical statements are the apostolicity of the church, oversight, and teaching that remains in the truth. The documents have treated these three themes with varying emphases. She concludes therefore that the work on apostolicity should seek "greater completeness."

The Lutheran–Roman Catholic Dialogue

Bilateral discussions between the Lutheran and Roman Catholic Church have taken place for over thirty years, notably with the international Lutheran–Roman Catholic Commission. I will briefly consider *Facing Unity* and then look in more detail at *Church and Justification* and *The Church as Koinonia of Salvation*.

Facing Unity: Models, Forms and Phases of Catholic–Lutheran Church Fellowship (1984)

This statement of the Lutheran–Roman Catholic Commission was preceded by *Ministry in the Church* (1981), which engaged in an expansive discussion of apostolicity, ordination, oversight, and teaching remaining in the truth. Throughout the text a pneumatological emphasis is apparent concerning ministry and in its conclusion it makes urgent the mutual recognition of ministries and suggests how such recognition might be achieved.

Facing Unity offers an overview of the various models of church union and concludes that "the unity we seek will be a unity in diversity," which allows both denominations to retain certain particularities and differences (#47). It points out the growth in mutual understanding, renewal of thinking about oneself and one another, and it asserts that the process of joint witness of the apostolic faith is manifested in the trinitarian and christological basis of the faith, and in the growing common understanding of the relationship between Scripture and tradition, the doctrine of justification, the church and sacraments, doctrinal teaching, etc. (#56–86). Thus it urges a "structured fellowship" to be established (#87–103) in which the "coexistence of ministries mutually recognized must be transformed into a common exercise of ordained

Apostolicity in Select Ecumenical Documents

ministry" with particular emphasis on the "common exercise" of the ministry of oversight (#92).

Building on *Ministry in the Church*, *Facing Unity* urges the "concrete implementation of the implications"[2] of its arguments and points out that especially with regard to *episcope*, both churches may learn from the practices in the early church (#104-116). We find reiterated what current ecumenical scholarship continually affirms:

> Members of the church participate in the election of their bishop and receive the person who is to exercise the apostolic ministry . . . *[T]he apostolic succession is not really to be understood as a succession of one individual to another, but rather as a succession in the church*,[3] to an episcopal see and to membership of the episcopal college . . . The responsibility of the congregation is not limited to the moment of ordination. Its full scope is illustrated by the exception that "one must deny one's consent even to bishops when it happens that they err and speak in a manner that contradicts the canonical text" [Augustine]. This means that the episcopé is not exercised in isolation but normally in concert with the community of the believers, i.e., within a diversity of ministries and services and in the synodal life of the local church (#110).

The ministry of oversight must serve the *koinonia* and is understood as personal and collegial and should always work in cooperation with the congregation. "Thus absolute sovereignty either on the part of the congregation or the bishop is excluded" (#114). Remarkably, the document then continues with a detailed framework of four phases for establishing a common ordained ministry (#117-149).[4] It emphasizes that any

---

2. Cf. O'Gara, "Apostolicity in Ecumenical Dialogue," 184.

3. My emphasis.

4. In order to demonstrate how far the discussion in the Joint Commission has already advanced, it is worth quoting from #118 in more detail. At the same time, it is discouraging to realize that *Facing Unity* was written over two decades ago, and the recommended steps (despite the *Joint Declaration*, 1999) are still far from being implemented: "The process leading to full realization of church fellowship as a structured community is, strictly speaking, a correlated and integral process involving reciprocally recognized ministries and the joint exercise of ministries, especially of the ministry of the episcopé. Fully spelt out, it has the following structure: An officially declared mutual recognition of ordained ministries opens the way by means of an initial act to the joint exercise of episcopé, including ordaining. A series of such ordinations would eventually lead to a common ordained ministry. The process could function at

step towards unity between the two churches must be seen as a step towards unity between all churches.

The Church and Justification (1993)

This document, also published by the Lutheran–Roman Catholic Commission, set out to examine the understanding of the church in the light of the doctrine of justification. It claims that a "consensus in the doctrine of justification—even if it is differentiated—must prove itself ecclesiologically" (#2).[5]

Like the previous documents it points out the trinitarian, christological, and pneumatological foundation of the church, and, similar to the *Dogmatic Constitution on the Church* in Vatican II, it employs biblical images of the church as God's pilgrim people, as the body of Christ, and as the temple of the Holy Spirit, whereby each biblical image highlights the trinitarian dimension (#51–62).[6] It considers the church as "koinonia/communion founded in the Trinity" (#63–65) and as recipient and mediator of salvation (#107–242). In this section the text also speaks about the significance of the doctrine of justification for ecclesiology, and it concludes:

> We may sum up by saying that in regard to all the problem areas discussed here . . . we may not speak of a fundamental conflict or even opposition between justification and the church. This is quite compatible with the role of the doctrine of justification in seeing that all the church's institutions, in their self-understanding and exercise, contribute to the church's abiding in the truth

---

the universal level, but could also be set in motion at local regional or national ecclesial levels. The process would thus have the following phases: — Preliminary forms of a joint exercise of episcopé . . . Initial act of recognition . . . Collegial exercise of episcopé . . . Transition to a common ordained ministry." These four steps are expanded upon in chapters 6–9 in the document.

5. Paragraph 2 continues: "Everything that is believed and taught about the nature of the church, the means of salvation and the church's ministry must be founded in the salvation-event itself and must be marked by justification-faith as the way in which the salvation-event is received and appropriated. Correspondingly, everything that is believed and taught about the nature and effect of justification must be understood in the overall context of statements about the church, the means of salvation and the church's ministry."

6. Cf. Burkhard, *Apostolicity Then and Now*, 183.

of the gospel which alone in the Holy Spirit creates and sustains the church (#242).[7]

One notes an echo of early writers like Hippolytus, Origen and Clement in the final line.

The document affirms that the Apostles, called by Christ, "are also the church's 'foundation'" (#44). Their witness is binding and normative, apostolicity "is an essential attribute of the church and the criterion par excellence of its faith, its proclamation, its teaching and its life" (#47). *The Church and Justification* reveals the primacy of communion/*koinonia* ecclesiology in both churches by their emphasis of the nature of the triune God as *koinonia*, of the believers' communion first with God and then with one another (#65), and of the role of the local churches, even if there remain differences in their understanding of local church (#63–106).[8] While, since Vatican II, Catholics have again come to appreciate the local church as having "all the qualities of the church of God" (#92), Lutherans now lay greater stress on the unity of the church, founded in the communion of the Trinity (#84–90).

The document also treats of the understanding of church as sacrament, and the hidden and visible church. These are honestly approached with nuanced agreements and left open for further discussion.[9] Some

---

7. O'Gara notes that two other publications had an influence on the drawing up of *The Church and Justification* (1983) from the U.S. Lutheran–Roman Catholic Dialogue, and *Lehrverurteilungen-kirchentrennend* (1988) of the German Protestant–Roman Catholic Ecumenical Study Group. The latter document notably deals with the doctrine of justification. Cf. O'Gara, "Apostolicity in Ecumenical Dialogue," 185.

8. Paragraph 79: "Catholics and Lutherans together understand that the communion with God mediated through word and sacrament leads to communion of the faithful among themselves. This takes concrete shape in the communion of the churches: the one holy catholic and apostolic church, the *una sancta* of the creed is realized in the *communio ecclesiarum* as local, regional and universal communion, and so as church fellowship." Paragraph 80: "There is only one church of God. In the New Testament the same word *ecclesia* signifies both the whole church (e.g., Matt 16:18; Gal 1:13) and the church of a region (e.g., Gal 1:2), the church of a city (e.g., Acts 8:1; 1 Cor 11:18) or of a house (e.g., Rom 16:5)."

9. Paragraph 134: "On the basis of the stipulations mentioned, there is agreement among Lutherans and Catholics that the church is instrument and sign of salvation and, in this sense, 'sacrament' of salvation. To be sure the reservations are taken seriously by both sides, and one must strive for a theological language that is unambiguous." Paragraph 147: "Catholics and Lutherans are in agreement that the saving activity of the triune God calls and sanctifies believers through audible and visible means of grace which are mediated in an audible and visible ecclesial community. They also

controversies still need to be worked out: the institutional continuity of the church, the ordained ministry as ecclesial institution, the teaching function of the church's ministry, the jurisdictional function of the church's ministry, which are addressed at length (#173–241). "Each of these areas relates to the . . . reciprocal questioning by Catholics and Lutherans: whether the Lutheran doctrine of justification diminishes the reality of the church; whether the Catholic understanding of the church obscures the gospel as it is explicated by the doctrine of justification" (#173).

The document concludes that signs and instruments of continuity and binding teaching always need to be in service of the Gospel and this ought not to be obscured. The doctrine of justification does not contradict an ordained ministry (#185), rather it must be the "yardstick for our understanding and exercise of the ministry" (#191). However, Lutherans affirm that the church exists where the Gospel is purely taught and the Sacraments properly administered according to the Word of God (CA 7)[10] and that bishops are instituted by *human* law with "the power of the Keys," which "according to the Gospel, is a power or commandment of God, to preach the Gospel, to remit and retain sins, and to administer Sacraments" (CA 28). Catholics, on the other hand, consider the episcopate a "divine institution" and apostolic succession an "orderly transmission of the ordained ministry" which "have developed as the expression, means and criterion of the continuity of the tradition in post-apostolic times" (#195). Thus by God's providence, the bishops are successors of the apostles. They continue the task of the apostles and are considered "essential" for the church to be church (#196). This difference of the Roman Catholic *esse* and the Lutheran

---

agree that in this world the salvation-community of Christ is hidden, because as a spiritual work of God's it is unrecognizable by earthly standards, and because sin, which is also present in the church, makes ascertaining its membership uncertain."

10. *Augsburg Confession* 7 (Abbreviated CA hereafter): "Es wird auch gelehrt, daß alle Zeit müsse eine heilige christliche Kirche sein und bleiben, welche ist die Versammlung aller Gläubigen, bei welchen das Evangelium rein gepredigt und die heilige Sacrament laut des Evangelii gereicht werden. Denn dieses ist genug zu wahrer Einigkeit der christlichen Kirchen, daß da einträchtiglich nach reinem Verstand das Evangelium gepredigt und die Sacrament dem göttlichen Wort gemäß gereicht werden. Und ist nicht Not zu wahrer Einigkeit der christlichen Kirchen, daß allenthalben gleichförmige Ceremonien, von den Menschen eingesetzt, gehalten werden, wie Paulus spricht Ephes 4: Ein Leib, ein Geist, wie ihr berufen seid zu einerlei Hoffnung eures Berufs, ein Herr, ein Glaub, ein Taufe."

bene esse remains a major point of controversy. Here the Catholic threefold ministry of bishop, priest, and deacon and the Lutheran emphasis of the one ministry, whereby the bishop is essentially no different in rank to the ordained pastor, is at stake. In this regard, Vatican II speaks of the *sacramenti ordinis defectum* (UR 22) that churches suffer that are not in communion with Rome, a point that naturally has been of considerable sensitivity in ecumenical discussions. However, the document points out that Lutheran and Catholic views on episcopacy are not so radically opposed, but rather the issue is about "a clear gradation" in the evaluation of this ministry, which can be and has been described on the Catholic side with predicates such as "necessary" or "indispensable" and on the Lutheran side with "important," "meaningful," and thus "desirable" (#197). It is this issue that keeps returning and has been discussed *ad infinitem* among ecumenists and therefore cries out to be solved—possibly with a differentiated consensus.

The document concludes that the "difference in the theological and ecclesiological evaluation of the episcopal office in historic succession loses its sharpness when Lutherans attribute such a value to the episcopate that regaining full communion in this office seems important and desirable, and when Catholics recognize that 'the ministry in the Lutheran churches exercises essential functions of the ministry that Jesus Christ instituted in his church' [*Ministry in the Church* #77] and does not contest the point that the Lutheran churches are church" (#204).

Both are teaching churches and maintain that the bishops have a special teaching function. For both, however, it is above all the Holy Spirit who enables the church "to continue and gives it authority to distinguish truth and error in a binding way" (#206).

The Church as Koinonia of Salvation: Its Structures and Ministries (2004)

The document is a statement of the tenth round of the U.S. Lutheran–Roman Catholic Dialogue. Inspired by the *Joint Declaration* both in content and method, this agreed statement applies the method of an "internally differentiated consensus."

It examines the interrelation between local, regional, national, and worldwide church structures and ministries in the light of seeing the church as a *koinonia* of salvation. The Gospel is understood as the message of justification by grace through faith, and *koinonia* is treated as "a lens through which to view ecclesiology and ministries of those ordained, within the whole people of God" (#7). The report proceeds from a more general reflection of *koinonia* ecclesiology to a review of the structures of *koinonia* in the two churches and its ministries. There is a brief discussion of apostolic succession and how it relates to ministries and finally arguments for "a fresh vision" (#8) and recommendations are put forward for greater mutual understanding, recognition and cooperation concerning ecclesial structures and ministry. While theologically rich, the document has a "practical" thrust in its concentration on church structures and ministry and, in particular, in its clear recommendations for both churches.[11] This in itself is a sign of progress, i.e., the process from reflection and discussion to concrete steps of increasing communion. The second part of the agreement is an extensive study of further biblical and historical evidence so as to deepen communion in ministries and structures.

What really matters here is how church ministries serve the *koinonia* of salvation. The document points out that Lutherans and Catholics have never disagreed on *koinonia* and it notes that "koinonia ecclesiology has many aspects but no uniform definition ... All structures and ministries, as instruments of koinonia, serve God's people" (#19). The document applies a method of pairing whereby similarities between church structures and ministries are ascertained, even if they are not symmetrical.[12] While for Lutherans—leaning on the theology of

---

11. One is somewhat reminded of the *Charta Oecumenica* with its concise, practical recommendations for increased cooperation between the Catholic Church and the churches of the Reformation, even if, of course, it is much shorter in length than the present document.

12. Paragraph 27: "Lutherans and Catholics each experience the church in a geographically local, face-to-face assembly where the word is preached and sacraments celebrated: the parish or congregation. In addition, for both of our churches this local assembly is not free-standing, but exists within a regional community of such assemblies, namely, a diocese or synod. These groupings reach to the national and international level, but the diocese or synod, as the primary regional community, forms the immediate institutional context of the life of the congregation or parish. Lutherans and Catholics differ as to whether the face-to-face assembly or the primary regional

Jerome—the office of proclamation of the Word and celebration of the sacrament are fully realized in the pastor, Catholics locate the fullness of ministry in the bishop (#54).[13] While Lutheran ecclesiology puts stress on the local congregation, Catholics emphasize regional structures and episcopacy.

The document develops an interesting notion that hopefully will be applied in advancing unity between the two churches: "A way forward beyond this contrast between the two traditions is to regard the regional/episcopal and the local/presbyteral difference as a *normative complementarity*, both in relation to ecclesiology and in relation to the doctrine of ministry. *The exclusive prioritizing of either the regional or the geographically local is a false alternative*" (#88).[14] The statement urges the churches to recognize that in both the one church of Christ and

---

community is the local church in the theological sense, but the institutional life of both traditions is shaped by this pairing."

Paragraph 33: "Lutherans and Catholics affirm together a variety of interdependent realizations of ecclesial koinonia: the congregation or parish (i.e., a face-to-face worshiping assembly gathered by word and sacrament), a regional community or grouping of congregations or parishes (the synod in the ELCA; the diocese in the Catholic Church), a multiplicity of national structures, and a worldwide organization."

13. Paragraph 56 is a concise summary of the medieval and Lutheran understanding of ministry and its historical consequences: "Peter Lombard, Thomas Aquinas, and many medieval theologians taught that bishop and priest belonged to the same order (*sacerdotium*). The Lutheran Reformers went further, and held that the distinction in dignity and power between bishop and presbyter was not established by divine law (*jure divino*) but by human authority (*jure humano*) . . . Whatever 'power' (*potestas*) is needed to 'preside over the churches' belongs 'by divine right to all who preside over the churches, whether they are called pastor, presbyters, or bishops.' [*Treatise of the Power and Primacy of the Pope*, 60f.] Since the congregation is the community gathered by word and sacrament which mediate salvation, the congregation must be church. In a situation of emergency, a church can provide for the needed ministry of word and sacrament by its own pastors ordaining clergy, since in principle a presbyter can do what a bishop can do, however matters may be ordered in non-emergency situations. On this basis, when the Catholic bishops would not ordain evangelical clergy, Lutheran churches within the Holy Roman Empire proceeded in the 1530s to ordain clergy with pastors as the presiding ministers. The Lutheran argument was complex, appealing both to ecclesiological claims about the powers of the church and to claims about the essential equality of presbyter and bishop. This argument reflects the idea that the presbyter could in a situation of necessity exercise all essential functions of the office of ordained ministry." See also Ickert, "Adiaphora, Ius Divinum," 209–25; O'Gara, "Roman Catholic Perspective," 226–46.

14. My italics.

the apostolic tradition are realized, and that in both apostolic ministry is "effectively," if maybe "imperfectly" carried out (#99).

Concerning a ministry that serves worldwide unity, the document states—somewhat diplomatically—that it is affirmed by Catholics and "not excluded by Lutherans." It is necessary thus for both denominations to discuss how this ministry can be "formed and reformed" (#70). Luther, even in his sharpest writings against the papacy, conceded that the pope might have a primacy of oversight concerning teaching and heresy in the church. In his direct and colorful words he affirms in his commentary on *Galatians* (1531–35): "All we aim for is that the glory of God be preserved and that the righteousness of faith remain pure and sound. *Once this has been established, namely that God alone justifies us solely by his grace through Christ, we are willing not only to bear the pope aloft on our hands but also to kiss his feet*" (#198).[15] Melanchthon, who is sometimes referred to as the "first ecumenist," added after his signature of the *Smalcald Articles*:

> But regarding the Pope I hold that, if he would allow the Gospel, his superiority over the bishops which he has otherwise, is conceded to him by human right also by us, for the sake of the peace and general unity of those Christians who are also under him, and may be under him hereafter.

This is evidence that even in the 1530s, when the *Articles* were published, Melanchthon and Luther still kept hopes for the church to be reunited and the papacy be kept under *iure humano*. These sentences by the two Reformers reveal something of the wholly tragic dimension of the Reformation that Luther and his friends had intended for the whole church, and which led to schism.

The text points out that the question of *iure humano* and *iure divino* needs further examination and that a reformed papacy must be subject to the Gospel and "not arbitrarily restrict Christian freedom" (#73–74).

In Section V (#75–81), "Ministry and the Continuity with the Apostolic Church," the document stresses "the strong commitment" in both denominations "to maintaining apostolicity in the Christian faith" (#75). It points out that apostolicity has been discussed in a narrow mechanistic and canonical sense in that apostolic succession has often

---

15. My italics.

dominated the discussion. What is important is the continuity of ministry, mission, and the message of the apostles, and this is primarily a gift of the Holy Spirit. Finally the text asks both churches to recognize "the real but imperfect communion among our ministers" and to put in place "appropriate forms of collaboration"(#122), which then follow in more specified detail.

To conclude: What strikes one about this document is that apostolic succession is only discussed *in nuce* and that apostolicity in both churches is presupposed and reaffirmed. Apparently the partners in dialogue did not consider it necessary to discuss this issue. The reason for this may well be that it has been elucidated on countless occasions in ecumenical statements and literature, and the common position is now rather clear: apostolic succession is not a historical pipeline but refers to the whole church and *is* realized in both churches, as *The Church as Koinonia of Salvation* affirms. In this way there has been a development from the initial documents towards a clearer vision of what is held in common, what remains to be solved, and of proposals for concrete steps towards church unity. Issues concerning episcopacy remain, in particular the notion of divine and human law, and the status of the bishop.

One would hope that the "kairos" now has come for these questions to be addressed at the highest ecclesial levels, i.e., between the Secretariat for the Promotion of Christian Unity in Rome and the Lutheran World Federation. This will demand further rethinking of ecclesial structures and ministry with the view to develop an agreed statement—similar to the *Joint Declaration*—on ministry and ecclesiology, and to describe the way forward in clear stages of mutual integration in praxis.

It is a much regretted fact that, since the *Joint Declaration* (1999), little if anything has changed in the concrete relations of both churches. This lack of reception must not only be addressed but, if further ecumenical statements on church and ministry are undertaken, a commitment towards receiving the documents by the respective churches should be the aim. Here the Porvoo agreement with its outline of steps towards communion might provide ideas for the Catholic and Lutheran churches on their stony path towards unity.

Part I: Apostolicity: Past, Present, Future

The Lutheran-Anglican Dialogue

The Meissen Common Statement was drawn up in 1988 between the Church of England, the Federation of the Evangelical Churches in the German Democratic Republic and the Evangelical Church in Germany. The more extensive *Porvoo Common Statement* appeared four years later in 1992 as an agreement between the Anglican Churches in Britain and Ireland and the Nordic and Baltic Lutheran Churches. Both documents in inspiration and content have drawn heavily from other bi- and multilateral dialogues. Both statements, especially Porvoo, have been influential far beyond their own confines and both are concise, dynamic, and with strong practical directions. Here one sees the realization of new possibilities, due to large consensus. In this way being confronted with these documents is an encouraging experience of ecumenism resulting in concrete reception and action.

The Meissen Common Statement (1988)

The shortest of all documents examined in this chapter, this statement was inspired by the celebrations of Luther's fifth centenary in 1983, at which Robert Runcie proposed closer ties between the two denominations in Britain and Germany. Already there had been advances after the Second World War in the partnership between Coventry and Dresden, and in theological conversations since 1964, with further steps through the Anglican–Lutheran European Commission (1982), the International Anglican–Lutheran Joint Working Group (1983), the Anglican–Reformed International Commission (1984), and with the groundbreaking document *Baptism, Eucharist and Ministry* (BEM). Official delegates were appointed in both churches to work out a "basis for closer relations." It started in 1987 in London Colney and finished in the former GDR city of Meissen in 1988. The statement was received in both churches.

The document begins by analyzing the role of the church as instrument, sign, and foretaste of the kingdom of God. Here it quotes relevant biblical sources and reveals a strong christological emphasis (#1–2). The church is a "divine," "holy," and "transcendent" reality and as a "human institution . . . shares all the ambiguity and frailty of the human condition" (#3). Thus the church is always in need of reform and renewal. The church is justified through grace by faith and is *koinonia*, the body of Christ "sharing in the life of the Trinity," and in that way destined to mission and service (#4–5). The document stresses that it is from the perspective of mission that unity is imperative; the church must be united to fulfill its task (#6). And so it affirms that it strives for "full visible unity," whereby this unity must be manifested in several aspects: the "common confession of the apostolic faith in word and life," sharing one baptism and celebrating one Eucharist, a "reconciled, common ministry," and "bonds which enable the Church at every level to guard and interpret the apostolic faith, to take decisions, to teach authoritatively, to share goods and to bear effective witness in this world" (#8). It goes on to affirm the unity already shared through the Scriptures, Creeds, the pre-Reformation tradition of spirituality, worship and theology, post-Reformation writings such as the Augsburg Confession, the Book of Common Prayer, as well as "a similar historical tradition of worship" (#9). It also points out that the two churches never condemned each other.

Regarding apostolic mission and oversight, the whole church plays its role: "We believe that all members of the Church are called to participate in its apostolic mission. They are given therefore various ministries of the Holy Spirit." The document describes the ordained ministry's task as being at the service of the whole people of God. Ordained ministry is "a gift of God" to the church and it is therefore "an office of divine institution" (#15).

Episcope (i.e., pastoral oversight) is "exercised in personal, collegial and communal ways," and the two churches consider it necessary to "safeguard the unity and apostolicity of the church" (#15). Further, the document asserts that episcopal succession, while being increasingly appreciated by the Lutheran and Reformed Churches, should not become a necessary condition for "full visible unity." Because of this difference in the understanding of episcopacy, the "full interchangeability" of ministers is not yet possible (#16). The document ends with the Meissen Declaration where both parties commit themselves to full, visible unity in several steps:

1. to continue official theological conversations . . . to encourage the reception of the theological consensus and convergence

already achieved and to work to resolve the outstanding differences....;

2. to establish forms of joint oversight so that our churches may regularly consult one another on significant matters of faith and order, life and work;

3. to participate in one another's worship, including baptism, eucharist and ordinations;

4. that authorised ministers of our churches may, subject to the regulations of the churches... carry out the tasks of their own office in congregations of the other churches when requested;
...

5. that the Church of England invites members of the member churches of the Federation of the Evangelical Churches in the German Democratic Republic and the member churches of the Evangelical Church in Germany to receive Holy Communion according to the order of the Church of England; the member churches of the Federation of the Evangelical Churches in the German Democratic Republic and the member churches of the Evangelical Church in Germany invite members of the Church of England to receive Holy Communion according to their respective orders. We encourage the members of our churches to accept the eucharistic hospitality extended to them and thus express their unity with one another in the One Body of Christ;

6. that whenever in our churches the people of God assemble for eucharistic worship, the ordained ministers of our churches, in accordance with their rules, may share in the celebration of the eucharist in a way which advances beyond mutual eucharistic hospitality but which falls short of the full interchangeability of ministers. Such eucharistic fellowship will reflect the presence of two or more churches expressing their unity in faith and baptism, and demonstrate that we are... striving towards making more visible the unity of the One, Holy, Catholic and Apostolic Church...

7. that whenever a bishop or minister accepts an invitation to take part in an ordination of another church this expresses the commitment of our churches to the unity and apostolicity of the Church. Until we have a reconciled, common ministry such participation in ordination cannot involve acts which by word or gesture might imply that this has already been achieved.

Apostolicity in Select Ecumenical Documents

This document, then, with its concrete steps towards full unity was agreed in 1988 and subsequently approved by the General Synod of the Church of England, the Federation of the Evangelical Churches in the German Democratic Republic and its member churches, as well as the Evangelical Church in West Germany and its member churches. Since then relations between the Lutheran Church in Germany and the Anglican Communion have grown and become closer, ranging from partnerships between parish communities in Britain and Germany to providing impetus for further ecumenical dialogues at the highest levels, notably the Porvoo agreement.

Porvoo Common Statement (1992)

Twelve churches were involved in issuing the Porvoo agreement, and some churches later signed the agreement: the Evangelical Lutheran Church in Denmark, the Estonian Evangelical-Lutheran Church, the Evangelical-Lutheran Church of Finland, the Evangelical-Lutheran Church of Iceland, the Evangelical-Lutheran Church of Latvia, the Evangelical-Lutheran Church of Lithuania, the Church of Norway, the Church of Sweden, the Church of England, the Church of Ireland, the Scottish Episcopal Church, the Church in Wales, the Lusitanian Catholic Apostolic Evangelical Church in Portugal (Anglican Communion), and the Spanish Episcopal Church.[16]

The Porvoo Statement has been influenced by, and results from, discussions between Anglican and Lutherans in the European Nordic and Baltic regions going back to 1909. Bilateral and other multilateral reports were consulted, notably Pullach (1973), BEM (1982), Helsinki (1982), Cold Ash (1983), Niagara (1988), as well as the Lutheran–Episcopal Agreement (1982) and Meissen (1988). These latter two have had concrete, practical implications as they have led to eucharistic hospitality, some degree of sharing ordained ministry, some occasional joint eucharistic celebrations, and commitment to common life and mission. The goal was to move from "piecemeal agreements" towards visible unity (Foreword).

---

16. For information about the Porvoo churches, see online: www.porvoochurches.org/index.html.

Part I: Apostolicity: Past, Present, Future

Chapter 1 (#1–14) sets the scene and looks at the historical and present common ground of these churches. In particular, it emphasizes the common mission. The second chapter (#14–28) discusses the nature and unity of the church. Here we find strong echoes from other documents: the trinitarian and christological basis of the church's unity and diversity, the notion of the church as communion and as sign, instrument, and foretaste of the eschaton, and, like Meissen, the stress on the transcendent, holy reality of the church as well as its frailty and its constant need of reform (#18, #20, #21–28). Chapter 3 (#29–33) reaffirms that the two denominations have never condemned one another and then declares in a summary account the "principal beliefs and practices" both hold in common (#32).

For our theme of apostolicity it is of particular interest what is said about the threefold ministry: "The threefold ministry of bishop, priest and deacon became the general pattern in the Church of the early centuries and is still retained by many churches, though often in partial form. '*The threefold ministry of bishop, presbyter and deacon may serve today as an expression of the unity we seek and also as a means for achieving it*'" (#32). The agreement here takes up Meissen and intensifies it:

> We believe that a ministry of pastoral oversight (*episcope*), exercised in personal, collegial and communal ways, is necessary as witness to and safeguard of the unity and apostolicity of the Church. Further, we retain and employ the episcopal office as a sign of our intention, under God, to ensure the continuity of the Church in apostolic life and witness. For these reasons, all our churches have a personally exercised episcopal office. (#32)

A comprehensive analysis of episcopacy as it serves the church's apostolicity follows (chapter 4). In this document, thus, we find a strong statement on episcopacy, and it leaves us in no doubt that both these Anglican and Lutheran churches consider episcopacy as necessary for safeguarding the apostolic church, its unity and continuity.

The final chapter contains the Porvoo declaration. The declaration is rather similar in form and content to the Meissen declaration. It asserts that this declaration should be "inaugurated and affirmed by three central celebrations of the eucharist at which all our churches would be represented," and it points out that this agreement as a move towards closer communion is not an end in itself but part of striving for a wider community on a worldwide level, including links with other world communions.

John J. Burkhard has noted that this text "has offered the most concentrated theological focus" on apostolicity.[17] Let us take a closer look. There are a number of strengths and a novel dimension in this statement. As in the other documents, Porvoo starts out with a clear assertion that apostolicity pertains above all to the whole church:

> Thus the whole Church, and every member, participates in and contributes to the communication of the gospel . . . [T]he primary manifestation of apostolic succession is to be found in the apostolic tradition of the Church as a whole. The succession is an expression of the permanence and, therefore, of the continuity of Christ's own mission in which the Church participates. (#38-39)

The document relates apostolic succession to, and clearly locates it *within*, apostolicity (#40). While the apostolicity of the whole church is prior, this priority "is embedded in a variety of historical expressions."[18] This is a strong and crucial point in the agreement, i.e., the analysis and affirmation of the relationship between apostolicity and apostolic succession. The ordained ministry's task is to gather and build up the community through preaching, the celebration of the sacraments, and through pastoral care (#41), while the bishops have pastoral oversight over the areas to which they have been called:

> They serve the apostolicity, catholicity and unity of the Church's teaching, worship and sacramental life. They have responsibility for leadership in the Church's mission. None of these tasks should be carried out in isolation from the whole Church . . . The ministry of oversight is exercised personally, collegially and communally. (#43-44)

Episcopal continuity is to be understood within the continuity of the whole church, and the episcopal office is "a visible and personal way of focusing the apostolicity of the whole Church" (#47). The ordination or consecration of a bishop signifies apostolic continuity.[19]

---

17. Burkhard, *Apostolicity Then and Now*, 193-96, at 193.
18. Cf. ibid., 194-95.
19. Paragraph 48 reads: "In the consecration of a bishop the sign is effective in four ways: first it bears witness to the Church's trust in God's faithfulness to his people and

Part I: Apostolicity: Past, Present, Future

One of the most difficult and sensitive matters in view of apostolic succession—namely, the question how episcopal churches can accept those churches that have genuine forms of *episcope* but have not kept the historical episcopate—is addressed, and, further, how these divergent positions can find reconciliation.[20]

> Faithfulness to the apostolic calling of the whole Church is carried by more than one means of continuity. Therefore a church which has preserved the sign of historic episcopal succession is free to acknowledge an authentic episcopal ministry in a church which has preserved continuity in the episcopal office by an occasional priestly/presbyterial ordination at the time of the Reformation. Similarly a church which has preserved continuity through such a succession is free to enter a relationship of mutual participation in episcopal ordinations with a church which has retained the historical episcopal succession, and to embrace this sign, without denying its past apostolic continuity. (#52)

This is one of the most remarkable and innovative passages in the text. What so far seems impossible to affirm between the Lutheran and Roman Catholic Church is here "solved" in one paragraph. The key word is "free." The churches have the *freedom* to accept each other's *episcope* as genuine, historical and adequate. Freedom is always associated with the Holy Spirit, and one cannot but sense that this paragraph has been inspired and is inspiring for any further ecumenical dialogue. What appeared impossible is transcended with unexpected, disarming simplicity: the dynamic freedom of the Christian, the freedom of one church to accept another. And this is no "flippant" freedom; it comes out of a *humility* of recognizing that "to the degree to which our ministries have been separated all our churches have lacked something of that fullness which God desires for his people (Eph 1:23 and 3:17–19).

---

in the promised presence of Christ with his Church, through the power of the Holy Spirit, to the end of time; secondly, it expresses the Church's intention to be faithful to God's initiative and gift, by living in the continuity of the apostolic faith and tradition; thirdly, the participation of a group of bishops in the laying on of hands signifies their and their churches' acceptance of the new bishop and so of the catholicity of the churches: fourthly, it transmits ministerial office and its authority in accordance with God's will and institution. Thus in the act of consecration a bishop receives the sign of divine approval and a permanent commission to lead his particular church in the common faith and apostolic life of all the churches."

20. Burkhard, *Apostolicity Then and Now*, 195.

By moving together, and by being served by a reconciled and mutually recognized episcopal ministry, our churches will be both more faithful to their calling and also more conscious of their need for renewal" (#54). There is no question here of one church imposing its ecclesiological understanding on another, or considering itself superior to the other; rather, the focus is on what is lacking when separation is upheld and what can be gained when separation is overcome. The assertion in #52 therefore is not a quick reconciliation whereby differences are denied. Rather the concrete desire to realize reconciliation for the greater good of both churches, out of a sense of lacking something if one does not, drives the partners. In this way the two churches have made visible progress by dealing with one another as sister churches, by acknowledging differences, and transcending them at the same time. In this way, too, as the Franciscan theologian, Henrik Roelvink, has noted, the agreement, although it does not consider universal *episcope*, "opens the way for a new analysis of the catholicity of the Church."[21] Thus the partners in dialogue confirm that they have reached "a new stage" in their journey of faith (#55). And so they express their shared belief

> that our churches should confidently acknowledge one another as churches and enter into a new relationship; that each church as a whole has maintained an authentic apostolic succession of witness and service; that each church has had transmitted to it an apostolic ministry of word and sacrament by prayer and the laying on of hands; that each church has maintained an orderly succession of episcopal ministry within the continuity of its pastoral life, focused in the consecrations of bishops and in the experience and witness of the historic sees. In the light of all this we find that the time has come when all our churches can affirm together the value and use of the sign of the historic episcopal succession. This means that those churches in which the sign has at some time not been used are free to recognise the value of the sign and should embrace it without denying their own apostolic continuity. This also means that those churches in which the sign has been used are free to recognise the reality of the episcopal office and should affirm the apostolic continuity of those churches in which the sign of episcopal succession has at some time not been used. (#56–57)

---

21. Roelvink, "Apostolic Succession," 353. Cf. also Burkhard, *Apostolicity Then and Now*, 195–96.

Part I: Apostolicity: Past, Present, Future

Finally the Porvoo declaration (#58) follows with a list of mutual acknowledgements. These include the common understanding of the church being one, holy, catholic and apostolic, the preaching of the word and celebration of the sacraments, the mutual recognition of ministries, personal, collegial and communal oversight, and the episcopal office as a visible sign at the service of the church and continuity of the church's mission. The churches then commit themselves

> (i) to share a common life in mission and service, to pray for and with one another, and to share resources; (ii) to welcome one another's members to receive sacramental and other pastoral ministrations; (iii) to regard baptized members of all our churches as members of our own; (iv) to welcome diaspora congregations into the life of the indigenous churches, to their mutual enrichment; (v) to welcome persons episcopally ordained in any of our churches to the office of bishop, priest or deacon to serve, by invitation and in accordance with any regulations which may from time to time be in force, in that ministry in the receiving church without re-ordination; (vi) to invite one another's bishops normally to participate in the laying on of hands at the ordination of bishops as a sign of the unity and continuity of the Church; (vii) to work towards a common understanding of diaconal ministry; (viii) to establish appropriate forms of collegial and conciliar consultation on significant matters of faith and order, life and work; (ix) to encourage consultations of representatives of our churches, and to facilitate learning and exchange of ideas and information in theological and pastoral matters; (x) to establish a contact group to nurture our growth in communion and to co-ordinate the implementation of this agreement.

While these commitments are very similar in content to the Meissen agreement, one discerns a growing emphasis on mutual church membership (iii), on the bishop's laying on of hands at episcopal ordinations (vi), on diaconal ministry (vii), and on joint consultation and common theological education (ix).

To conclude: the consensus in this agreement is more than substantial, and it is clearly more advanced than the dialogue between Roman Catholics and Lutherans, or between Roman Catholics and Anglicans. With the affirmation of apostolic succession as embedded in the apostolicity of the whole church, it is possible for both churches to affirm the sign of succession as of "value and use." At the same time it contains a differentiated consensus regarding the valuation of episcopacy. I agree with Harding Meyer when he asserts, in the context of the Porvoo statement, that a "valid solution" to the problem of *episcope* can only be brought about "in the direction of a new common sharing in the ecclesial reality of the episcopal office" while accepting a "partial, though clearly perceptible difference in the valuation of this office and its exercise."[22] What has been achieved with this agreement is a unity in diversity "transposed from the level of doctrines to the level of structures and ecclesial realities."[23] In this way it opens possibilities for further dialogues between the Roman Catholic, Anglican, and Lutheran churches, and with other churches. For the unity between and among these three churches to come about, one hopes that the Catholic Church will be inspired before too long to choose a similar freedom and acknowledge the Lutheran and Anglican churches as "proper" sister *churches*, i.e., as those in which apostolic *episcope* has been exercised and preserved, even if in somewhat different forms or emphases than in the Church of Rome. In so doing all three churches will be enriched and grow in apostolicity. Ultimately it would enable altar and pulpit fellowship, and the exchange of ministers. We are a long way from this, but the Porvoo agreement so far seems one of the most hopeful documents to forge a way forward between these churches.[24]

The document has made a groundbreaking contribution to the concept of apostolicity, *episcope*, and apostolic and episcopal succession. It is in this agreement that encouraging, concrete, and quietly radical ideas for real steps towards church unity can be gleaned.

---

22. Meyer, "Apostolic Continuity," 181–82. See also M. Tanner for a fine analysis of the document and who has noted the "holistic" manner in which the Porvoo statement treats apostolicity. "The Anglican Position on Apostolic Continuity," 114–25.

23. Meyer, "Apostolic Continuity," 181.

24. See also Paul Avis' insightful analysis and commendation of the Porvoo statement as a "transconfessional" agreement, which forges unity while allowing for difference. Avis, *Reshaping Ecumenical Theology*, 200–203.

3

Looking Ahead: Possibilities and Challenges in Ecclesiology and Ecumenical Dialogue

WHERE DO WE GO from here? What can be said about the task of thinking about the marks of the church, in particular apostolicity, in the wider context of contemporary ecclesiology and the ecumenical quest for reconciliation and unity? In this chapter I want to raise a number of issues, not so much as to come up with clear-cut conclusions, but rather as points in ongoing ecumenical-ecclesiological debate. Firstly, I will examine some methodological issues in ecumenical dialogue. This is necessary as method obviously has a direct impact on arriving at agreements on remaining issues. Taking into account what has been established in the preceding chapters, I will offer some reflections and suggestions concerning future considerations in ecumenical ecclesiology.

Reception

One of the most difficult concerns in ecumenical dialogue is the question of reception. Reception is a multi-layered process; it can mean full, partial, or non-reception. It involves a church's reception of a document into its own life, its dogmas and confessional texts; it includes a reception process in which documents are put into practice on all theological, ecclesial and ecumenical levels; it entails a reception procedure whereby a church must decide on a document's binding and legal authority; it requires an official response with a preliminary commentary on, and evaluation of, the document; and finally it demands the implementation, i.e., the continued application of the theological and spiritual contents of the document on all levels of church life.[1] This obviously is a long, drawn-out process, stretched over years, and often churches simply do not seem to consider it imperative to act on reception.[2] In short, the problem is that the many documents worked out in painstaking fashion are not put into practice in the churches. In his survey of texts, mainly from the Lutheran-Roman Catholic dialogue, Udo Hahn speaks of the sobering fact that a number of documents, from the *Malta Report* (1972) to *Church and Justification* (1994), have not been received, even if some efforts were undertaken, mostly by the Vereinigte Evangelische Lutherische Kirche in Deutschland (VELKD).[3] Likewise *Baptism, Eucharist and Ministry* (1982), *Church Unity in Word and Sacrament* (1984) and *Lehrverurteilungen—kirchentrennend?* (1986) have not been officially received, even though BEM has been widely studied and has received responses from various churches. Not only is this an entirely frustrating situation for ecumenists, it also actively prevents progress on the ground. In fact, one could go so far as to suggest that such non-reception and lack of interest in reception is an offense against, and serious omission in, the apostolic task of teaching, proclamation, and pastoral service in the church, as well as against the ecumenical aim that the church may be truly one, holy, catholic, and apostolic. One cannot reiterate that there is no alternative to ecumenism, as John Paul II and other church officials have, and ignore on official church levels decisive, painstaking theological work undertaken towards church unity. Apostolicity today—as in the earliest epoch of the church—demands precisely this: attention to any work that furthers

---

1. Goertz, *Dialog und Reception*, 40–41.

2. Given the proliferation of ecumenical statements over the last decades, it is not even surprising that churches do not take the time to bother with reception, especially when they are initially willing to do so and then realize that partner churches in dialogue do not bother either.

3. Cf. Hahn, *Das kleine 1x1 der Ökumene*, 106–17. Goertz, *Dialog und Rezeption*, 193–96. "Mit einer Ausnahme stammen sämtliche Voten von Seiten der VELKD bzw. der evangelischen Kirchen. Die römisch-katholische Kirche hat sich bisher zu keinem der bilateralen Dokumente verbindlich geäussert. Lediglich zum Lima-Dokument liegt eine offizielle Stellungnahme von 1987 vor. "

the goal of visible unity in the one church of Christ. This applies to documents drawn up between the Lutheran, Catholic, and Anglican churches, as much as to any other bi- or multilateral ecumenical statements. This also implies that a genuine willingness to the possibility of *change* is involved in the path to unity. If such willingness is not truly sought, ecumenical documents have little value.

Walter Kasper, well aware of this discrepancy between theory and praxis, has urged people to realize what is already possible—and this is not inconsiderable: to engage in spiritual ecumenism, which, he insists, is at the heart of the ecumenical quest.[4] At the same time he does not pretend that spiritual ecumenism is the panacea for all ecumenical problems. *De facto*, however, what could be the norm remains the exception. We do not regularly share services with those of other denominations; pastors of one denomination rarely preach—maybe once a year in the Week of Prayer for Christian Unity—in other churches. We still have predominantly denominational schools and theological faculties, whereas we could have far more interdenominational schools and faculties. The religious knowledge of people of one church about another often remains in the realm of projection, myths, or misinformation. Of course, all of this is not the whole picture, and there has been considerable progress in some quarters, but it could be far more advanced.

It is clear that this situation has direct repercussions on apostolicity, on the apostolicity of the whole church (worship, proclamation, prayer, faith life, pastoral activities, mission, etc.), on ecclesial structures and oversight, and on theology. All of these are part and parcel of an apostolic church. The lack of reception hinders and limits striving towards unity, towards a greater understanding of, and life in, apostolicity, in particular the notion of the apostolicity of the whole church, as favored by most ecumenists today. As a result, building up the one body of Christ through the various ministries (1 Cor 12; Eph 4:11–16) is lacking in enthusiasm.

---

4. Cf. Kasper," Es gibt keine Alternative," 52. Kasper, *That They May All Be One*, 155–72.

Differentiated Consensus

The method of a differentiated consensus has had a significant impact on recent documents, notably the *Joint Declaration*, as well as on *The Church as Koinonia of Salvation* and the Porvoo agreement, even if the method features less explicitly in the latter two. A differentiated consensus allows for and even welcomes difference on the level of theological perceptions and church life, and at the same time it can transcend difference in a larger consensus. Different views can be compatible and even complementary with one another and thus can be integrated into a more comprehensive picture.[5]

One of the dangers in ecumenical dialogue has been, on the one hand, the denial of differences in an—often genuine—enthusiasm for ecumenical progress.[6] On the other hand, there are those who are only too keen to dissect ever more differences, which in themselves would not constitute any significant obstacles to any agreement on essentials. The method of a differentiated consensus can contribute to some extent to solving this problem and thus has consequences for the notion of apostolicity in the church. This type of consensus reflects something of our postmodern mindset in the best sense as it allows for plurality, historicity, the limitations of narratives and concepts, while at the same time enabling a common ground of agreement.[7] The consensus might be likened to a good marriage or close relationship. The partners have a solid common basis, a far-reaching agreement on important views, beliefs, and convictions. Yet they are perfectly aware of their own history and make up, of their weaknesses, strengths, and differences that cause tensions at times but can also attract, enrich, and enliven the relationship. Indeed it would be rather unrealistic and boring if two people, two Christians, or two churches for that matter, were in absolute unison on everything. Not only is this an impossibility anyway, as every individual, group, or church has its own characteristics, but it would mean an artificial homogeneity and a limitation which simply do not reflect the expanse of charisms among the people of God that Paul insists are foundational to the apostolic church. Since the Catholic

---

5. See Birmelé, *Kirchengemeinschaft*, 105–17.

6. On this problem, cf. also de Mey, "Call to Conversion," 1–10.

7. Cf. Burkhard on the connection between the postmodern situation and contemporary ideas on apostolicity. *Apostolicity Then and Now*, 159–64, 249–50.

Church (Vatican II) advocates a legitimate diversity even amongst its own local churches, such recognition and cherishing of diversity will be essential to agreements between different denominations. Hence, this method of ecumenical dialogue markedly fosters the notion of unity in diversity, a notion that has been accepted by all churches as a model. It thereby enriches our understanding of the church and its structures and lends vibrancy and freedom to theological-dogmatic expression and in church life. It could thus be instrumental and advantageous in accelerating ecumenical progress. Facets that are essential are distinguished from those which need less attention or can simply be left as they are.

One would suggest that this method of a differentiated consensus be used in future bi- and multilateral agreements not only between the Anglican, Lutheran, and Roman Catholic Churches but also among other churches as it makes real progress possible.

Trilateral Agreements?

The large-scale agreement achieved between the nordic Lutheran and Anglican Churches through Porvoo and the consensus achieved in the *Joint Declaration* between the Catholic Church and the Lutheran Church could inspire trilateral agreements, whereby a tripartite commission could aim at a differentiated consensus on remaining issues, in particular, on the thorny questions of papacy, oversight, and church structures. Equally, and preceding tripartite documents, further bilateral commissions could be set up with the specific task to conclusively tackle the outstanding problems concerning *episcope*. However, if these commissions were established, it should be under the auspices of the highest church officials who would *commit themselves a priori* to enter processes of reception.

Otto Hermann Pesch echoes these sentiments when he mentions that after all the decades of ecumenical dialogue in which each and every topic regarding ministry has been discussed, the Roman Catholic and Lutheran churches surely should be ready for a second differentiated consensus, i.e., a joint declaration on ministry.[8] Rightly he wonders

---

8. Pesch, "Hermeneutik des Ämterwandels?," 417–18. "Gibt es denn zu diesem Thema ein einziges Argument—sei es pro, sei es contra Konvergenz—das in der theologischen und Kommissionsdiskussion der letzten Jahrzehnte noch nicht vorgebracht

whether the lack of reception of ecumenical texts in the churches is due to "strictly theological reasons." André Birmelé, similar to Pesch, has also called for exploring the possibility of a differentiated consensus on ecclesiology between the Lutheran and Catholic Church.[9]

A Priori Commitment to Reception

When one engages with the documents issued between the three denominations, it does not seem too early to suggest that the time has come to expect that future documents ought to be undertaken *on request of, and with the imprimatur from, the highest ecclesial levels*. This would be a momentous hermeneutical and practical change from documents being prepared with the *hope* of reception to *reception being granted a priori*, even if this could imply that documents would have to be reworked several times. One should expect that church leaders consider this an essential and urgent task to commit to such an approach—and thereby to end the stagnancy in progress and the lip service paid to ecumenism.

Comparative Ecclesiology

In the second volume of his *Christian Community in History*, Roger Haight expounds the idea of a comparative ecclesiology.[10] This method, which is likely to become of increasing relevance to (ecumenical) ecclesiologists, also has direct implications for investigating the theme of apostolicity. Haight comments that "the church has become a multi-coloured tapestry of ecclesiologies, . . . so that it is simply no longer possible to think that a single church could carry the full flow of Christian life in a single organizational form."[11] This statement with its

---

worden wäre? Und ist tatsächlich die Lage in dieser Frage nicht auch reif für einen "differenzierten Konsens"? Ist nicht soviel gemeinsamer Bekenntnisstand gegeben, dass die verbleibenden Unterschiede und Gegensätze (in Theorie *und Praxis*!) "tragbar" sind, die Gemeinsamkeit nicht aufheben?"

9. Birmelé, "Zur Ekklesiologie der Leuenberger Kirchengemeinschaft," 60.

10. Haight, *Christian Community in History*, 2:7. I thank Gerard Mannion for raising my attention to Haight's work.

11. Ibid.

acknowledgment of a plurality of organizational structures might lead one to imagine that Haight advocates diversity and difference rather than unity. However, he proceeds with a rigorous comparative template in his examination of ecclesiologies from the Reformation to our day, and asserts that the "theoretical goal" in his study is not a stress on differences, "but rather, after having displayed them [the ecclesiologies] in their difference, to see each one as part of the one tradition of the whole church."[12] In some sense Haight is working from a future premise, i.e., as if the actual unity in reconciled diversity of the one church had already happened. He analyzes ecclesiologies from Luther and Calvin to the present day, and acknowledges all of these as being part of the whole tradition of the church. Thus he is able to throw light on how we can comprehend the apostolic church: one church made up of various churches all of whom offer ecclesiological insights that contribute to, and make up, our understanding of the church. With his method there is a genuine balance between the local and the universal church; neither attains dominance over the other. Churches can retain their own confessional identities, yet they belong to the one church. Haight therefore appears to be taking *Lumen Gentium*[13] one step further: not only are there local churches within the Roman Catholic tradition but all churches are local, and all churches belong to the universal church. His may be an idealistic perspective and certainly belongs to our hopes for the future, but it does offer ways forward in ecumenical ecclesiology.

Comparative ecclesiology then takes seriously the pluralist situation in which we find ourselves today. It emphasizes respectful dialogue as an imperative in the face of such plurality. Moreover, it acknowledges the plurality of theologies that has always existed in the church, as Rahner already observed decades ago. Thus in Haight's opinion, all true theology must be ecumenical, a fact that becomes ever more urgent in our day of denominational and religious pluralism. Comparative theology, Haight argues, "consists in analyzing and portraying in an or-

12. Ibid., 2:6.

13. *Lumen Gentium*, par. 13: "Moreover, within the Church particular Churches hold a rightful place; these Churches retain their own traditions, without in any way opposing the primacy of the Chair of Peter, which presides over the whole assembly of charity and protects legitimate differences, while at the same time assuring that such differences do not hinder unity but rather contribute toward it. Between all the parts of the Church there remains a bond of close communion whereby they share spiritual riches, apostolic workers and temporal resources."

ganized or systematic way two or more different ecclesiologies so that they can be compared."[14] As the church is divided into a plurality of churches, this comparative method is the "only way to understand the whole church." Haight therefore, unlike official Roman Catholic teaching, but like many other Catholic ecclesiologists, acknowledges other churches, i.e., Protestant churches, as *church* and in this way implicitly the preeminent concept of the importance of apostolicity of the whole church.

However, one would suggest that, as with all methods, there are strengths and limitations within this method. Even with the best of intentions, one's own horizon will color one's hermeneutic, and therefore might on occasion lack objectivity. Any theologian who acknowledges personal adherence to a particular denomination will be in "danger" of prejudice or preferences, even if these are minor. On the other hand, a truly ecumenical author might at times supply a more objective reading on another denomination than a member of that church. Anyone who applies this method must necessarily be aware of such problems from the outset.

Biblical Foundations and Church Structures

What strikes one with regard to the ecumenical statements discussed in chapter 2 is the frequently detailed and impressive examination of the biblical foundations of the church. However, neither the New Testament writers nor the early thelogians provide us with a definitive church structure. Above all, Jesus himself did not give us any instructions on how his church should develop and operate. Thus from a hierarchical, episcopal church, like the Roman Catholic Church, to non-episcopal churches, Pentecostal churches, and democratically run fellowships, various forms of church or Christian communities have existed and survived (for a longer or shorter time) through Christian history. Certainly it is an ironic truth that small fellowships, which have no bishop-priest-deacon hierarchy, often have led admirable, committed, and wholly convincing Christian lives, a fact that is rarely acknowledged or analyzed in ecumenical documents, and thus might well be a point to be explored in the discussion of church structures. In

---

14. Haight, *Christian Community in History*, 2:4.

future dialogues, this, as one might put it, "variety" in church structures must bear on any decisions to be made between two or more churches. The fact that Jesus did *not* tell us how his group of followers should be organized, as well as the fact that other writers, especially Paul, reiterate the importance of the various gifts of equal worth that make up the one body, and, moreover, the supreme idea of God as Trinity, i.e., God as relationship and love, give us some important clues about the apostolicity of the whole church and about its structure. If God is relationship in Godself, this surely must have bearing on how Christians and churches relate to one another. Above all, it implies respect, openness, relationality, humility, and concern for the other.

All of this should contribute to a certain freedom in devising appropriate church structures in a unified church. In the context of apostolicity this applies especially to the question of the *esse* or *bene esse* of the episcopate. However, I want to clearly point out that I am *not* advocating a relativist stance, whereby any church structure could be envisaged.

In future bi- and multilateral texts *all* relevant biblical and patristic references will have to be taken into account, so as to arrive at the most comprehensive picture. Any reduction or selectivity in order to insist *a priori* on the superior authority of one's own tradition's ecclesiology can only lead to prejudiced, unbalanced views and thus to non-progress. In this way tripartite or even multilateral agreements may well be feasible in arriving at broader perspectives.

Episcopate and Apostolic Succession

Let us now look again at the early church and its various notions about an apostolic church and apostolic succession. Most of the bilateral texts examined in our study start out by affirming what the churches have in common: the Scriptures, the trinitarian, christological, and pneumatological foundations of the church, adherence to the same creeds and to the authority of the early theologians in ecclesiological matters. However, if the Bible does not provide us with a definitive concept of *episcope*, episcopacy, and church structures, the early theologians do so even less. From the origins of Christianity we witness a variety of ecclesiological accentuations, and this constitutes a—perhaps *the*—fundamental problem that still faces us today in our quest for church unity.

Although the monarchical episcopate and tightening of leadership developed in the second century in the face of persecutions, heresies, and need for self-protection, a historical chain of episcopal succession cannot be verified; in fact, as we have seen, most theologians now dismiss such a notion as crude and unsustainable. As Jervell and Burkhard have shown, the Twelve were not a college who took on leadership in the church, and from whom all subsequent bishops descended in one line.[15] The Twelve are symbols of Christ and thus symbols of unity, apostolicity, holiness, and oneness; even if they, too, had struggles and disagreements among themselves, and therefore were prone to fallibility like the rest of Christendom. It is their *teaching of the good news of Jesus Christ* that remains *the binding content* of the apostolic faith handed on in each generation.

In the light of theological-historical scholarship it is therefore simplistic and tendentious when Benedict XVI explained in an address to a general audience that "the link between the College of Bishops and the original community of the apostles is understood, above all, in the line of historical continuity. Therefore, continuity is expressed in this historical chain. And in the continuity of the succession the guarantee is found of perseverance in the ecclesial community, in the apostolic College, gathered by Christ around him."[16]

Although this is the official position of the Catholic Church, confirmed in the Vatican II documents, one wonders why a theologian like Ratzinger presents this "historical chain" and "apostolic College" gathered by Jesus as "fact" when it has been disproved by ecclesiologists of various denominations. While he acknowledges that "this continuity . . . must also be understood in the spiritual sense, as the apostolic succession in the ministry is considered as the privileged place of the action and transmission of the Holy Spirit," he does not significantly develop this point of pneumatic succession in this address, nor does he provide any references to the ecumenical search for a common understanding of apostolic succession. Rather his reading here is selective; he refers to Ignatius of Antioch and Irenaeus in backing up his address. He omits

---

15. Cf. also on the issue of office (*Amt*) and apostolic succession, Wenz, "Das kirchliche Amt-evangelisch," 376–85.

16. Benedict XVI, cited in Vatican City, May 10, 2006.

that Irenaeus speaks of both the succession of bishops and presbyters, which confirms that the two terms were used interchangeably.

Reductionist readings of this kind obstruct ecumenical progress. Even if this address was not for theologians but, rather, for a general audience, one would have expected a more nuanced, constructive, and ecumenical approach.

The Holy Spirit and Apostolicity

The pneumatological aspect is a central, often undervalued, dimension in the search for a comprehensive understanding of apostolicity. We saw earlier, that some of the foremost church fathers—based on numerous biblical sources—emphasize the role of the Holy Spirit in the notion of apostolicity, notably Origen, Clement of Alexandria, the *Traditio Apostolica* (Hippolytus), and Augustine. This surely needs further exploration. The pneumatic-charismatic criterion in apostolic succession offers considerable possibilities, as it is based fundamentally in the freedom of the divine *ruah* to blow where s/he wills, and it respects the gift of individuals and groups within the people of God. Naturally this can also imply dangers, namely those of extreme individualism and even arbitrariness. Yet, one must trust that church leaders and the faithful will discern what belongs to genuine apostolicity and what does not. If it is the divine will that the Spirit should reign among the people of God, it is the task of overseers to try to facilitate the Spirit's floating in the body of Christ and not to unnecessarily hinder the Spirit's power and freedom.

Apostolicity, as Eberhard Jüngel and the ecumenical documents examined remind us, is above all the church's faithfulness to the early Christian apostolate, i.e., its task and mission to proclaim the Good News in thought, word, and deed from generation to generation.[17] Similarly, Wolfgang Beinert pointed out, over thirty years ago, that apostolicity is the criterium for all genuine theology, as apostolicity is the concrete form of the christological self-interpretation of the faith community.[18] What essentially matters thus is the proper and faithful handing on of Christ's Gospel in every age. Whether this is primarily granted through

---

17. Jüngel, "Credere in ecclesiam," 23.
18. Beinert, "Die Apostolizität der Kirche," 161–81.

the teaching, proclamation and pastoral work of the presbyter/priest, or by the bishop is secondary. The binding *traditio* of the content of the Good News constitutes the essence of apostolicity and is primary to those who mediate the message; i.e., the succession of the Gospel is primary to the succession of bishops and priests. As Porvoo tells us, the special task of oversight and the succession of bishops must be seen as embedded *within* the apostolicity of the whole church.[19] Apostolic succession is a sign of apostolicity, but it "does not by itself guarantee the fidelity of a church to every aspect of the apostolic faith," nor does it "guarantee the personal faithfulness of the bishop" but it is always a "challenge," "summons," and "commission" to "realize more fully, the permanent characteristics of the Church of the Apostles" (#51). It remains a challenge for the churches to work out a comprehensive—in parts differentiated—consensus on apostolic succession, even if there is, as the documents reveal, already considerable agreement. This is especially so as there is an increasing openness among some Lutheran theologians towards rethinking episcopacy and considering the role of the papacy in a new light.[20]

Role of Bishops and Mutual Recognition of Ministry

Already in 1984 *Facing Unity* developed a detailed framework in four phases of how to establish a common ordained ministry in the Roman Catholic and Lutheran Churches and thereby achieve visible unity. Over a quarter of a century and several documents later, this has not happened. With Porvoo, the steps towards a common ministry, and thus visible *koinonia* between Anglicans and Lutherans, are already much further advanced. In Porvoo we now have an agreement on the recognition of mutual ministries, as well as a clear mandate for bishops to be present at each other's ordinations:

> (v) . . . to welcome persons episcopally ordained in any of our churches to the office of bishop, priest or deacon to serve, by invitation and in accordance with any regulations which may

---

19. For a good analysis of apostolic succession in the Porvoo agreement, see Tjørhom, "Apostolic Continuity and Apostolic Succession in the Porvoo Common Statement: A Challenge to the Nordic Lutheran Churches," 126–37.

20. Cf. Lindbeck, "Lutheran Understanding of the Ministry," 588–612.

> from time to time be in force, in that ministry in the receiving church without reordination; (vi) to invite one another's bishops normally to participate in the laying on of hands at the ordination of bishops as a sign of the unity and continuity of the Church. (#58)

Agreement was made possible in Porvoo, specifically through the differentiated consensus regarding the understanding of episcopate. In this way Porvoo is a generous document, one that transcends the "problem" of episcopacy in a gesture of dogmatic freedom giving priority to the aim of unity.

In a search for a proper balance between an ecclesial understanding of the priesthood of all believers and the need for an episcopate, one would urge that—as with Porvoo—the Catholic and Lutheran Church and the Anglican and Catholic Church will come to similar conclusions. This would be a milestone in church history in which dogma and pneuma, church teaching and in-spiration, would merge and create a new step, based at the same time on solid historical theological grounds. What otherwise constitutes a living tradition? The *esse* and *bene esse* would no longer be divisive but be accepted in a genuine and differentiated consensus. All three partners would acknowledge the historical episcopate as present in each other's churches, even, if in a time of extreme pressure and lack of choice occasional presbyteral ordinations occurred in the sixteenth century. It should be acknowledged that these were *legitimate*, as Luther did not arbitrarily decide this by himself, but based his reasoning on St. Jerome's writings about ordination in the early church.

Imperative of Bishops' Authentic Apostolic Witness

We must also look ahead. If all of this was agreed upon, it is still a fact that there are deeper underlying issues. For Protestants the notion of a hierarchical, strongly episcopal church and the power associated with the papacy continues to be a difficult and dividing issue. In reality, individual bishops and high-ranking church leaders at times may be looked upon with suspicion due to repeated and sometimes gross abuses of power. However, bishops can also earn admiration if they live convincing, humble Christian lives in word and action. In fact, it is above all by living a life of integrity, by acting as empathetic pastors, courageous spokespersons and good theologians that they gain respect. This includes the challenging task of cherishing the tradition of church teaching while engaging with the believers' concerns in ever-changing contexts. The same applies, of course, to any minister from deacon to pope. This need for faithfulness in word and action of those entrusted with *episcope* is mentioned in ecumenical documents, but in a more peripheral mode. While it is acknowledged that episcopal ordinations do not guarantee the proper passing on of the Gospel, it would be worth exploring this in a more positive way.

What do we expect of a bishop, what qualities ought she or he display, what kind of training should they accomplish, what ought to be their primary aims? Do they truly live exemplary apostolic lives? Of course, here we enter rather dangerous terrain, as such assessments are never wholly objective and betray some of the assessors' own ideas of the qualities a bishop should embody. Maybe for the moment it would suffice to say that in the ministry of clergy, including bishops, word and action must reflect each other. And one might beware of those who demonstratively angle for leading positions in the church; they may not be the best messengers of the apostolic faith. As Luther noted, "the deed interprets the word."

Recognition of the Papacy?

A further key problem in apostolicity is that of primacy, in particular the role of the bishop of Rome and the papacy. Some Lutherans for the sake of unity would be cautiously open to a new recognition of the papacy; others, aware of the arduous path to freedom from the dominance of a papal church, are strongly against such a possibility. This question has been discussed in all documents and, as we saw, there is greater appreciation now among Anglicans and Lutherans of the role of Peter and leadership in the church. However, serious obstacles have still to be overcome. If a trilateral commission were set up between the Anglican, Lutheran and Catholic Churches to produce an agreement on ministry, the role and function of the papacy would have to be worked out. Obviously, openness to serious reform of the papacy would be required. John Paul II invited leaders of other churches to meet with him

Part I: Apostolicity: Past, Present, Future

concerning this issue. One would hope that such meetings will happen in the future—and not to exchange niceties but to tackle the thorny issues! For example, a question such as whether the Catholic Church could envisage a female pope, bishop or priest seems at present a million miles away from official magisterial thinking—even if not from the minds of many Catholic theologians and lay people. Another question concerns the divine or human institution of the papacy. Further, the issue of infallibility would have to be resolved. *Pastor Aeternus* says:

> [W]e teach and define as a divinely revealed dogma that when the Roman Pontiff speaks EX CATHEDRA, that is, when, in the exercise of his office as shepherd and teacher of all Christians, in virtue of his supreme apostolic authority, he defines a doctrine concerning faith or morals to be held by the whole Church, he possesses, by the divine assistance promised to him in blessed Peter, that infallibility which the divine Redeemer willed his Church to enjoy in defining doctrine concerning faith or morals. Therefore, such definitions of the Roman Pontiff are of themselves, and not by the consent of the Church, irreformable.[21]

Lumen Gentium reads:

> But the college or body of bishops has no authority unless it is understood together with the Roman Pontiff, the successor of Peter as its head. The pope's power of primacy over all, both pastors and faithful, remains whole and intact. In virtue of his office, that is as Vicar of Christ and pastor of the whole Church, the Roman Pontiff has full, supreme and universal power over the Church. And he is always free to exercise this power. The order of bishops, which succeeds to the college of apostles and gives this apostolic body continued existence, is also the subject of supreme and full power over the universal Church, provided we understand this body together with its head the Roman Pontiff and never without this head. This power can be exercised only with the consent of the Roman Pontiff. (#22)

Such absolute notions of the status of the pope and papal power will hardly be acceptable to Lutherans, Anglicans, or any other Protestant churches for whom the authority of the Bible remains supreme. It may

---

21. Abridged from Vatican Council I, *Pastor aeternus*, ch. 4, par. 9.

Looking Ahead: Possibilities and Challenges

require an ecumenical council or synod to establish a revised notion of the office of the pope, and as yet it also is far on the horizon.[22]

Two Steps Ahead, Three Steps Back?

On the other hand, despite these major unresolved issues, more progress could be made. If the Anglican and Lutheran Church have reached large consensus on ministry in the Porvoo, Meissen, as well as in North-American and Canadian agreements, if the Roman Catholic–Anglican Commission was able to publish *The Gift of Authority*, and if the Lutheran–Catholic dialogue devised concrete steps for merg-

---

22. For a considered assessment of the current discussion on papacy between Catholics and Lutherans, see: Ickert, "Recent Lutheran Reflections," 247–66. See also Manfred Kock, "Das Papsttum aus evangelischer Perspektive": "Die grundsätzliche Frage, ob der Papst iure divino das Oberhaupt der Kirche sei, ist wohl für beide Seiten der entscheidende Punkt. Gerade diese Frage kann nicht offengelassen werden, weil daran die Lehrvollmacht und der Iurisdiktionsprimat des Papstes über die gesamte Kirche hängen. Mit dem Zugeständnis schonender Behandlung in Lehr—und Rechtsfragen ist uns evangelischen Kirchen nicht gedient. Am entscheidenden Punkt bleibt es auch nach diesem Denkmodell [Fries/Rahner] bei strikt hierarchischen Macht—und Entscheidungsstrukturen. Eine grundsätzlich *verpflichtende* Einbindung der päpstlichen Vollmacht in kollegiale und synodale Strukturen ist nicht in Sicht, wenn dem Papst diese Vollmacht iure divino zukommt, und zwar ihm allein—aus sich, nicht aber auf Grund der Zustimmung der Kirche. Die von Rom zu beantwortende Frage ist, ob die römische Kirche, ihre eigene Amtsstruktur als verpflichtend betrachtend, zugleich einer anderen Kirche die Freiheit zugestehen kann, diese Amtsstruktur lediglich als eine mögliche Form kirchlicher Struktur zu verstehen. Die zwischen den Anglikanern bzw. der Church of England und der Evangelischen Kirche in Deutschland geschlossene Vereinbarung hat den historischen Episkopat der Anglikaner als Zeichen der Treue zur Apostolizität der Kirche, nicht aber als ausschließliche Garantie verstanden. Das ermöglicht Kirchengemeinschaft zwischen bischöflich verfassten und synodal verfassten Kirchen. In diesem Kirchengemeinschaftsmodell steht die in Gottes Treue begründete Sukzession des Evangeliums über der Amtssukzession. Dieses Modell ist zwischen römisch-katholischer Kirche und den Kirchen der Reformation nicht in Sicht. Daher wird man sagen müssen: Einen wirklichen Durchbruch zur Gemeinschaft der Kirchen haben wir bisher nicht. So dankbar wir sind für die Gemeinsame Erklärung zur Rechtfertigungslehre, . . . in der Frage nach der Kirche und was sie von Gott her konstituiert, sind wir nach wie vor deutlich auseinander. Das soll uns allerdings nicht daran hindern, vielmehr eher noch ermutigen, in der kirchlichen Praxis und im gemeindlichen Leben die Möglichkeiten von Gemeinschaft, die wir haben, auszuschöpfen und wo es geht, auch auszuweiten . . . Kirche im eigentlichen Sinn ist eine, die sich vom Dreieinigen Gott zu Glaube, Liebe und Hoffnung berufen weiß und diesem Ruf zu folgen trachtet. Alle, die eben dies tun sind Schwesterkirchen."

ing in *Facing Unity* and has established a differentiated consensus in the *Joint Declaration* on *the* issue which centrally brought about the Reformation, then it is indeed difficult to comprehend how significant development in ecumenical church praxis is not actively furthered, especially among Lutherans and Catholics. Certainly, it is quite incomprehensible that the *Joint Declaration* has not lead to any significant change in the relations between the two denominations. While church leaders still emphasize the ecumenical imperative, there is a palpable sense of frustration, especially on the side of the Evangelische Kirche Deutschlands, as the Catholic Church still denies the reality of being fully *church* to denominations not in communion with her. Such condescending *anti*-ecumenical notions certainly do nothing to advance the common search for unity.

Models of Church Unity

What is more—and this is one of the most crucial difficulties in terms of apostolicity and of worldwide ecumenism—a definitive model of church unity has not yet been worked out, neither between the churches under consideration, and less so for a worldwide united church.[23] Naturally the question here is whether there should or ever could be one model. *The Nature and Purpose of the Church*, issued by Faith and Order (WCC, 1998) goes a considerable way to clarify "what the churches can now say together about the nature and purpose of the Church" (#4), but it also leaves us in no doubt about remaining issues to be solved: the understanding of the church as sacrament, a shared idea of what "visible communion" as well as "diversity" entails, the relationship between local and universal church and how authority is exercised on different levels, ministry, apostolic succession, forms of *episcope*, and understanding of sacrifice in relation to the Eucharist.

In the light of this situation it is not obvious what shape the *koinonia* between the Anglican, Lutheran, and Roman Catholic Churches will take, even if their ecumenical statements point out that there should be full visible unity. This is a more comprehensive type of unity than a fel-

---

23. For a good reflection on the present state of multiple solutions and agreements see Root, "Once more on the Unity We Seek," 167–77. See also other articles by Arx, Sagovsky, and M. Tanner in the same book, *The Unity We Have*, on related questions.

lowship of churches, as, for example, with the Community of Protestant Churches in Europe (Leuenberg Fellowship). As we can see from *Facing Unity* and Porvoo, a merging in ministry is intended. Nevertheless, as mentioned earlier, it would be a great impetus for the three churches (and others) to work out together a clear concept through bi- or trilateral agreements concerning the establishment of a common ministry and church structures. In trying to reach such an agreement, the milestone contribution of BEM should not be undervalued as a guide and preliminary sketch for a more detailed comprehensive outline for a common ecclesiology.[24] Moreover, as Porvoo illustrates, the method of differentiated consensus could enable and significantly advance such an agreement. This includes the central issues regarding the role and rank of bishops, the problem of the pope's institution (*ius divinum* or *ius humanum*),[25] and collegiality and synodality.

Women's Ordination and Gender Equality in the Church

The role of women in the church is of such far-reaching consequence that in itself it may provide a definitive obstacle to unity. It is inconceivable that those Lutheran and Anglican Churches that ordain women will revoke the ordination of women in the future in order to reach unity. John Paul II made clear that this issue is not open for discussion in the Catholic Church. Yet, of course, it continues to be discussed and is becoming ever more urgent.

A further issue is the treatment and the ordination of gay and lesbians. For example, European and other countries increasingly recognize same-sex marriages. Thus a bishop, female or male, may be married to someone of their own sex. This scenario is worlds apart from the Catholic rule of an exclusively male, celibate priesthood, not to mention bishops and popes. These are considerable differences and much water will flow down the Tiber before agreement on such issues will be found.

In short, as long as the Catholic Church and other churches (including the Orthodox churches, and certain Lutheran and Anglican churches, etc.) reject gender equality in ordained offices, the aim of

---

24. Cf. Burkhard, *Apostolicity Then and Now*, 187–92.

25. Cf. Ickert, "Adiaphora, Ius Divinum, and Ministry," 209–25; O'Gara, "A Roman Catholic Perspective," 226–46.

church unity is suspended, unless a differentiated consensus was found on this issue. However, this would hardly be a proper solution as it could imply that there might not be any change for a long time into the future for women in those churches that reject women's ordination.

Inner-Denominational Differences

Another, not inconsiderable, issue regarding apostolicity and unity is the fact that there are not only differences *between* churches but also *within* churches. Whether in the three churches under examination or in others, theological spectra are now so diverse that it is no longer possible to say "a Catholic holds . . ." or "a Lutheran believes . . ." One hundred years ago such statements, by and large, were still applicable. Today, however, many Catholics have given up adherence to a number of official teachings of their church and have adopted, as one might put it, "Protestant views" on certain ethical, ecclesial, and theological matters. Many Protestants, on the other hand, have become more open to sacramentality, high church liturgy and celebration, pilgrimages, etc. and to the positive aspects of the chair of Peter, especially in light of the papacy of John XXIII and John Paul II, which could not but impress most Christians, even if they may not have shared all these popes' views. While for some eucharistic hospitality and intercommunion are not to be realized until full unity is achieved, for others it has become part and parcel of their faith practice, both among Catholics and Protestants. Thus denominational-theological and ecclesiological parameters are increasingly less distinct. In themselves many of these are positive signs that ecumenism *is*, in fact, *progressing and alive* while it also evidences that ecumenism does not seamlessly progress but necessarily entails complexity, unclarity, and pain. However, against the background of postmodern pluralism, inner-denominational divisions are a fact to be reckoned with in ecumenical dialogue. It provides both difficulties and opportunities as the gap between lived ecumenism and official teaching is fast growing.

Looking Ahead: Possibilities and Challenges

Churches' Mutual Recognition

Mutual respect and the acknowledgement of Protestant churches as *church* are fundamental to ecumenical dialogue. Mutual agreement cannot occur if one church regards itself superior to others. It is unfortunate and has had repercussions for the whole ecumenical dialogue that the Catholic Church still claims that in her subsists the true church. Despite the best intentions and a notable desire on the Catholic side to be open to ecumenical progress, one cannot but notice in some ecumenical documents an underlying tendency to "satisfy" Catholic "demands," even if a "return" ecumenism is now rejected by *all* partners in dialogue. On the surface this tendency is often not immediately apparent, but occasionally it can be sensed. For example, a leaning towards Catholic issues is particularly noticeable in *Communio Sanctorum* (2000), and, for that matter, it has received a lot of criticism.[26] This paper was the first major ecumenical statement issued by the German official bilateral working group of Lutheran–Catholic dialogue since the *Joint Declaration*. It will be important in future dialogues between the churches to make room for progress whereby *both* sides gain, but also truly have to be prepared to let go of some long-held perceptions, if full visible unity is desired. Without doubt this will include painful steps.

"Rehabilitation" of Martin Luther?

A significant step in this direction would be Martin Luther's official rehabilitation by the Catholic Church, as proposed by, amongst others, Catholic theologian Otto Hermann Pesch. Luther was excommunicated as a heretic in the sixteenth century. One would hope that before 2017 his condemnation and excommunication will be renounced. This unprecedented, radical step would be an utterly crucial and symbolic act, one that would give new impetus to all ecumenical endeavours and cement our faith in the church being one, holy, catholic, and apostolic. Luther and all Reformers—starting with Jan Hus and others who anticipated the Reformation—would then be regarded as re-instated members of the Catholic Church. This would not be a gesture of weakness on the Catholic side, but one of true greatness as it would show that

---

26. See the EKD's response to *Communio Sanctorum*.

a church can admit its own failures and appreciate and acknowledge loyal criticism. This, of course, was all that Luther ever intended. In fact, it seems a bizarre situation to conduct ecumenical dialogues between churches when one side is still officially considered to be based on the teachings of a heretic. Certainly, Luther has been *implicitly* reinstated as he is now read with appreciation and admired also among Catholic theologians. However, an *explicit* reinstatement is still pending. Is it too much to hope that a future pope might consider such a momentous gesture? Of course, it would also create at once other major questions: If Luther, Calvin, et al. were reinstated, what would it mean for all the members of Protestant churches? Would and could they still be considered "*separated* brethren" and sisters? Taking such a step to its full conclusion, separation would no longer make any sense. Obviously, the questions and consequences of this giant step would be enormous.

The "Normative Meaning of Factual Faith" and the Apostolicity of the People of God

Already in the 1970s Karl Rahner prophetically claimed that from a dogmatic point of view church unity was possible; yet he lamented the stagnancy in ecumenical development.[27] His observations are entirely, almost uncannily, up-to-date. This confirms, on the positive side, his status as one of the greatest theologians of the twentieth century (and in church history), and, on the negative side, the slow pace in ecumenical progress.

Rahner offers some pertinent reflections, which are hardly ever seriously expounded upon in ecumenical dialogue, namely on the difference between what is actually believed among the people of God in a church, and what is officially taught in that church. In the context of apostolicity, one could say that there are at times considerable differences between what the people of God consider as constitutive for an apostolic church and what is officially taught in this regard. Rahner rightly notes that what the believer actually receives in his or her own church is basically to be found in all churches: belief in God, the ac-

---

27. Cf. Rahner, "Ist Kircheneinigung dogmatisch möglich?," 119–34. Cf. Rahner, "Die eine Kirche und die vielen Kirchen," 93–104. See also Lennan, "Ecclesiology and Ecumenism," 128–43, esp. 139–40.

Looking Ahead: Possibilities and Challenges

knowledgement of Jesus Christ as saviour, forgiveness of sins, prayer, and hope for eternal life. These aspects have essentially shaped the faith of people in all churches, even if in varying forms and emphases. Unless they are explicitly orthodox in their faith traditions, for most of the laity concerns about ecclesiological differences between denominations therefore usually are less impinging or "worrying" than for theologians or church office holders who work on the level of theology, church history, and magisterium. Most of the faithful have little precise knowledge of intricate doctrinal differences between the churches and indeed often these do not interest them either, probably because they simply do not carry much importance for them. This is why they frequently do not perceive any ecclesiological problems (e.g., with a shared Eucharist), while the theologians and officeholders continue to dissect issues that they perceive as church-dividing.

Prophetically, Rahner noticed that in the church of the future, the traditional points of controversy will still play a role, but what would essentially matter to people are existential questions about the very substance and foundations of faith. In this situation, he noted, it would be possible to discuss the traditional dividing issues in a much more "relaxed manner," and always in the greater context of the innermost meaning of the Christian faith.[28] At the same time he was far from advocating a relativist stance, a difference-denying ecumenism, and he was fully aware that there must be room for those who try to fully live by the rules and dogmas of their church, in particular the Catholic Church. Yet he raises an important point by advocating the "normative meaning of factual faith," the theology of the people, as one might put it, as a possibility and necessity in guiding our search for unity. Rahner noticed that an exploration of this difference between what is actually believed and what is officially taught plays hardly any role in contemporary ecumenical dialogue. On the ground it does, but not in the dialogues of church leaders and theologians.[29]

This state of affairs has implications for our understanding of apostolicity. One look at the countless documents published over the last fifty years generally confirms Rahner's observations. Yet the texts also express *something* of his hopes. In the documents and numerous

---

28. Rahner, "Die eine Kirche und die vielen Kirchen," 96–102.
29. Rahner, "Ist Kircheneinigung dogmatisch möglich?," 121.

articles on apostolicity stress is laid upon the apostolicity of the whole church; this includes foremost the people of God and then the tiny percentage of theologians and church leaders. However, while the people of God are mentioned in all the documents, their *actual* faith life—hence their *(f)actual apostolicity*—is not examined or taken seriously as a basis in further dialogues. A religious-sociological study among churches would be of revelatory significance for how *de facto* apostolicity is lived and understood among contemporary believers, even if the very terms "apostolic" or "apostolicity" in themselves may not have much meaning for them.

We may not like to admit it, but it seems true to say that, in fact, most *episcopoi* and even theologians do not consider it worth undertaking such investigations as they/we—and not the people—are academically trained in theological matters and thus always "know more and know better." Naturally, such analyses would be large-scale undertakings as such studies would have to be conducted in local churches. But it would prove that those who conduct dialogues are serious about the apostolicity of the *whole* church, and that "the people of God" does not merely connote a "politically correct" theological term. With insights gained from such studies—which could be started in local, national contexts—ecumenical dialogue, in general, and a commonly worked-out understanding of apostolicity, in particular, would become a more "holistic" enterprise, in which insights from the actual life of faith of the people of God could be integrated with church teachings into a credible, comprehensive systematic and practical theology of apostolicity and ecclesiology.

Such a study would be of special significance to the question of eucharistic sharing, which at present is perhaps the most pressing example of what Rahner refers to as the "factual faith" of the people that comes from below, and is hardly taken account of in official dialogues. In order to reach new perspectives on issues such as apostolicity, ecumenical bilaterals, and multilaterals, one could appropriate the hermeneutical principles that liberation theology introduced several decades ago: 1) to be informed and guided by and investigate the faith and social/cultural context of the people; 2) to confront these results with church dogmas, confessions, and academic theology; and 3) to draw some synthetic and hopefully inspiring conclusions.

Looking Ahead: Possibilities and Challenges

Of course, this cannot always be done, nor is it essential in relation to all ecclesiological and ecumenical issues. Official dialogues need to be continued as they have built on one another. But such an approach might be employed and tried out on certain, mutually agreed themes, and it likely would offer new insights. Not only would the outcomes be interesting in themselves, but such undertakings could instil new life into the ecumenical movement on the whole, both on the ground and on the theological (academic) level. Moreover, it would transcend the lip service so often paid to the importance of the people of God. It could also further the development of shared theological projects by theologians of various denominations, as advocated in the *Charta Oecumenica*.

Conclusion

Engagement with the various issues mentioned in this chapter would not only advance ideas on apostolicity but in themselves constitute concrete aspects of apostolicity, including the "apostolicity of life" that refers to the whole church and that has been mentioned in recent ecumenical theology as a fuller and more concrete way of perceiving the task of the apostolic church.[30] Reflections and explorations on the apostolicity of life would also allow more radical, imaginative, creative ventures, something that often seems lacking in ecumenical documents. One cannot deny the "yawn factor" in reading ecumenical agreements with their repetition and their lack of inspiring, exciting content.

In fact, those documents that have occasioned actual progress are also those that are more inspiring than others, precisely because of their new methods, dynamism, courage, freedom, and their commitment to reception, i.e., the partners in dialogue commit themselves to a genuinely new stage.

At the same time one must admit, of course, that some painstaking work is indispensable to drawing up ecumenical documents. The breath of fresh air, so urgently needed, however, is only rarely to be noticed. If it is theology's task to think about revelation, faith, and the church in every age, then this implies creativity and courage to possibly

---

30. Burkhard, *Apostolicity Then and Now*, 40. See also *Ökumene des Lebens als Herausforderung*.

Part I: Apostolicity: Past, Present, Future

revise one's own views for the sake of greater truth and unity among the churches.[31] This applies to both theologians in the academy and to church leaders. In fact, Rahner's voice again rings a prophetic tone when he wrote, many years ago (!), that church officeholders should not pretend that they cannot do anything because theologians are unable to find agreement.[32] Indeed.

Progress lies in all our hands, but significantly also with those whose life-task it is to be signs of unity, apostolicity, catholicity, and holiness. While theologians and ecumenists have found abundant agreement (on paper), it is for bishops et al. to take such agreements seriously and ensure that they be discussed and received. It is a sad irony that those who are supposed to protect the church's unity often appear content to anxiously and complacently uphold separations, while at the same time engaging in rhetoric on the importance of unity. Maybe it is high time for church leaders and all people of faith to ask for God's forgiveness for our continued divisions and to seriously focus on the way ahead.

---

31. In this context of theology's task to both retrieve and transpose doctrines see O'Gara's perceptive analysis in chapter 10 of her book, *Ecumenical Gift Exchange*, 162–71.

32. Rahner, "Ist Kircheneinigung dogmatisch möglich?," 134.

PART II

Unity, Diversity, and Ecumenical Praxis

4

Denominations: Churches in (Post)modernity—The Lutheran Church (A Case Study)

UNITY IN DIVERSITY HAS been a key concept in twentieth-century ecumenical debate. The universal church of Christ exists in the diversity of churches and faith communities, the tension always being manifested in the question of how much unity we need and how much diversity is desirable in the life of the church. One of the most significant, while not unproblematic, post-Reformation and post-Enlightenment developments has been the emergence of denominations, i.e., the many churches and Christian groups, largely associated with the development of Protestant churches in North America from the seventeenth century onwards. Today, the Roman Catholic and Orthodox churches are usually also referred to as denominations.

As my own background is Lutheran, I have a particular interest in the historical development of Lutheran churches inside and outside of Europe and their ecumenical situation in, and relationship with, the larger ecclesial contexts of today. In the following, I therefore want to examine the meaning of denomination and denominationalism and analyze this concept in particular regarding the history and contemporary life of the Lutheran churches in Europe and North America. (However, as I have not lived in the United States or Canada I necessarily have to rely on relevant literature by North American scholars.) Further, the question in the overall context of this book is to reflect on

Part II: Unity, Diversity, and Ecumenical Praxis

how the notion of denomination impacts on the church as apostolic, ecumenical, and radical.

Context

Before I will engage with the subject, it seems appropriate to say a few words about my own Lutheran background. I was brought up as a member of the Nordelbische Evangelisch-Lutherische Kirche (North Elbian Lutheran Church), in the far north of Germany, one of the twenty-two member churches of the Evangelische Kirche Deutschlands (EKD), a fellowship of Lutheran, United, and Reformed Churches.[1] The Evangelische Kirche (EKD) and the Katholische Kirche constitute the two main churches in Germany, with almost equal membership (at present ca. 25 million members in each Church). The Nordelbische Kirche also belongs to the Vereinigte Evangelisch-Lutherische Kirche Deutschlands (VELKD), founded in 1948, and comprising eight independent local Lutheran Churches (Landeskirchen), which in turn are under the umbrella church of the EKD.[2]

A resident in Ireland since 1985, I have been a member of the Lutheran Church in Ireland over the last two decades. This church has existed for over three hundred years. Largely a diaspora church, it is part-funded by the EKD, with a lively, open, broadly "liberal" (for want of a better word) congregation. Inter-marriages between Catholics and Lutherans in this church are common, and in its orientation it is an ecumenical, international church, with weekly communion services in German, including Lutheran liturgy, eucharistic hospitality, and an English-speaking branch, also with communion services.[3] The commu-

---

1. "The territories of the 22 EKD member churches correspond in many cases to the borders of the kingdoms, dukedoms and principalities of the Napoleonic era and are a vestige of the much older *cujus regio, ejus religio* principle, that is, 'whose rule, their religion.' The Federal Republic of Germany is comprised of 16 federal Länder or states. Their borders do not coincide with those of member churches . . . . Following the war, in 1948, the German regional churches adopted a constitution and formed the Evangelical Church in Germany (EKD). A fellowship of Lutheran, Reformed and United churches, the EKD is a public-law corporation, as are its member churches." Online: www.ekd.de.

2. These Lutheran *Landeskirchen* include: Bayern, Braunschweig, Hannover, Mecklenburg, Nordelbien, Sachsen, Schaumburg-Lippe, Thüringen.

3. For more info, see online: www.lutheran-ireland.org.

nity has an understated yet real sense of pride in its tradition. Naturally, belonging to a diaspora church heightens awareness of one's own tradition, its strengths and weaknesses, and its relationship to other churches.

As I wrote my doctorate at, and have been teaching in, a Catholic institute for over fifteen years, while belonging and being actively involved as an auxiliary minister in the Lutheran Church in Ireland, my own perspective is therefore from living and working ecumenically, primarily in both a Catholic and Lutheran context, in a small country on the European periphery. Situated geographically and culturally between Europe and the States, Ireland itself has undergone enormous changes since the late 1980s and has become multireligious, multiethnic, and multicultural, especially in Dublin.

From Postage Stamp to World Religion: An Initial Search for a Definition of "Denomination"

Consulting Wikipedia on the term "denomination," one finds the following: "Any name can be considered a 'denomination' of the thing being named."[4] Some subheadings follow: "Denomination (currency), denomination (postage stamp), protected designation of origin, a protected product name, usually by region of production." One then checks on "religious denomination" and is told that it includes the Christian, Jewish, Islamic, Hindu, and Buddhist denominations. Informed that "religious denomination" basically comprises any religion and church under the sun, one might then move to Wikipedia's offering on "denominationalism": "the division of one religion into separate groups, sects, schools of thought or denominations." So then, onto Wikipedia's "List of Lutheran Denominations": several hundred Lutheran churches appear, spanning all continents, including illustrious ones mostly unheard-of in Europe.[5] Finally, the website of the Lutheran World Federation, headquartered in Geneva, lets the interested reader know that the LWF

> is a global communion of Christian churches in the Lutheran tradition. Founded in 1947 in Lund Sweden [in the aftermath of

4. Online: http://en.wikipedia.org/wiki/Denomination.
5. Online: http://en.wikipedia.org/wiki/List_of_Lutheran_denominations.

Part II: Unity, Diversity, and Ecumenical Praxis

the Second World War] the LWF now has 140 member churches in 79 countries all over the world representing over 68.5 million Christians . . . LWF member churches confess the triune God, agree in the proclamation of the Word of God, and are united in pulpit and altar fellowship. The LWF confesses one, holy, catholic, and apostolic church and is resolved to serve Christian unity throughout the world.[6]

What Constitutes the "Church"?
Luther and the Augsburg Confession

In Luther's pre-Enlightenment time the word denomination was as yet unthought-of in ecclesial and ecclesiological contexts. Luther speaks about the "church," "congregation," and "holy Christendom":

> Thus the word Kirche [church] means really nothing else than a common assembly, and is not German by idiom, but Greek [as is also the word ecclesia]; for in their own language they call it kyria, as in Latin it is called curia. Therefore in genuine German, in our mother-tongue, it ought to be called a Christian congregation or assembly [eine christliche Gemeinde oder Sammlung], or, best of all and most clearly, holy Christendom [eine heilige Christenheit].[7]

Luther urged his followers *not* to name their church after him. We should call it the "Christian Church," not the "Lutheran Church," a fact that adherents of the Lutheran confession have happily and consistently ignored. Luther with his strongly christological theology would have wished that Christians would always refer to Christ; it is his church to which we belong. With Luther's aim of reforming the *whole* church, naming a church after a reformer would have meant polarization, division, and exclusion. Indeed, for Luther this would have been a contradiction in terms.

According to him, then, the church is not a place of power, a hierarchy, or a building, but primarily the gathering (congregation) of

---

6. Online: http://www.lutheranworld.org/Who_We_Are/LWF-Welcome.html.
7. Luther, *Large Catechism*, "The Apostles' Creed," art. 3.

believers around Word and sacrament.[8] The Augsburg Confession's definition of what constitutes the church is minimal:

> Article VII: Of the Church. Also they teach that one holy Church is to continue forever. The Church is the congregation of saints, in which the Gospel is rightly taught and the Sacraments are rightly administered. And to the true unity of the Church it is enough to agree concerning the doctrine of the Gospel and the administration of the Sacraments. Nor is it necessary that human traditions, that is, rites or ceremonies, instituted by men, should be everywhere alike. As Paul says: 'One faith, one Baptism, one God and Father of all', etc. (Eph. 4:5–6).
>
> Article VIII: What the Church Is. Although the Church properly is the congregation of saints and true believers, nevertheless, since in this life many hypocrites and evil persons are mingled therewith, it is lawful to use Sacraments administered by evil men, according to the saying of Christ: 'The Scribes and the Pharisees sit in Moses' seat', etc. (Matt. 23:2). Both the Sacraments and Word are effectual by reason of the institution and commandment of Christ, notwithstanding they be administered by evil men.[9]

Church, Confession, Congregation, Denomination: An Attempt to Clarify Terms in English- and German-Speaking Contexts

In a way, the term "denomination" intrigues. It intrigues when one starts to actually think about it, which is something one usually does not. Quite the contrary; in theology and ecclesiology we take this term for granted. We use it frequently and with considerable ease. The ease of use, it seems to me, is due to a mostly comfortable—and occasionally uncomfortable—vagueness regarding its meaning and implications. Using this term signifies above all a key notion in (post)Enlightenment modernity, namely tolerance. Tolerance is essential to the emergence of

---

8. Wengert, *Harvesting Martin Luther's Reflections*, 15.
9. *Augsburg Confession*, art. 7–8.

Part II: Unity, Diversity, and Ecumenical Praxis

denominations and denominationalism, as it has come to connote the peaceful co-existence of different churches, notably in North America.[10]

"Denomination" is not a specifically theological or ecclesial word; yet, more often than not it is used as an equivalent for "church." In Wikipedia's "List of Lutheran *denominations*," several hundred "*Churches*" are listed.[11] Why, thus, does Wikipedia choose the heading "List of Lutheran denominations" when, in fact, in what follows, it would be just as appropriate to call it "List of Lutheran Churches"? In this case both words seem synonymous.

Denomination as a term is prevalent in English-speaking contexts. It is used in German, but rarely so. On the website of the Evangelische Kirche Deutschlands (EKD), the word "Denomination" is explained thus: "Latin and English term for church mainly used in Great Britain and USA, and which in Germany has 'Konfession' as its equivalent."[12] However, while this definition goes some way to explain the term, it is not quite as straightforward as the explanation above might imply. There are some differences in meaning between "Konfession,"[13] as used in German, and "denomination." Checking up on "Konfession" on the same website, one reads that "Konfession" today is generally synonymous with "Church." Thus: Denomination = Confession = Church? Yes, and sometimes no. "Konfession," the EKD website notes, includes the "great Christian Confessions"—"Protestants (Lutherans, Reformed, Anglicans), Catholics, Orthodox and Pentecostal Churches."

"Konfession" in its original meaning implies that churches are based on confessions of faith (*Bekenntnisse, Glaubensbekenntnisse*).[14] The Lutheran Church has been a strongly confessional church. Its numerous writings are held in the *Lutheran Book of Concord* (1580).[15] Yet,

10. Cf. Carlin, "Denomination Called Catholic," 18–21.

11. My emphases.

12. "Lateinische und englische Bezeichnung für Kirche, die hauptsächlich in Großbritannien und in den USA anzutreffen ist, in Deutschland gleichbedeutend mit Konfession gebraucht wird." Online: www.ekd.de

13. "Der Begriff Konfession (lat.: Bekennen des Glaubens; Bekenntnis) wird heute meist als Synonym für Kirche gebraucht. Die großen christlichen Konfessionen bilden Protestanten (Lutheraner, Reformierte, Anglikaner), Katholiken, Orthodoxe und Pfingstkirchen." Online: www.ekd.de.

14. Cf. Holeton, "Religion without Denomination?," 38.

15. *The Book of Concord* contains the Apostles' Creed, Nicene Creed, Athanasian Creed, the Augsburg Confession, the Apology [Defense] of the Augsburg Confession,

"denomination" today not only refers to churches or communions that regard themselves as explicitly confessional (Catholic, Anglican, some Reformed and Orthodox), but also includes new Pentecostal Churches and other ecclesial communities, and sometimes it is even used for other religions, as we saw earlier. The term "denomination" is therefore used in considerably broader contexts than what "Konfession" originally and customarily would imply. Essentially, then, denomination can indicate both—the worldwide Lutheran (or Anglican, Reformed, Catholic, etc.) Church/Confession/Communion and actual regional Lutheran (or Anglican, Reformed, Catholic, etc.) churches.

A North American friend made me aware of a further simple, yet important, aspect of common linguistic usage. Apparently, when a North American is asked to which *denomination* s/he belongs, s/he would answer Lutheran, Catholic, Episcopalian, etc. In German-speaking everyday contexts one would normally ask, however, to which *church* they belong, and less frequently (usually in official documents or in an official context) to which *confession*. In this case, denomination, confession, and church would thus be equivalent. It seems, further, that when North Americans are asked to which *church* they belong, what is usually meant is the *local congregation*, i.e., the actual local church in one's village or city of residence. In German this question would translate as to which *community/congregation* (*Gemeinde*) one belongs. Here may be the most significant difference in terms of usage of "church," "denomination," "confession," and "congregation" in the respective Anglo/American and German contexts.

Barry Ensign-George comments that "denomination" is a "middle term" between church and congregation.[16] In a Lutheran context this would appear to mean that all the local Lutheran churches as well as

---

the Smalcald Articles, the Treatise on the Power and Primacy of the Pope, the Small Catechism, the Large Catechism, and the Formula of Concord. The final words in the Book read: "Since now, in the sight of God and of all Christendom [the entire Church of Christ], we wish to testify to those now living and those who shall come after us that this declaration herewith presented concerning all the controverted articles aforementioned and explained, and no other, is our faith, doctrine, and confession, in which we are also willing, by God's grace, to appear with intrepid hearts before the judgment-seat of Jesus Christ, and give an account of it; and that we will neither privately nor publicly speak or write anything contrary to it, but, by the help of God's grace, intend to abide thereby . . ." (*Solid Declaration of the Formula of Concord*, 12, 40).

16. Ensign-George, "Denomination as Ecclesial Category," 4.

some mergers and Lutheran church fellowships are denominations, e.g., Evangelical Lutheran Church in Tanzania, Evangelical Lutheran Church in America (ELCA), and the Vereinigte Evangelish-Lutherische Kirche Deutschlands (VELKD).[17] Despite some significant differences in church practice, liturgy, and especially in theological, social, and ethical convictions, ranging from the far "left" to the far "right," Lutheran churches broadly adhere to the Lutheran Confessions. Metaphorically speaking, the Bible, Creeds, and the Book of Concord constitute the fundamental confessional stem, while the denominations (local/regional churches or church fellowships) are the branches. At the same time, when we speak of the "Lutheran denomination," what is, in fact, more often than not meant is the stem, i.e., the Lutheran "Konfession," or the worldwide Lutheran Church. Therefore, it seems, denomination can imply both—the Lutheran Church/Confession as such, as well as regional churches, or affiliations of churches. Thus while, as Ensign-George writes, denomination frequently constitutes a "middle-term" between congregation and church, and denominations are "a primary mode of trans-congregational structure and life within the church today," it is obvious that the term denomination not only connotes regional churches but also the worldwide Lutheran Church/denomination/confession.

"Protestant" Churches: Which Denominations Do They Include?

A further, although less problematic, aspect of unclear terminology arises regarding the usage of the very term "Protestant" church. I want to consider this briefly, especially from a Lutheran context. Which churches belong to and are regarded as "Protestant" churches is not always clear. Protestants, i.e., non-Catholics, have often disliked the term as they originated as a reform movement and see themselves fundamentally as part of the universal one, holy, catholic, and apostolic church, which they confess through reciting the ancient Christian creeds during services. Anglicans, due to their history, often emphasize that they are not "Protestants." In Germany, those who belong to the Evangelische Kirche would rarely refer to themselves as "Protestant,"

17. Cf. footnotes 1 and 2 in this chapter.

but rather as "evangelisch." But this is not to be confused with "evangelical" in its English meaning. Rather, these Christians belong to the fellowship of Lutheran, United, and Reformed churches that the EKD comprises. In an English-speaking context, hence, I would not refer to myself as "evangelical" but as Lutheran. Moreover, in British/American ecclesial contexts, Anglicans/Episcopalians and sometimes even Lutherans may not necessarily be referred to, or like to refer to themselves, as "Protestants." Some Lutherans consider themselves "evangelical Catholics."[18] On the other hand, the usage of the term "mainline Protestantism" usually refers to those churches that trace their tradition to the magisterial Reformation, i.e., to Luther and Calvin.

Even if the use of "Protestant church" usually appears quite straightforward it obviously is not quite as clear as it might be. Moreover, "Protestant" was at times used and perceived even as a pejorative term in the past.

Denominationalism: Voluntarism, Tolerance, Diversity, Confusion

The lack of precision concerning definitions of, and clear distinctions between, "denomination," "confession," and "church" is likely to remain into the future. This problem of confused terminology seems to be further underpinned by Ensign-George when he notes how denominations are "unable to provide compelling accounts of their own existence," having "no meaningful internal coherence." Or, as Charles Long, professor emeritus of Religions, University of California, points out, denomination/denominator is most commonly "thought of in terms of a mathematical metaphor."[19] Long, too, like most other scholars who have reflected on the concept of "denomination,"[20] notes the vagueness regarding the self-understanding of denominations:

---

18. Cf. Cimino, "Evangelical Catholics," 81–101. On the notion of "evangelical catholicity" and its ecumenical relevance, and with particular focus on Philip Schaff's theology, see also von Kloeden, *Evangelische Katholizität*.

19. Long, "Question of Denominational Histories," 102.

20. See the articles included in Mullin and Richey, *Reimagining Denominationalism, Interpretive Essays*.

> [T]he denomination, is expressive of a seemingly endless proliferation of religious orientations that do not fit neatly into the older Troeltschian classification of church-type and sect-type ... [T]he religious body as a denomination simply suggests that aspects of religion are common without having to give any definition as to what this entails ... It is a way of having a religion without being forced to say what it is.[21]

Denominations are a particular North American phenomenon. They arose during the Enlightenment and could develop in the context of a democratic, capitalist, and pluralist society and culture.[22] Denominations emerged on a voluntary basis, which presupposes and implies tolerance as well as a sense of purpose.[23] Not only have they proliferated in North America, but the boundaries between them apparently are becoming ever more fluid with the result that people are ever more confused as to what is constitutive of their own denomination.[24] Thus church members increasingly switch denominational affiliations, also referred to as "church shopping." This seems to be particularly the case when people relocate and have to find a new local congregation. For example, an Episcopalian/Anglican or even a Catholic congregation in a local neighborhood with a broad outlook and an ecumenical atmosphere might provide a welcome "home" for a newly arrived Lutheran, who might find her/his local church being too far away, not find him/herself on a wavelength with the new local community and their way of worship, or simply dislike the local Lutheran pastor. While this "switching" seems to be far more prevalent in the U.S., it is becoming more evident also in the European context, although not at all as strongly. Also, of course, there is a much greater denominational variety in the States. One would suggest that the fact that churches in North America are independent of the State (i.e., no church tax, as in Germany, for example) would contribute to a sense of independence and flexibility when choosing one's local congregation.[25]

---

21. Long, "Question of Denominational Histories," 101–2.

22. Richey, "Denominationalism," *Dictionary of the Ecumenical Movement*, 294–95.

23. Ibid., 295.

24. Cf. Wuthnow, *Christianity in the Twenty-first Century*, 24–29.

25. I thank Martin Sauter, head of the Church Council, Lutheran Church in Ireland, for his comments.

Denominations: Churches in (Post)modernity—The Lutheran Church

Such "switching" has both positive and negative implications. On the positive side, flexibility of moving from one denomination to another obviously reflects the modern sense of tolerance that fostered the emergence of denominations as well as the ecumenical developments over the last century and our contemporary pluralistic *Zeitgeist*. As prejudices against, and misinformation about, one another's denominations recede, and as the ecumenical quest has created attitudes of increasing openness and curiosity, it does not surprise that followers of Christ are more ready to join other congregations that they find congenial to their own religious outlook and experience. Of course, this raises the issue of denominational double-belonging as such, and as a possible stage towards church unity. On the negative, or at least more problematic, side, this openness to dual or even multi-belonging will increase confusion about and challenge one's theological/ecclesiological convictions and tradition and thus one's denominational identity. While believers tend to have somewhat vague ideas about the history and doctrines of their own denominations, such knowledge becomes even more blurred and puzzled in our contemporary contexts of cultural, ethnic, and religious pluralism.

And yet, when one actually consults the denominations'/churches' websites, the sense of confusion and the apparent lack of providing accounts of themselves is countered by the churches' mission statements and their eagerness to say who they are. Many church websites are actually rather informative and clear. Today they are, in fact, a significant source of mission, as church websites will often be the first point of contact and reference for a prospective new church member. For anyone who cares to know about Lutheran churches (and I imagine the same applies to other denominations), the respective church website will usually list at the very top of its links "Who we are" or "What we believe." Having checked various such websites, it is obvious that the churches take great care in presenting what they see as constitutive of their faith tradition and history. For all Lutheran churches, despite their differences in outlook and historical emergence, this will include: adherence to the Bible, the Apostles', Nicene, and Athanasian Creeds, the Augsburg Confession, Luther's Small (and Large) Catechism, and the other writings contained in the Book of Concord. This is the—very considerable—confessional basis.[26] In praxis, however, the vast major-

---

26. A rather interesting Lutheran website is: http://www.lutheranchurch-canada.

Part II: Unity, Diversity, and Ecumenical Praxis

ity of Lutherans has never read all, or even just a few, of these works. Moreover, we now live in a radically changed world to that of the sixteenth century, and Lutheran churches have developed and revised some of their teachings.

One imagines that the same discrepancy between a clearly laid out theological/confessional basis and a prevalent lack of knowledge of one's own tradition is equally apparent in other denominations.

Denominations and Their Internal Divisions

A further difficulty for denominations in attempting to present a clear understanding of themselves today is the awareness of increasing intra-denominational divisions, as mentioned briefly in the previous chapter.[27] While a concept of what it entailed to be a Lutheran, Anglican, Roman Catholic, or Presbyterian was a more clear-cut exercise until the early twentieth century, such clarity no longer exists. A manifestation of this is the denominational double or multi-belonging mentioned above. For example, a "liberal" Catholic and a "liberal" Lutheran may indeed share more common ground today than a liberal member and an emphatically conservative member of the same church. Similar scenarios are found in other denominations where divisions between "right/conservative" and "left/liberal" are increasingly felt, even though these terms, of course, are flawed in themselves. Indeed, one needs to be aware that these (polarizing) outlooks are (often far too) general, and many nuances of convictions can be found in between.

In the context of the Lutheran churches, this, relatively recent, problem is noted by several Lutheran writers. As Christa Klein remarks:

> Coincidental with the loss of interest in American Lutheran history is the division of Lutherans on the future course of

ca/CTCR/LCC-ELCIC.pdf: "Where Canada's Lutherans stand." It consists of two texts running parallel to one another, issued by the Lutheran Church-Canada (which is close to the LC-Missouri Synod) and the Evangelical Lutheran Church in Canada (close to the ELCA). In these texts both churches describe their church organizations, present a confession of faith, and include summary accounts on various church positions—mission statements, ecclesiology, sacraments, worship, ecumenism, homosexuality, abortion, etc.

27. On the problem of intra-denominational conflicts and possible solutions see van Driel, "Church and Covenant," and Flanagan, "Communion Ecclesiology," 62–75 and 141–60 respectively, in Thiessen (ed.), *Ecumenical Ecclesiology*.

American Lutheranism ... Lutherans were wracked by the same tensions, albeit to a lesser degree, that absorbed most other denominations. The political right and left, theological liberalism and strains of fundamentalism, the charismatic movement and the rise of managerial styles of leadership all found nourishment in American Lutheranism.[28]

Differences: European and North American Lutherans

Reading the various contributors to *Lutherans Today, American Lutheran Identity in the 21st Century*,[29] as well as other writers who have reflected on Lutheran history in the United States, a European would be struck by the diversity of Lutheran groupings and theological outlooks that developed in North America, including significant tendencies towards pietism, biblical fundamentalism, and puritanism.

Mark Granquist, Luther Seminary, St. Paul, Minnesota comments how Lutheranism in the U.S. is largely a story of "synodical mergers and the march to ever larger and more complex denominational structures."[30] While in the mid-nineteenth century "over one hundred synods" existed in "twelve major groupings," "today 95 percent of the 8.5 million American Lutherans are members of the two largest denominations, the Evangelical Lutheran Church in America (5.1 million members) and the Lutheran Church–Missouri Synod (2.6 million members)" as well as the "Wisconsin Evangelical Lutheran Synod (400.000 members)." "A dozen or so of very small Lutheran groups," mostly "dissenters from previous mergers," can be added.[31] Granquist points out how mergers have been regarded as the work of the Holy Spirit uniting Christians of Lutheran confession, but, he points out, such a romantic view of Lutheran denominational history is "greatly flawed" as it does not take into account the numerous problems and costs associated with mergers, leading to "hard feelings and disenchant-

---

28. Klein, "Lutherans, Merger and the Loss of History," 19–20. See also Cimino who, like Klein, and with reference to Wuthnow, remarks on the inner divisions in the ELCA. "Evangelical Catholics," 96. See also Wuthnow, *Restructuring of American Religion*.

29. Cimino, ed., *Lutherans Today, American Lutheran Identity in the 21st Century*.

30. Granquist, "Word Alone and the Future of Lutheran Denominationalism," 62.

31. Ibid.

ment" and exposing "theological and ecclesiastical cracks that are endemic to American Lutheranism."[32]

While tensions and new or revised alignments are no strangers in European Protestant churches, and, more particularly, in the fellowship of churches of the EKD, differences in theological outlook among German Lutherans would generally not be as striking as they have been in North America. In Germany, a small independent Lutheran Church (Selbständige Evangelisch-Lutherische Kirche) exists with about thirty-six thousand members. It would be regarded as "conservative," with a strong emphasis on the Lutheran confessional writings, and with certain elements that would be closer to traditional Catholic teachings, such as the understanding of ordination (a modified understanding of *in persona Christi*), the non-ordination of women, the role of personal confession, and no intercommunion with "mainstream" Lutherans (even though that has changed in recent times and depends on local contexts). The SELK has links with the Missouri Synod, the Lutheran Church in Lithuania, and in Latvia. But given its very small membership, it plays an insignificant role in Germany. Most Germans today would hardly know that the SELK exists. However, it has to be said that in this church, too, theological and ecclesiological differences make themselves felt. For example, it appears that many of its members would like to see women ordained and are unhappy with the church's links with the LC-MS.

What makes the SELK significant to our theme is its historical origin. It emerged from the "Old Lutherans," i.e., those who, in the 1830s and 1840s, refused to join the Prussian Union, decreed by Friedrich Wilhelm III in 1821, which was a union of Protestant and Reformed churches in Prussia. In disagreement over the new liturgical agenda (book of worship) that the King had ordered, many Lutherans dissented, especially over the issue of the Eucharist. They felt that the real presence in the Eucharist was no longer proclaimed. This dissent led to their suppression, and, in turn, many, in search for religious freedom, emigrated to North America and Australia where they founded new Lutheran denominations. While mainline European Lutherans today might be puzzled how denominations, such as the LC-Missouri Synod, could emerge, it is these historical events, as well as the history, theo-

---

32. Ibid., 62–63.

logical outlook, and ecclesial organization of Scandinavian Churches, including certain Pietist leanings that explain the rise of the Missouri Synod and other such Lutheran Churches in North America.

The Emergence of North American Lutheran Churches as Denominations

Most North American scholars who have reflected on denominations and denominational history remark on how these were seen as somewhat embarrassing subjects by scholars working in universities. In modern, scientific, open, ecumenical university environments, writing about one's church and its tradition was regarded as irrelevant, parochial, defensive, lacking objectivity, and thus was not considered a subject for respectable scholarly engagement.[33] Yet, the need for proper academic works on denominational histories with attention to developments in contemporary historiography has been repeatedly noted.[34]

Jaroslav Pelikan—one of the foremost twentieth-century historians of Christianity, a Lutheran, and later a member of the Orthodox Church—in an article entitled "American Lutheranism: Denomination or Confession?" (1963), attempted to make some future predictions about American Lutheranism. He noted that a "foliation of theological diversity within some sort of confessional unity" was "closer to the tradition of Lutheranism than is the identification of confessional unity with uniformity that many Lutherans in this country [U.S.] would regard as normative."[35] And he points out that American Lutheranism had been influenced both by its ethnicity, being almost exclusively of Nordic stock and "by a Pietism that could be either confessionally rigid or confessionally indifferent without surrendering its distinctive

---

33. Several writers refer to this problem, e.g., some of the contributors to *Reimagining Denominationalism*, including N. T. Ammerman, C. Klein, and R. Richey. See also Tygart and Blaikie from a sociological perspective: Tygart, "On the Inadequacies of the Utilization of the Concept of 'Denomination,'" 87–90; Blaikie, "Comment," 79: "In spite of the fact that the concept 'denomination' (or religious affiliation) has been extensively used in all types of sociological research, little advance appears to have been made in its theoretical elaboration and empirical specification."

34. Bowden, "The Death and Rebirth of Denominational History," 17–30.

35. Pelikan, "American Lutheranism," 1608.

character."³⁶ This strengthening of Pietist traditions that had been brought from Europe was not limited to the Lutheran churches in the U.S., but became determinative for a "large part of the rest of American Protestantism." Pelikan emphasizes that the "coalescence of Puritanism and Pietism" was a hugely neglected area of enquiry in North American church history. Thus, he notes, someone who knows Lutherans only from a European perspective or from the "generalizations about it by Ernst Troeltsch and Karl Barth" would be surprised indeed how "Puritan and theocratic" Lutheran churches in the States could become. However, Pelikan concludes that American Lutheranism would predictably "adapt itself ever more completely to its American Protestant environment during the coming decades, and that eventually, for better or for worse, it will become a denomination."³⁷ This is an interesting and a slightly puzzling conclusion. The very last words would imply that up to this point Pelikan, and others for that matter, would have regarded the Lutheran Church in America in terms of being a "confession" or "church," but not yet as a denomination. What exactly he understands by "denomination" he does not specify, but what it might imply appears to be captured indirectly in his insistence that Lutherans "have nothing to lose but our [their] isolation."³⁸ This is a rather important point, and one that is consistently re-echoed by others, such as Todd Nicholl, Christa Klein, and Mark Noll regarding Lutheran history in North America—its noted "isolation" and "difference." Becoming a "denomination" essentially would imply being challenged by, and living in close dialogue with, other denominations, rather than pursuing an inward-looking attitude of seclusion and separation. Pelikan points out that North American Lutherans had indeed learned much and changed through their encounter with other denominations. However, these positive developments were concurrent with more negative ones. As Pelikan remarks, "at least a confessional isolationism kept its contact with the fathers if not with the brethren, but this new denominationalism runs the risk of following the most shallow contemporary fads in the church even while it still stands off reciting its formulas of discord."³⁹ Thus the "most damaging feature of such denominational-

36. Ibid., 1608.
37. Ibid.
38. Ibid., 1609.
39. Ibid.

ism" could be that it might drain "Lutheran theological vitality." Pelikan urged that Lutherans in future should be "faithful to the text and open to modern thought"; they should take seriously their relationship to other denominations, especially the Catholic Church to which they have a "special responsibility"; and they should become "simultaneously more Catholic and Reformed" instead of seeking only Lutheran unity by clutching their "confessions desperately to . . . [their] breast," thus losing "both Catholic substance and Protestant principle."

Denomination with a Difference

In an important article, "The Lutheran Difference," Mark Noll, professor of history at the University of Notre Dame, writes that impressions about U.S. Lutherans can be "wildly contradictory."[40] When traced through some of their own memoirs and literature, they could be seen as "mildly exotic," "tragic," "interesting," but above all as being "on the fringe."[41] However, as a social group, they appear to have been "pretty ordinary"—mostly middle class, voting predominantly Republican (this may have changed in the most recent election), with 80 percent of Lutherans living in the Midwest.

Most Lutherans emigrated to North America later than those of other mainline Protestant churches, notably between 1840 and World War I, with over 5 million Germans and almost 2 million Scandinavians.[42] Two distinct aspects were hugely influential in shaping their identity—hanging on to their old-world languages and a strong confessional basis. "Gottes Wort und Luthers Lehr' vergehen nie und nimmermehr" (God's word and Luther's teachings will never ever pass away). This was the motto of *Der Lutheraner*,[43] a Lutheran journal founded by C. F. W. Walther in 1844.[44] Such triumphalist language,

---

40. Noll, "Lutheran Difference," 31.

41. "Perhaps the shy Norwegian bachelor farmers populating Lake Wobegon Lutherandom symbolize Lutheran reticence about itself." Cimino, "Introduction," in *Lutherans Today*, x.

42. Noll, "Lutheran Difference," 32. Germans were the largest ethnic group in the USA.

43. This was a newsletter written entirely in German and published in St. Louis, Missouri.

44. Ibid.

Part II: Unity, Diversity, and Ecumenical Praxis

which might occasion a smile today, evidences the sense of pride and religious identity that Lutherans brought to the New World.

Despite such strong confessional belonging, Noll observes how, as a social group, Lutherans have been largely "inconspicuous" in the U.S., almost surprisingly so he maintains, given their strong cultural-theological background, ranging from Luther, Melanchthon, the "irenic" Book of Concord, to Bach, Kierkegaard, and Bonhoeffer.[45] Holding on to their confessions and language, Lutherans were "insulated from American life for a long time."[46] These two elements made them "different." Interestingly, both Todd Nicholl and Mark Noll challenge American Lutherans: they ought to make a specific Lutheran contribution to America. For example, despite their large numbers, with nearly "four times as many Lutherans as Episcopalians, nearly three times as many as either Presbyterians or Jews, and almost as many Methodists,"[47] Lutherans have been seriously under-represented in American national politics. Noll wonders whether the ELCA may have something "authentically Lutheran to contribute," noting, at the same time, Klein's conclusions about "denominational leaders fleeing from distinctive Lutheran doctrines like two-kingdom theology in their haste to be relevant to ... American life" as not being encouraging. While one would sympathize with those who find the two-kingdom theory problematic (and which also has suffered the grossest misinterpretations), it is indeed a challenge whether Lutherans—in the States and Canada, and elsewhere—can offer something distinct and beneficial to contemporary faith and society—distinct in the sense that it is specifically Lutheran, and beneficial in that it must be of wider ecumenical, theological, social, political, or cultural significance.

The mergers of the Lutheran Church of America (LCA) and the American Lutheran Church (ALC), which led to the Evangelical Lutheran Church of America (ELCA), is considered a mixed blessing; it has been remarked how Lutheranism thereby lost some of its distinctiveness.[48] Noll makes several suggestions as to what elements in Lutheran teaching may be of relevance in the future: history as being

45. Ibid., 33.

46. A comment by Winthrop Hudson in his book *American Protestantism* (1961), quoted in Klein, "Denominational History," 307.

47. Noll, "Lutheran Difference," 33.

48. Noll refers to a comment by Peter Berger. Cf. Noll, "Lutheran Difference," 36.

important to faith, a long view of history that might prevent against too much fluctuation and instability, a rightly interpreted two-kingdom theory, a "noble theological tradition," the theology of the cross,[49] and the "Lutheran gift of ambiguity"—"the paradoxes . . . *simul justus et peccator*, Law [sic] and gospel as two sides of the same thing."[50] Significantly he notes: "Rarely have American Christians considered Luther's tension with culture, which saw him committed to Christian activity, but always with the sharpest reservations."[51] In the face of Naziism and other totalitarian, or exploitative, unjust cultures, including neo-capitalism and its deep failures, Luther's call for Christian cultural involvement *and* critical distance, may indeed still have something to say to Western civilization! Nicholl observes that Lutherans may have resources to be explored for mission in "the contemporary United States," in modern politics, understanding of faith, science and liberal education, church order, and ministry.[52]

Conclusion: Towards the One Body of Christ

The history of Lutherans in North America emerges as having been shaped by many strands, struggling to find unity—and not always quite succeeding—while also being ecumenically minded, and becoming denomination(s) alongside others. Synods, splits, and mergers are part of it.

From a European perspective, the fact that two large Lutheran denominations (ELCA and LC-MS) exist side by side is perhaps strangest of all. In addition, over the last forty years, a "dramatic growth of parachurch groups, renewal movements, and caucuses within and on the edges of denominational life" has happened in North America, and Lutherans are no exception.[53] This is a sign of the diversification among

---

49. Cf. ibid., 37–40.
50. Noll, "Americans Lutherans," 21. See also Nicholl, "Lutheran Venture," 162: "An often uncritical acceptance of nineteenth-century confessional theology and the twentieth-century pre-occupation with denominational affairs, mergers, and an increasingly retrospective ecumenism has severely limited the American Lutheran imagination."
51. Noll, "Americans Lutherans," 21.
52. Cf. Nicholl, "Lutheran Venture," 159–64.
53. Cimino, "Introduction," *Lutherans Today*, x–xi.

and across denominations, including an accommodation of the "seeker culture," the growing pick-and-choose *à-la-carte* way of living one's faith within a denomination while also getting involved in movements and events of other denominations and faith groups.

Is the Lutheran Church a denomination? Obviously, yes. Yet, the idea of "denomination," while recognizing the church's diversity, implies, as Ensign-George argues, partiality and permeability vis-à-vis the one, holy, catholic, and apostolic church of Christ, which most of those belonging to denominations confess at worship each Sunday. Nor is "denomination" much used when Lutheran Churches refer to themselves. In the German context, where there are essentially two large churches (the Evangelische Kirche Deutschlands and the Catholic Church), the term "denomination" is hardly used at all, even though in the last decade there has been a rise of small independent churches and trans-denominational movements in Germany and other parts of Europe.

Lutheran Churches worldwide refer to themselves as *church*. Mark Hanson, presiding bishop of the ELCA, in an article, "The Future of Denominations: Asking Uppercase Questions" rightly points out that "denomination" is not found in the Bible; rather it is a "phenomenon of history and context."[54] According to him, denominations are needed, but not as competing in the supermarket of religion, with institutional survival as their primary aim. With reference to his colleague, Charles Miller, Hanson declares that "'whither denominations' is a lowercase question, while the question of the mission to which God calls us is the uppercase question . . . What kind of church serves God's mission in the world today?"[55] This is what essentially matters. For Hanson the biblical images of the vine and branches and being members of the one body of Christ are powerful pointers towards understanding that mission—the body metaphor being "the classic illustration of unity in diversity."[56] And so he notes the danger of denominations defining themselves by issues that divide them—thus dividing the body of Christ—rather than seeking to focus on the "gospel, faith and mission that unite them." Hanson therefore suggests that Lutheran identity should be thought of "in terms

---

54. Hanson, "Future of Denominations," 7.
55. Ibid., 9.
56. Ibid., 10–11.

of what we bring as *a part of* the body of Christ, even as we are open to receiving the gifts of others."[57] Like Nichol and Noll, he emphasizes that the strengths of Lutheran faith lie in "justification by grace through faith," "the priesthood of all believers," "the freedom of the Christian," and, in particular, its paradoxical, dialectical emphasis—law *and* gospel, *simul justus* et *peccator*, "creation as good *and* fallen," Jesus "human *and* divine, crucified *and* risen," "God hidden *and* revealed," and "faith *and* reason in healthy tension." These are gifts that Lutherans can bring to the whole body of Christ, the church universal.

Naturally, every denomination has its own strengths and can offer these to fellow Christians. Is it, however, realistic to think that denominations will be only too eager to adopt the strengths of other denominations as their own? Indeed, how do we assert something as being a "strength" or "weakness" in the first place? Who can judge? In an ideal world, one could imagine that the strong points of each denomination would be ascertained, then the churches would agree to all of these, and, finally, the one church—wholly reformed—would result, denominations would cease, and we would be one church again. The reality, however, with the existence of hundreds of denominations, including the Catholic and Orthodox churches, and the world of ecumenism itself disparate and wholly unclear which model of church unity to adopt, looks very different. While the unity of the one church of Christ must always remain our (eschatological!?) hope and aspiration, it seems that denominations are here to stay for a while to come.

But when focusing on the ecumenical aim of unity in diversity, could we envisage that denominations might be cherished as *local/regional churches*, and that churches will increasingly recognize each other as *church*, agree on fundamentals, including the full acceptance of each other's ministry, enjoying altar and pulpit fellowship? Differentiated consensus agreements, such as Porvoo, may be a good guide to seek such unity in diversity.

There are voices who speak of the possible demise of the mainline denominations. Indeed, they may be threatened by the rise of Pentecostal churches and new ecclesial movements. In the face of this Hanson's asks: "How will those called to serve denominations respond to the growing evidence that people in this culture seek meaning in life,

---

57. Ibid., 12.

want faith to matter, and seek to be part of a church that makes a difference not only in their lives but also in the life of the world?"[58]

If churches cannot respond to such questions and give convincing witness to their Christian faith and confessions in the social, religious, intellectual, and ethnic contexts in which they find themselves, then, indeed, there seems little hope or reason why they should survive.

Luther's dictum "A Christian is the most free lord of all, and subject to none; a Christian is the most dutiful servant of all, and subject to every one" may be a prophetic starting point—not just for Lutheran denominations but for all those who believe in the one, holy, catholic, and apostolic church. To bring something of Christ's radical message of God's kingdom of love, freedom, and justice into this world surely must remain the task of, and the bond between, all Christian denominations into the future.

58. Ibid.

5

Ecumenism in Praxis: Critical Observations on the Week of Prayer for Christian Unity

IN THIS CHAPTER I will consider the emergence of the Week of Prayer for Christian Unity as one of the oldest and most significant events in the ecumenical quest for church unity. This annual event has played a central role in ecumenical praxis through the twentieth century and continues into our own day. However, one might argue that it is increasingly becoming a pleasant if unexciting "institution" rather than a challenging impetus for ecumenical progress. While it celebrates the church's unity in diversity, my concern is to ask how it could become once again a driving force for unity and lead to renewed ecumenical commitment and apostolic witness between parishes, dioceses, and denominations.

Jesus' prayer for his disciples that they ought to be one in John 17 is a poignant reminder that conversion is at the heart of what it means to follow Christ. It is this prayer on which all prayer for Christian unity is based and from where it takes its inspiration. Ecumenical engagement requires an openness to (self-)correction, reform, and conversion. Naturally, this cannot mean that members of the various churches should deny deep and long-held convictions. Authentic dialogue on ecclesial doctrines entails moments when frontiers seem impossible to cross. Yet, if one is not prepared to enter new ground, dialogue becomes impossible and change and progress cannot occur.

Part II: Unity, Diversity, and Ecumenical Praxis

In this light I will set out to discuss the annual Week of Prayer for Christian Unity. In the following I will outline the history and theology of the Week of Prayer, the notion of spiritual ecumenism, and then consider the Week's achievements and my central question: Has the Week become a "comfortable institution," or does it continue to serve as a real challenge and force for Christian unity? I will finish with some suggestions for future church initiatives in our ecumenical quest.

The History of the Week of Prayer

Traditionally, the Week of Prayer is celebrated throughout the Churches from January 18–25. In the southern hemisphere, Christians hold the Week around the feast of Pentecost. The Octave has several roots. Chronologically, it can be traced back to nineteenth-century Anglican circles, especially the Oxford Movement, as well as to the Evangelical Alliance founded in 1846 in London by 921 participants of various denominations.[1] The Alliance, one of the oldest movements for church unity and still in existence today, consists of a loose union of members from churches in Europe and North America. At the time, the Congregationalist Free Churches, in particular, expressed an interest in forming a non-binding union that would bring to expression the desire for unity in faith beyond the level of the independent parish.[2] In London, these evangelical Christians stated their wish that the week after the first Sunday in January should be designated for prayer amongst Christians "for the one Church of Jesus Christ," thereby celebrating and realizing the unity that exists by the fact that all belong to the one Christ.[3]

An "Association for the Promotion of the Unity of Christendom" was founded in 1857 by two Catholics, Ambrose Phillips de Lisle and A.W. Pugin, and by the Anglican, Frederick George Lee. Its aim was to further prayer for the re-establishment of the "visible unity of Christianity."[4] The Association brought together Roman Catholics,

---

1. No name given, "Prayer for Unity," 251. See also Heller, "Gebetswoche für die Einheit der Christen," 110–11.
2. Vogt, "Evangelische Allianz," 90–91.
3. "Prayer for Unity," 251–52.
4. Heller, "Seele der ökumenischen Bewegung," 313.

Orthodox, and Anglicans.⁵ However, Pope Pius IX did not approve of it, and in 1864 Roman Catholics were forbidden to become members of the Association. He may have felt the time was not yet ripe for this move.

In 1895 things began to improve. Pope Leo XIII ordered that each year Catholics should pray on the days between the Feast of the Ascension and Pentecost for "reconciliation with our separated brethren."⁶ Although it did not receive much resonance, at least papal concern was shown for a rapprochement of Catholics with Christians of other denominations. Some Anglican groups shared the call for prayer, notably the Anglican priest Lewis Thomas Wattson (1863–90), who, deeply inspired by the desire for church unity, was to assume a pivotal role in promoting the Week of Prayer.⁷ Together with Lurana White, an Anglican nun, he founded *The Society of the Atonement* in 1898 as a branch of the family of Franciscan Orders in Graymoor in the States, and from 1908 took the name of Paul James Francis Wattson.⁸ John 17 was inspiration for him, and he proposed the Octave to be held between January 18 (then the Feast of the Chair of Peter) and January 25 (Feast of the Conversion of Paul). This Octave was first inaugurated in 1908 and in the following year Pius X gave his blessing.⁹ By this time Wattson had changed ecclesial allegiance and had entered the Catholic Church. It was Benedict XV who extended the Octave to the whole Catholic Church, an event which has been approved by each pope since. Initially, it was hoped that the Week of Prayer would lead all "separated brethren" to be reunited under the Roman Catholic Church. However, a simple notion of "home to Rome" was, of course, insensitive and could not work. Subsequently, a more objective attitude of a desire towards unity became operative among Catholics.

Some events and forerunner movements that would eventually combine into the World Council of Churches coincided with and partly influenced the history of the Octave. The international, interdenomina-

5. "Prayer for Unity," 252.

6. Ibid. Heller, "Seele der ökumenischen Bewegung," 313.

7. "Prayer for Unity," 252.

8. Heller, "Seele der ökumenischen Bewegung," 313. Curtis, *Paul Couturier and Unity in Christ*, 59.

9. "Prayer for Unity," 252. In the following paragraphs I am relying mainly on this article for information.

Part II: Unity, Diversity, and Ecumenical Praxis

tional world missionary conference (later the International Missionary Council [IMC]) took place in Edinburgh in 1910. Another root in the genesis of the Week of Prayer was the work of the Faith and Order Movement. In 1920 the preparatory committee for the first world conference of Faith and Order proposed a Week of Prayer for Unity to be held annually around Pentecost. The Life and Work Movement started with the eminent ecumenist Nathan Söderblom, Archbishop of Uppsala, in 1925. During this time, too, the Malines Conversations (1921–26) took place in Belgium between Anglicans and Roman Catholics under Cardinal Mercier, and a new more irenic atmosphere took hold. Faith and Order met for the first time in Lausanne in 1927.[10] The WCC, finally, was founded in Amsterdam in 1948.

These events in both Roman Catholic and Protestant circles form the background to Abbé Paul Irénée Couturier's (1881–1953) milestone contribution to the history of the Week of Prayer.[11] A French priest, of "profound humility and at the same time unparalleled audacity,"[12] he spent most of his life in Lyons. He worked with Russian Orthodox refugees and became a hugely influential leader in the ecumenical movement, notably as the driving force behind the Week of Prayer and as the founder of Le Groupe des Dombes (1937). The discussions among this small independent ecumenical group of French Catholic and Protestant pastors and priests, held annually at the Abbey of La Trappe Les Dombes near Lyon, were later to prove influential on some key ecumenical texts, e.g., the *Decree on Ecumenism (UR)* and *Baptism, Eucharist and Ministry (BEM)*.[13] One of their central convictions was that ecumenical progress could only come about through continual conversion.

Couturier's interest in ecumenism was roused after a stay in the Benedictine monastery at Amay-sur-Meuse in 1932 (from 1939 at home

10. For the history of the World Council of Churches, see van Elderen, *Introducing the World Council of Churches*.

11. For literature on the life of Paul Couturier, see Villain, *L'Abbé Paul Couturier*; and Curtis, *Paul Couturier and Unity in Christ*. Curtis points out that his own book is largely based on Villain's book. A conference was held on Couturier's significance, the proceedings of which were published as *The Unity of Christians: The Vision of Paul Couturier*.

12. Bobrinskoy, "Theological Basis of Common Prayer," 274.

13. For information on the Groupe des Dombes see Curtis, *Paul Couturier and Unity in Christ*.

in Chevetogne).[14] In 1933 he received a letter from Wattson who might therefore be attributed with having been influential on Couturier's famous idea of "spiritual ecumenism,"[15] a notion that became of central importance in the *Decree on Ecumenism* in the documents of Vatican II, and that continues to be vital in ecumenical life and theology.[16] Couturier introduced a Triduum Prayer for Christian unity at Lyons in 1933, which was followed by an octave of prayer from January 18–25 in 1934. Inspired by John 17, Couturier felt profoundly the separation of Christians, which in turn convinced him that unity could only be furthered through a renewal of spiritual life. Although he remained loyal to the teachings of his church, he was acutely aware that the idea of a return to Rome could and would never work with non-Catholics. Couturier, "the grand apostle and pioneer of spiritual ecumenism,"[17] proposed the universal Week of Prayer for Christian Unity. It was he who finally formulated the intention of the Week and thereby enabled all Christians to pray together. Such prayer would not mean a return to Rome but rather to "pray for the unity God wills, by the ways and means he wills."[18] At first, some Catholics were reluctant to support it since to them the original Octave seemed watered down.[19]

In 1940 the Faith and Order Movement recommended that the dates for the Week of Prayer, "which had remained unchanged since 1920,"[20] ought to be observed in January so as to coincide with the Catholic Octave. In an apostolic letter in 1959, John XXIII endorsed the Week. The Second Vatican Council, especially the *Decree on Ecumenism* (1964) with its emphasis on prayer for unity, thus enabled a much closer cooperation between Couturier's successor P. Pierre Michalon in Lyon and the Secretariat of Faith and Order in the World Council of Churches. By 1966 complete agreement was reached concerning preparations for the annual celebrations of the Week. In that year the WCC

---

14. The monastery is set up in two groups, the Western and the Eastern (Greek and Slavonic) rite.

15. "Prayer for Unity," 253.

16. See, for example, Kasper's article "Spiritual Ecumenism" in Kasper, *That They May All Be One*, 155–72.

17. Kasper, *That They May All Be One*, 156.

18. Couturier cited in Congar, "Theology of Prayer for Unity," 269.

19. Heller, "Seele der ökumenischen Bewegung," 314.

20. Fey, *Ecumenical Advance*, 2:322.

and the Pontifical Secretariat for the Promotion of Christian Unity held a consultation at which it was decided that in future the materials for each Week of Prayer should be prepared by a common workgroup. In 1973 a new method was introduced. An ecumenical group of one particular country is invited to prepare a basic draft on a biblical theme and then an international work group with WCC-sponsored participants of the Protestant, Orthodox, and Catholic Church edits the materials in such a way that they can be used worldwide. The texts are then sent to the WCC member churches and to Catholic dioceses in the various countries which can contextualize and use these in their own situation. A further small step was achieved in 2005 when the text was not only prepared, but also for the first time jointly published between the Faith and Order Commission of the WCC and the Pontifical Council for Promoting Christian Unity.

The Theological Foundation of Prayer for Unity

Ecumenism is founded on Jesus' prayer in John 17 for his disciples shortly before the beginning of his passion. Christ exhorts them to keep and to grow in unity and thus witness their faith in him: "I ask . . . that they may all be one. As you, Father, are in me and I am in you, may they also be in us, so that the world may believe that you have sent me" (John 17:21). Here, Jesus prayed emphatically for continued unity among his disciples. In fact, John 17 is his only explicit prayer for the unity of his followers.[21] Such unity ought to reflect the unity between him and the Father. The people of God are to make apparent something of the inner-trinitarian perichoretic love in their life as a Christian community. We are taken into the trinitarian unity by trying to emulate its unity. In this way ecumenical theology is grounded in trinitarian theology, in our faith in the triune God. This applies in a special way to the Week of Prayer, as precisely in its focus on prayer it takes up Jesus' prayer, which manifested his concern for his followers in unparalleled intensity. Christ interceded for his disciples and continues to intercede for his followers (Rom 8:34). It is God's love that Christ received "before the foundation of the world" (John 17:24) and into all eternity, which he wishes to be at work among the disciples. As Christ is the head of

---

21. Bobrinskoy, "Theological Basis of Common Prayer," 276.

Ecumenism in Praxis: Critical Observations on the Week of Prayer

the Christian community we are to strive continually towards greater community through prayer.

The prayer in John 17 and the promise of the Holy Spirit in John 14 epitomize what is required of Jesus' followers time and again, to pray to God in Christ and to call on the Holy Spirit to be present so as to enable and effect unity. *Epiclesis* is central to the ecumenical quest, especially when Christians pray together for unity and celebrate the unity they already have. Christ promised the sending of the Paraclete, the Comforter, to be with his people in the time when he would no longer be with them. "And I will ask the Father, and he will give you another Advocate, to be with you forever. This is the Spirit of truth . . . You know him, because he abides with you, and he will be in you" (John 14:16–17). This promise of the presence of the Holy Spirit amongst Jesus' friends is at the heart of the farewell discourse.[22] It is the Spirit who continues the work of the Son and who must be present in our endeavour for the visible unity of all believers and churches. It is through the Spirit that the disciples will be guided into truth (John 16:13, 17).

The Spirit who is truth will glorify the Son. It is Christ's wish that his followers will see and receive his glory. "The glory that you have given me I have given them, so that they may be one, as we are one . . ." (John 17:22–23). The Orthodox theologian Boris Bobrinskoy noted that the entire farewell discourse "places us in the framework of this glorification, which is both accomplished and yet to be completed . . ."[23] (John 14:31–32). The disciples will "know" through the presence of the Spirit that Jesus is in his Father and they in Christ, and Christ in them (John 14:20).

However, Christ is aware that his followers' unity is always at risk in the world, that when he has left them they will be under threat "in the world" to which he has sent them (John 17:18). Therefore they need divine protection. He asks the Father to sanctify them in the truth. As Jesus knew, rivalry and jealousy, human discord and weakness were present among his friends, too; thus his prayer is urgent. Hence the "supreme injunction of the farewell discourse is the commandment of love."[24] "Love one another, as I have loved you" is Jesus' profound wish.

---

22. Ibid., 278.
23. Ibid., 277.
24. Ibid., 280.

Part II: Unity, Diversity, and Ecumenical Praxis

In his prayer, the meaning of this love is established, i.e., love as communion and unity. Such love is at the heart of his prayer and forms the foundation for Christian living, for the church community and thus for any ecumenical endeavor. Christ's disciples must form a *comm-unity* in order to be witnesses of faith in the world. They do not belong to the world; they may be hated by the world, yet they must witness Christ *in* and *to* the world. Thus it is God who needs our unity. Without unity in which the Spirit prevails, the world will not recognise the God of and in Jesus Christ, the triune God.

Spiritual Ecumenism

The term spiritual ecumenism has become central to the ecumenical movement. This notion has been prevalent for decades, starting with Abbé Couturier, whom Yves Congar named the "father of spiritual ecumenism."[25] With his momentous influence, the Week of Prayer was to become a universal event in the Christian churches. Couturier believed that it is essential first of all "to touch the hearts of men [and women] in order that souls may have a chance of mutual understanding."[26] Ecumenical progress and true unity cannot be established without Christians coming together to pray. This is what comes before and must accompany any ecumenical work. Above all, it is one of the fundamental means of celebrating the unity that we already possess. The late German Bishop Erich Eichele pointed out that it is important to remember that praying for unity does not mean that we pray for something that we do not possess, but rather that we need to "prevent the unity which does exist . . . from being paralyzed through indifferent coexistence, obstinate separation or hostile animosity."[27] While undoubtedly this is true and deeply important, more radical ecumenists might argue that it is one aspect of ecumenical prayer to which concrete prayer for and persistent engagement dealing with thorny, unresolved questions must be added.

Couturier's view is reflected in one of the central passages (par. 7, 8) in *Unitatis Redintegratio* (1964): "There can be no ecumenism

---

25. Curtis, *Paul Couturier and Unity in Christ*, 51.
26. Ibid., 50.
27. Eichele, "Reflections on the Universal Week of Prayer," 292.

worthy of the name without a change of heart . . . This change of heart and holiness of life, along with public and private prayer for the unity of Christians, should be regarded as the soul of the whole ecumenical movement, and merits the name 'spiritual ecumenism.'"

Walter Kasper, in his role as head of the Pontifical Council for Promoting Christian Unity, continually emphasized spiritual ecumenism as being intrinsic to the ecumenical quest. He has pointed out that in order to get the ecumenical aim revitalised, we must "return to the very first impetus of the ecumenical movement . . . [to] spiritual ecumenism."[28] It demands prayer, conversion, repentance, key experiences and actions that are "greater and stronger than human undertakings and academic debate."[29] What is crucial is a genuine ecumenical spirituality, not one that is happy to operate on a superficial or pseudo level, but is grounded in the Bible, in Christ, in Christian truth, guided by the Holy Spirit and deepened through theological reflection. In this way trust and friendship can be established by people of different denominations that in turn leads them to a greater, more truthful, understanding of the other.[30] Here dialogue that neither coerces the other nor shies away from focussing on, what Kasper calls, the "hard core" of our "institutional ecclesiological differences" becomes possible. Prayer is at the heart of this dialogue, and thus the Week of Prayer is an important and fundamental facet in ecumenical activity. However, Kasper also rightly notes that ecumenical spirituality "is not a magic formula which will easily solve ecumenical questions and the present ecumenical crisis."[31] Nevertheless, prayer, repentance, and conversion remain a prerequisite to and accompany all ecumenical progress.

---

28. Kasper, *That They May All Be One*, 156.

29. Ibid.

30. See also on ecumenical spirituality Augustin, "Ökumene als geistlicher Prozess," 522–50.

31. Kasper, *That They May All Be One*, 161. "Spiritualities . . . carry the danger of syncretism . . ." They "can also be appropriated for political reasons and aims, giving the Christian faith not only a national but also a nationalistic, chauvinist or ideologically pseudo-spiritual character. In some forms of religious fundamentalism this danger is all too obvious."

Part II: Unity, Diversity, and Ecumenical Praxis

The Week of Prayer:
From Challenge to "Institution" and Beyond

The universal Week of Prayer, when first developed over half a century ago, gave great impetus and hope to the ecumenical movement. Christians of one confession who hitherto would have looked suspiciously at those of another, or, worse, would have been taught that it was positively a sin to attend a service in a church other than their own, were now encouraged once a year to explore and celebrate their common faith with believers of other traditions. Ecumenical writing of that time is filled with gratitude and enthusiasm for this annual event. It helped to remove prejudices and create new friendships and contacts.

"An ever widening support"[32] for the Week reigned in the 1960s; it was perceived as "a week in which we repent and listen to what the Lord's will is for us, in the present state of contradiction between our oneness in Christ and our disunity as churches."[33] In 1967 Bobrinskoy noted that in "recent years this Week has become a spiritual institution in the various Christian communions, and it has now come to be *an increasingly significant event* at parish level since Vatican II."[34] In those years of hope and of an ecumenical spring the Week was achieving what it intended. Having become the universal Week of Prayer in 1948, it is clear that about twenty years later in the sixties it continued to be perceived as a life-giving event in the ecumenical world, gaining increasing popularity.

Forty years later we find ourselves in a changed situation. Widespread frustration and, increasingly, anger that despite countless dialogues and common statements, endless ecumenical meetings, and prayer, the common sharing of the Eucharist by Catholics and Protestants is still forbidden from the Catholic side (apart from exceptional cases),[35] is making itself felt. To add to the dilemma, *Dominus Iesus* (2000), in particular, caused hurt and anger among Protestants as well as among many Roman Catholics.

---

32. "Prayer for Unity," 260.
33. Eichele, "Reflections on the Universal Week of Prayer," 294.
34. Bobrinskoy, "Theological Basis of Common Prayer," 275. My emphasis.
35. The encyclical on the Eucharist (2003) by the late John Paul II strongly reiterated that a common Eucharist is only permissible when full unity is established.

Ecumenism in Praxis: Critical Observations on the Week of Prayer

On the other hand, only a few months prior to the controversial *Dominus Iesus*, Catholics and Lutherans celebrated the *Joint Declaration on Justification* (1999), a milestone in ecumenical relations, and a binding agreement between the two churches. Further, *In One Body through the Cross, The Princeton Proposal for Christian Unity* was published by an ecumenical study group of U.S. theologians in 2003,[36] and the substantial common statement of the tenth round of the U.S. Lutheran–Roman Catholic Dialogue, *The Church as Koinonia of Salvation: Its Structures and Ministries*,[37] was issued in 2004. The Anglican–Roman Catholic International Commission (ARCIC) released a common statement on Marian theology entitled *Mary: Grace and Hope in Christ*.[38] Also progress between the Roman Catholic and Orthodox churches has been fostered in recent times under John Paul II and his successor. John Paul's *Ut Unum Sint: On Commitment to Ecumenism* (1995) here also must be mentioned, with its emphasis on spiritual ecumenism, i.e., conversion and prayer, and his call to church leaders to discuss with him the role of the bishop of Rome. These are a few hopeful signs on the largely fragmented ecumenical horizon, even if, apart from the justification statement, the documents are not officially binding for the churches involved.

The situation then is not one of general, steady progress, but progress in pockets here and there, with sometimes painful and unnecessary regressions, leading to frustration and resignation. The world of ecumenism, if not at a stand still, has for many certainly lost its élan, its attraction, and its momentous impact of half a century ago. For ecumenists it is difficult to keep going, and in reaction, in part, to recent unhelpful official Catholic statements and, in part, to the need for ecclesial and individual identity in a scattered world with both fundamentalism and relativism at its extremes, there is an increasing danger among denominations of a retreat into confessionalism. *Deo gratias* there are some for whom the scandal of division still remains a burning issue that demands on-going effort and commitment.

So what is happening concerning the Week of Prayer? Naturally, it is impossible for any one writer to ascertain what exactly is going

---

36. Braaten and Jenson, *In One Body through the Cross*. See also a critical analysis of this document by de Mey, "Call to Conversion," 1–10.

37. Online: www.usccb.org/seia/koinonia.htm.

38. The document was issued on May 16, 2005, in Seattle, as the "Seattle Statement."

Part II: Unity, Diversity, and Ecumenical Praxis

on worldwide. I am writing in the Irish context. It is therefore mainly against this background that I will try to voice some observations.

In countries in the northern hemisphere there has been a general decline in participation in the Week of Prayer over the last fifteen to twenty years.[39] This goes hand in hand with the general crisis in the ecumenical movement. High expectations have not been fulfilled, especially in relation to Eucharistic communion. Many have simply become impatient, while others seem quite content to leave things as they are, partly out of fear of change and partly out of complacency.[40]

Around Ireland the Week is still celebrated each year in various venues. The opening services are joyful, festive events that are carefully prepared with considerable thought and liturgical acumen. What one cannot but notice, however, is the age bracket. Approximately 75 percent of the attendants at these services are above the age of sixty. This is the generation of Vatican II, of the ecumenical spring, who remain devoted to the ecumenical quest. Some young people in their teens and twenties may be specially invited, not least to instill a sense of future hope for church unity. This age profile says a lot about the state of the church in general and ecumenism in particular. The increasing popularity that Eichele and Bobrinskoy gladly noted about the Week and about ecumenical progress is no longer apparent. The enthusiasm for the Week seems to have evaporated and now it appears to be more of an annual *event of duty* one must get on with rather than a week one looks forward to with genuine joy and excitement. The Week of Prayer has become a comfortable institution where we are *reminded* of the ecumenical cause, but seemingly have lost the radical passion to make new things happen. During the Week we share prayers, liturgy, tea, buns, and pleasantries, and then, for the most part, retreat back into our own denominations for another year. This may sound cynical, but, unfortunately, it appears to be true. How many still consider the Week a vibrant ecumenical force? How many of us genuinely look forward to it each year? For some it is still a real concern, especially those who volunteer to be involved in and prepare it, but of those ministers and priests who are obliged to attend the various services during the Week, how many really see it as an *essential and fundamental* part of their ministry? How

---

39. Cf. Heller, "Seele der ökumenischen Bewegung," 318.
40. Ibid.

many draw life from it and follow it up by ongoing ecumenical activities in their parishes all year round?[41]

By now the reader will sense my own ambiguous sentiments in relation to the Week. I have to admit that I do not greatly look forward to the Week, and this has to do primarily with the sad fact that ecumenical progress on the level of concrete ecclesial reception is happening at less than a snail's pace with the occasional reverse gear. What gives me hope and encouragement, however, is the work and the freedom of the Holy Spirit. She blows happily where she wills, at times delightfully undisturbed by rules and regulations. She breathes in the faithful of all traditions, many of whom, at a rapidly increasing rate, can no longer see a problem with eucharistic hospitality and intercommunion.

Ecumenism *is* working; it is alive and well amongst the people of God, even if there are those who apparently wish to control and hold back the divine power of unity in the Holy Spirit. It is among many of the lay faithful that ecumenism becomes a transforming spiritual and prophetic force. The Week of Prayer can continue to play a significant role if we are willing not to rest with it but foster further actions as "offsprings" from it. Prophetic voices and activities are imperative in these times when the whole ecumenical movement has become complex, confused, and difficult to survey, on the one hand, and stagnant on the other. In the following, I want to make a few suggestions about how this might happen.

The encouraging and important aspect about the Week is the fact that it is and has long been accepted and celebrated by the majority of the historic churches. It therefore constitutes an important link between the WCC and the Roman Catholic Church, which should not be underestimated.[42] Even if one might feel cynical at times about the lack of real enthusiasm with which it is now "kept," as one might put it, it *can* continue to function as a high point in spiritual ecumenical activity. One cannot ignore something that is already firmly established. But the

---

41. For example, an interesting survey, conducted by the Irish School of Ecumenics, Trinity College, Dublin, in 2009, revealed that clergy on the island of Ireland, when asked how much time in percentage should be spent annually on ecumenical activities, generally thought that less than 10 percent was appropriate, while 48 percent of lay people have never been involved in any ecumenical activities. See Ganiel, *21st Century Faith*.

42. Cf. Heller, "Seele der ökumenischen Bewegung," 316.

important issue here is whether priests, pastors, et al. will content themselves with just that or whether they are prepared to give new life to the Week to further and promote flourishing ecumenical fellowship.[43] For example, each year the faith leaders in a given community, parish or diocese, or just between two neighbouring congregations, could decide to introduce one or more particular ecumenical engagement(s). These could include:

- Encouraging the faithful to attend services/masses of neighbor communities *once a month* and building up personal friendships with the faithful of those neighboring churches. This would be a huge step forward as it would make people clearly aware that *we are*, in fact, *in a time of transition* towards full unity.
- Joint ownership/sharing of church buildings of different denominations. There are a few places where this is already operative. One would hope that such ownership will become much more common in future—and not primarily for reasons of "rationalization" and financial necessity!
- Ecumenical Bible study groups that meet on a regular basis.
- Ecumenical prayer groups, rituals, and services.
- Common celebration of offices (e.g., matins, lauds); *agape* meals.
- Involvement in social/community/aid work: ecumenical pastoral teams for visiting the aged and the sick in hospital and at home; meals on wheels; common fundraising for development projects in the southern hemisphere; common charity projects.
- Common engagement in environmental issues.
- Shared pilgrimages and outings.
- Regular mutual invitations to parish feasts, leisure activities, etc.
- Mutual invitations to celebrations of common and separate Christian feasts (e.g., Christmas, Annunciation, Easter, Pentecost, Trinity, Reformation Day [October 31], All Saints, All Souls, etc.).

These are some possibilities. Most important in all of this would be the shift of emphasis from coming together for worship once a year to

---

43. Ibid., 316–19.

meeting on a far more frequent basis. This would concretize the ultimate ecumenical aim: visible unity. It would foster the unity we already have, can have, and will have in fullness one day. It makes real that this "one day" is not a never-never, but a reality which is *in reach*. Of course, such ecumenical ventures are already established in some parishes to a greater or lesser extent. But they are wholly dependent on whether the respective clergy consider it a priority. If the churches would commit themselves from the required annual Week of Prayer to *monthly and weekly activities*, a massive step would be made towards full unity. In this context it must be said that the *Charta Oecumenica* (2001), like so many other statements, still awaits realization "on the ground" in the European churches.[44] Naturally, such commitment in order to work must be freely chosen and encouraged in each church. Decisions "from above" that end up being taken on grudgingly and lacking in enthusiasm would only lead to what one senses at present about the Week of Prayer. In that way it is of fundamental importance that all church leaders/clergy must freely pledge and actively foster renewed ecumenical commitment.

Further, services and masses could take on a much greater ecumenical dimension with some simple changes. For example, in Germany both the Protestant and the Catholic hymnbooks have many hymns in common. Churches could agree on one common hymnbook. Also, the member churches of the World Council of Churches and the Catholic Church could have one common lectionary so that all "mainline" churches would share the same biblical readings/themes each Sunday. In fact, it is surprising that this has not already happened. Moreover, at the prayers of intercession, each community should not only pray for the faithful, clergy, and leaders of its own church, but also always for members and leaders of other (neighboring) churches. In fact, this has been recommended in the *Charta Oecumenica*. Again, it is surprising that such prayers are still an exception rather than the rule.

All of the above suggestions entail little or nothing for which new ecclesial agreements are required. Basically, all of these activities can happen *now*. When asked what we *can* do during the time of transition, Cardinal Kasper, on a visit to the Lutheran Church in Dublin in 2004,

---

44. Cf. *Charta Oecumenica*, which was drawn up specifically as a sign and encouragement of active ecumenical commitment among European Churches.

Part II: Unity, Diversity, and Ecumenical Praxis

simply stated that we should do *all* the things that we already can do.[45] Of course, as stated earlier, this could be an evasive answer in relation to unresolved issues Yet, it actually is a reminder that indeed we can do a lot more than what so far has been realized.

While I agree with Kasper on this matter I want to finish this chapter with a question as a point for discussion. Could the Week of Prayer become a renewed and intensified spiritual force of and for unity if it would include—among other imaginative celebratory elements in its liturgy/worship—the celebration of Holy Communion at its annual (opening and/or closing) services? Countless Christians would be delighted if this was the case. If the Pontifical Council for Promoting Christian Unity and other churches and ecumenical bodies were to encourage eucharistic sharing during the Week, it would be a concrete and significant symbolic step towards visible unity. As for the Orthodox churches, such a step would most likely be opposed, even if some individual members might not see it as a problem. Some may also object that such a step was never envisaged by those who first conceived of the idea of the Week of Prayer, and thus runs counter to the Week's original *raison d'être*, namely to celebrate what we *already* have in common as churches. Others may argue that after so many decades of ecumenism and the celebration of the annual Week of Prayer, it may well be time to introduce a new step in its life and history. While the question arises whether shared Holy Communion during the Week would be feasible at all, it seems to me it is at least worth consideration. For the Catholic Church it would be a definite sign towards sister churches that it continues to be committed to the advancement of the ecumenical quest. Official Catholic teaching on this matter insists that shared Holy Communion will be the fullest expression of unity, and therefore can only be celebrated when visible unity is established. Many Protestant churches, on the other hand, see it as an expression on the way towards unity. However, as the Week in some sense *anticipates that full unity*, it may be an opportunity to give more tangible expression to that anticipation during the Week's celebrations. While I do not expect that this idea will be commended by either the Pontifical Council for Promoting Christian Unity or by the WCC, I suggest that it might at

---

45. Cf. also Kasper's article "Es gibt keine Alternative zur Ökumene," where he develops this idea under the heading "ecumenism of life," in *Sich regen bringt Segen*, 52–53.

least be given consideration. The ecumenical quest, in general, and the Week of Prayer, in particular, have a history of over one hundred years. Is it not time for some significant, radical, new steps of progress?

The Spirit is known to surprise. May She surprise us at the annual Week of Prayer and fill it with new vigour, prophetic imagination and enthusiasm, and with a real and renewed sense of Christ's command that Christians *ought to be one*.

PART III

Towards a Radical Church

6

A Theology of Liberation: Dorothee Sölle

Introduction

UNITY IN THE CHURCH is not only urgent *ad intra*, so as to give witness to what the church is meant to be, but also *ad extra* so as to give authentic witness to our faith and to face together with people of other faiths the gravity and expanse of the world's problems. We find ourselves in a world marked by the grossest injustice, by ever-increasing discrepancies between rich and poor, war, hunger, and looming ecological disaster. In the West, the realization of the enormity of these global problems accompanied by the feeling of individual powerlessness has led to apathy and cynicism in many quarters. While such reactions are understandable, Christians whose lives ought to be guided by faith, hope, love, and justice are continuously challenged to counteract such resignation.

What it means to be a committed, radical Christian in modern times has been exemplified by a number of outstanding Christian thinkers, pastors, and ministers—Martin Luther King, Dietrich Bonhoeffer, Oscar Romero, and by liberation and feminist theologians in the Americas, Europe, and elsewhere. It includes also the countless unsung heroes who have devoted their lives in mission for the gospel.

In this chapter, I will reflect on Dorothee Sölle, who was a theologian, scholar of literature, political activist, and feminist. As such she has been an outstanding example of a modern and sometimes controversial "apostle," mediating between faith praxis and theology, the church and the public, political engagement and mysticism.

Part III: Towards a Radical Church

She is remembered for her unceasing siding with those on the margins and for her outspoken critique of political issues and the churches. For her to be a Christian and not to be politically involved—working for justice, peace, liberation, women's rights, and the environment—would have been a contradiction in terms. Hence her theology and spirituality were shaped by action and contemplation, theological reflection, and resistance of anything that opposes the Christian faith in the kingdom of God.

In the following I will focus briefly on Sölle's biography and then consider some of her central theological themes as an introduction to her life and work, which in her case are essentially and deeply intertwined.[1]

Biography

Dorothee Sölle (née Nipperdey) was born in Cologne on September 30, 1929, into a well-educated "liberal protestant"[2] family with three brothers and one sister. She studied philosophy and ancient languages in Cologne and Freiburg (1949–1951). In 1951 she changed to study Protestant theology and German in Göttingen, completing a doctoral dissertation on literary criticism entitled "Studies in the Structures of Bonaventure's Vigils." She married the painter Dietrich Sölle in the same year. After teaching German and religion for six years at a girls' school, she became a freelance writer on theological and literary subjects for journals and the radio from 1960 to 1965. She also worked as an assistant at the Institute of Philosophy at the Technische Hochschule in Aachen. In 1964 her marriage ended in divorce. From 1964 to 1967 Sölle worked at the Institute of German Studies at Cologne University. In the following years, and coinciding with the politically exciting years of the late sixties, she became involved in politics, speaking out against the Vietnam War, the Cold War, and the arms race. Notably, she organized the "political evensongs" ("politische Nachtgebete") in Cologne. These were liturgical prayer services that were attended and supported by left-wing, mostly Christian, intellectuals and opposed

---

1. Cf. Mawick on the occasion of Sölle's seventieth birthday: "Gott will nicht allein sein."

2. Sölle, *Gegenwind*, 54.

A Theology of Liberation: Dorothee Sölle

by the bishops at the time. Here she met her second husband, Fulbert Steffensky, a Roman Catholic Benedictine monk and priest, theologian, and later professor of religious education at Hamburg University (until 1998). In 1971, Sölle completed her post-doctoral work (Habilitation) in Cologne and taught theology as an associate lecturer in Mainz from 1972 to 1975. However, despite the fact that she had thereby fulfilled the academic requirements to be appointed professor and had widely published, she was never offered a chair of theology in Germany. Sölle maintains she did not really regret this exclusion. The reasons for this are probably twofold. As both a woman and as an outspoken, politically engaged writer and Christian she obviously proved too threatening for the academic theological establishment. In fact, for some of her radical political comments and criticism of the church she received hate mail and was denounced by some leading members in the Evangelische Kirche in Germany.

While the honor of a professorial chair was denied to her in her own country, she held a post of professor of systematic theology at Union Theological College in New York from 1975 to 1987. She received the Theodor Heuss Medal in 1974, an honorary doctorate from the Faculté Protestante in Paris in 1981, a fellowship of the Lessing Prize in Hamburg (1981), and the Droste Prize of poetry in Meersburg in 1982. In 1985 she took part in an action of civil disobedience against the Pershing II missile base in Mutlangen and was found guilty of "provoking unrest." In 1988 she was involved in a similar action for peace at a U.S. poison gas depot in Germany and was again found guilty of "attempting to provoke unrest."

In 1987/88 and in 1991/92 she was visiting professor at the University of Kassel and at the Protestant faculty in Basel respectively. She also held an honorary chair at the University of Hamburg in 1994. In 1997 Sölle received an honorary doctorate from the Episcopal Divinity School in Cambridge, Massachusetts. A mother of four children, she lived in Hamburg. Sölle died on April 27, 2003.

Sölle published over thirty-five works ranging from her first book *Christ the Representative: An Essay in Theology after the Death of God* (1967)[3] to her substantial book on mysticism *Mystik und Widerstand—*

---

3. German original: *Stellvertretung. Ein Kapitel Theologie nach dem "Tode Gottes"* (1965).

Du stilles Geschrei (1997)[4] and her biographical memoir *Against the Wind* (1999).[5] Given her background in German studies, she engaged in interdisciplinary literary-theological studies. Dominant themes in her books are political and liberation-theological issues, mysticism, religious experience, the experience of suffering, atheism, personal reflections, poetry, and meditations. Many of her works have been translated into English.

Theology, Prophecy, and Politics

Throughout Sölle's writings, social and political awareness, a radical stance for the oppressed, is intensely felt. Sölle's lived faith and her theological writing go hand in hand. Thus her theological method and style of writing occasionally are somewhat unusual. The more conceptual arguments are interrupted by poetry and storytelling, which are often highly politically engaged.[6]

For Sölle, to be politically on the left is axiomatic for a Christian. To be radical has a political and a theological dimension, i.e., for her it meant to grow both in "revolutionary consciousness" and in "piety" in the hope of becoming more and more Christ-like. Matthew 6:33 became *the* inspiration for her work for several decades, namely to strive first for the kingdom of God and for God's righteousness.

When people wondered whether she was a Marxist, she would feel impatient, thinking that it is quite impossible to read Amos and Isaiah and omit Marx or Engels. As God sent prophets who proclaimed that to know God means to do justice, it would, in her opinion, be ungrateful to God if one were not to appreciate those who have spoken for justice throughout history. In a time when it is obvious that capitalism seems neither able to nor wants to get rid of the hunger in the developing world, this is especially important to remember.[7]

Her interest in Christian dialogue with Marxism and Socialism was a personal journey, which was influenced by the realization that

---

4. English translation: *The Silent Cry: Mysticism and Resistance* (2001).

5. German original: *Gegenwind* (1999)

6. See, for example, her book: *Im Hause des Menschenfressers, Texte zum Frieden* (1981).

7. Sölle, *Gegenwind*, 94–95.

A Theology of Liberation: Dorothee Sölle

our economic system fails to work for two-thirds of the humans on the planet, as well as by the post-war rearmament of Germany and the ensuing peace movement.[8] While she came from an educated middle-class family with a liberal outlook, she discovered that this was not enough, and that a more radical stance towards justice needed to be taken. However, with a clear sense of realism, she naturally wondered whether and to what extent she, as a middle-class intellectual, was actually in any way capable of aligning herself with people of the working classes. Further, a central question for her was whether, in fact, a Christian can be a socialist. Was it possible to be a socialist without being an atheist? She points out that with liberation theology—which expounds a faith free of "an opium of the people"—these questions have become obsolete. Significantly, she adds that it is not the critique of religion but the critique of the "idol of the free market" that will remain from Marx' thought.[9]

Sölle's involvement with political groups on the left has been an open one. What was important to her and those around her in the political evensongs in Cologne (1968–1972) and elsewhere was to find an identity through terms like "agape," "love of neighbor," and "solidarity."[10] It is important to note that in this way Sölle's outlook and involvement has always been concretely ecumenical, not only through her taking part in the political evensongs but also through her work in liberation theology and pacifist groups, and through her interest in mysticism and spirituality. In fact, people who have met her were often surprised to find out that she was not Catholic but Lutheran.[11]

Sölle's Vision of God: From Omnipotent Ruler to Co-Sufferer

Sölle writes that she basically went through three different stages in her understanding of God, which in turn influenced her own faith and way of doing theology. Having grown up with the idea of an almighty Father God, who rules the world in majesty and glory, Sölle sought from an early stage to distance herself from this concept by using the metaphor

8. Ibid., 96.
9. Ibid., 98.
10. Ibid.
11. Boschki and Schuster, *Zur Umkehr fähig*, 80.

Part III: Towards a Radical Church

of the "death of God."[12] The controversial "death of God" theology became popular in the 1960s with theologians like Sölle in Germany and Thomas Altizer, Paul van Buren, and William Hamilton in the States. While interests among them differed, their basic assumption was that the traditional understanding of God could no longer make sense as people turned away from the institutional churches and from Christian faith. Moreover, they tried—as Nietzsche had already done—to radically question a naïve understanding of God as an idol-like figure, a kind of super-Father who runs the world from above. Such a God is neither the God of the New Testament nor the God of a mature, critical faith.[13] For Sölle, the issue was, in particular, how to conceive and speak of God after the holocaust, after Auschwitz. Essentially this meant for her a breaking-away from the theist notion of God's omnipotence to a God who becomes co-sufferer with us:

> The metaphor of the "death of God" means for me consciously to give up the notion of God's omnipotence as a theological and ethical impossibility. In the light of Auschwitz God's omnipotence seemed and still seems (!) to me a heresy, a misunderstanding of the idea of God.[14]

Thus Sölle, similar to Moltmann in his theology of hope, developed the idea of God in which the crucified Christ is at the center, i.e., an affirmation of suffering love.[15] The question and difficulty that thus arose for her was whether power is intrinsically and always bad or evil. Can anything positive be said about power? Here the third stage of her notion of God unfolds in that she began to conceive of Christ's and our own resurrection as a participation in the divine power. She points

---

12. Sölle, *Gott denken*, 244.

13. Sölle later gave up the death-of-God metaphor as it occasioned considerable difficulties. The term was often misunderstood and her critics and opponents who may not even have read any of her works would maintain that Sölle advocated the idea of the death of God in her theology. Cf. Boschki and Schuster, *Zur Umkehr fähig*, 45–47. Sölle commented: "Ich habe später diese spezielle Metapher nicht mehr verwendet. Aber daß die Weltenlenker-Metapher nicht reicht, und daß das der falsche Gott ist, den man sich gemacht hat, das würde ich nach wie vor sagen . . . Aber es ist klar, daß damit nicht der Gott der Bibel gemeint ist, sondern eben etwas anderes, was man aus ihm gemacht hat. Gottesideologie könnte man das nennen."

14. Boschki and Schuster, *Zur Umkehr fähig*, 45–47. (My translation). For a full treatment of the subject, see her book *Christ the Representative*, especially 150–52.

15. Sölle, *Gott denken*, 244.

A Theology of Liberation: Dorothee Sölle

out that this notion had to do with her becoming involved in liberation theology. Sölle came slowly to realize that there is another type of power than the imperial one, namely *that* power which comes from a relationship with life, a power that believes in sharing, "which distributes itself" and "involves others."[16] In this context she emphasizes that it is especially Jewish thought, e.g., the Talmud, which has influenced her idea of participation in God, as there the notion of the human being created in the image of God is especially developed. Hence humans can act like God—the *imitatio dei*. As the God of the Bible is essentially a God of covenant and relationship, a God who wants to be with God's people, she rejects the—very male—idea of an omnipotent, omniscient, omnipresent God who has no need of anyone, an independent God. It is not just we who need God but, she insists, God needs us. God is no longer seen as the one who is above us but in us. We do not stand before God in utter helplessness but are liberated into community with God. Transcendence Sölle describes as "radical immanence"; immanence and transcendence are not opposites but "are related to the same thing, the same one creation." The difference between them is that "transcendence concentrates and makes holy every phenomenon of immanence to which it is applied."[17] In the past the relationship between immanence and transcendence was conceived in hierarchical terms (the transcendent is higher, greater, more spiritual and supremely true, i.e., *above* the physical, bodily, contingent, immanent). In modern theology it is conceived of in dialectical or paradoxical terms, especially in Protestant theology. Sölle points out that the dialectical/paradoxical, however, does not go far enough in trying to overcome the hierarchical notion. While in Christianity God's immanence—through the incarnation—was never denied, God's transcendent "male side," she insists, has always been regarded as "higher, more true, more real, than God's immanence."[18]

---

16. Ibid., 245.
17. Ibid., 249.
18. Ibid., 248–49.

Accepting the Cross—Following Christ

The cross, the suffering of God in Christ, is central to Sölle's understanding of the divine and to her faith and spirituality. She provides an important clue in relating a personal experience of a talk by Miguel d'Escoto, a Maryknoll priest, which she once attended. For d'Escoto, Martin Luther King was "the greatest saint of our time" who influenced him more than many others.[19] King thus became a role model for this priest. He made d'Escoto feel ashamed in that King had made himself free of everything to give his life entirely to God. Yet d'Escoto maintained that most important of all was grace, *that* grace that made King the person he was. When d'Escoto realized this he also remembered a prayer: "Lord, help me to understand the mystery of your cross. Help me to love your cross and give me the power and grace to take it up, as you show it to me."[20] And he added that this is possible.

The need to fully give oneself up for God, to lay everything in the hands and will of God *now* is essential. It is only in this way that we can overcome our fears and become truly liberated. Finally, d'Escoto pointed out that the most wonderful attitude we can develop towards the cross is that we learn to perceive it "with joy . . . because life is love."[21] Sölle renders d'Escoto's speech at much greater length. What is relevant in our context is that her vision of faith in Christ, and the meaning Christ can have for us today, is included therein:

1) What matters is acceptance of the will of God and to radically follow Christ so that Christ becomes visible in us. She is aware that here she echoes Luther who would concern himself not so much with Christ's nature, but rather stressed Christ's will, and what the God-Man accomplished for us. 2) The consequence that arises thus is the readiness to suffer for Christ's sake, for the kingdom; it entails taking on the difficulties and hardships that this road implies. 3) Finally, it is important not only to accept the cross but to begin "to love" the cross, precisely because it is a sign of being one with God.[22] This is what resurrection faith means for her, the love between Father and Son, which is inde-

---

19. Ibid., 168.
20. Ibid., 169.
21. Ibid., 170.
22. Ibid., 172.

structible. For Sölle, the "most simple, so to say demythologised, . . . formulation of the resurrection" is that "they were unable to kill Christ, . . . the significance of his life, his Spirit, the work of his disciples, this oneness with God's will lived and still lives today. Redemption without the Cross is not that redemption whereby we become one with love."[23]

For Sölle, then, it is love—suffering love—that is at the center of the Christian message and of her mystical spirituality. For her it means to be willing to take one's own stand, not to go with the masses, to live in precarious situations, with anxiety and difficulties.[24] The more we speak out against injustice, the more difficult our life becomes in a society of injustice. For her "to choose life is to embrace the Cross."[25]

Sölle therefore advocates a Christology "from below." She points out that the deeply rooted docetism in theology has not yet been overcome in the wealthy countries. Instead of seeing Christ as a real person who truly lived and walked the earth, who "wept, sweated, hungered and had fears," the tendency in the West has been to glorify him rather as the risen God, who never quite fully became a human being. She holds that it is in liberation theology that this view has been radically changed. Here Christology from below at last is truly realized. She remarks: "Spanish-European patriarchal culture had celebrated Christ as the 'salvador del mundo' and at the same time identified with the oppressors."[26] Now in Latin American liberation theology we find, instead of the "glorious *kyrios*," the poor one: "the child out of wedlock, the refugee . . . the rebel, who is considered a criminal."[27] There is thus a "unique identification of the poor Jesus of the Gospels and life in the slums."

For Sölle such strong identification with Christ in the face of evil, torture, hunger, and oppression seems the only way to live one's faith, to find any sense in it. The benign *ruler* of heaven, the savior with whom we will be united only in the *eschaton*, and who was used as an opium for the people rather than proclaimed as a liberator who sides with the marginalized, is anathema for this theologian. Her understanding of

---

23. Ibid., 173.
24. Ibid., 174. Sölle notes: "To be a Christian at the end of this millennium becomes more expensive and costly."
25. Ibid., 176.
26. Ibid., 151.
27. Ibid., 151.

Part III: Towards a Radical Church

Christ, of the Cross, and of the resurrection, and hence her faith, is one that essentially has been shaped by, and lived out of, the insights and real-life experience of a theology of liberation.

Mysticism and Resistance

In 1997 Sölle published a substantial new work, *Mystik und Widerstand— Du stilles Geschrei*.[28] If Sölle's interests have been liberation theologies, religious experience, social-political action, and personal reflections in poetry and narrative, it follows quite naturally that she should concern herself at length with mysticism.

Her book is divided into three main parts: "What Is Mysticism?," "Places of Mystical Experience," and "Mysticism Is Resistance." In the first part, Sölle considers various elements that contribute to mystical experience, such as ecstasy. She looks at various authors, including C. S. Lewis, Buber, as well as Sufi mysticism. Notably, she attempts to come to a real understanding of the meaning of mysticism, taking into account the language of mysticism, and she outlines a possible mystical journey for today. In the second part, Sölle considers nature, eros, suffering, community, and joy as places of mystical experience whereby she discusses contributions ranging from Job to St. John of the Cross and D. H. Lawrence, the poet Ingeborg Bachmann, and the Buddhist monk and writer Thich Nhat Hanh. In the final section, she discusses liberation and freedom, self and selflessness, possession and the giving up of possessions, power and powerlessness, and "liberation mysticism." Here, Martha and Mary, St. Francis, Dorothy Day, Mahatma Gandhi, Dom Helder Camara, Dag Hammarskjöld, and others figure in her reflections.

At the beginning of the work, Sölle states that religion is fundamentally made up of three elements: the institutional, the intellectual, and the mystical. In Christianity, the institutional, or "Petrine," dimension pertains to the life and work of the church, to tradition and memory. The intellectual, the "Pauline," aspect is the analytical-speculative, while the mystical element is concerned with the emotional-intuitive life of believers.[29] Sölle points out that it is this mystical dimension that

---

28. Sölle, *The Silent Cry: Mysticism and Resistance* (2001).
29. Sölle, *Mystik und Widerstand*, 15.

A Theology of Liberation: Dorothee Sölle

"keeps a hold on her." In other words, it is God's love that she wants "to live, understand and spread." Divine love and its realization in the world is for her at the heart of the mystical experience. Not only does God love us, but, she insists, love, real love, needs to be mutual: "That humans love, protect, renew and save God sounds megalomaniac or even crazy for most people. But it is precisely this craziness of love by which the mystics live."[30]

Sölle has felt strongly drawn to mysticism. Here, as she says, she has found a less dogmatic and less male spirituality than was the case in German Protestantism. To truly yearn for God, to deeply need God in one's life, this was often interpreted as a misleading enthusiasm. She quotes the German writer Johann Gottfried Herder who noted that without enthusiasm nothing truly great comes into existence. It is the experience of the mystic, becoming one with God, being filled with God, eating and breathing God, as Buber wrote, which, Sölle insists, is central to our life as believers.[31] These images are expressions of the desire for and experience of union and oneness. Yet, she comments, the sexual-ecstatic dimensions implied in these images should not simply be reduced and trivialized as substitute expressions of an unlived sexual drive.

To need God is the greatest perfection in the human being, she concludes. Without mysticism, without an intense desire for God, we become consuming and producing agents who have neither a need of, nor an ability to be with, God. Mysticism, she notes, differs from (ecclesial) orthodoxy in that it proclaims that humans have a potential for divinization (Gottfähigkeit), and it differs from the orthodoxy of science in that it affirms our dependence on and need for God. While, in general, Protestants, with their insistence on the sharp divide between the human and the divine, have been apprehensive about notions of human perfection and *theosis*, it must be said, however, that through the Christian tradition thinkers, especially in the Orthodox tradition, have dwelt on, or at least have alluded to, the possibility of divinization, holiness, and sanctification. St Athanasius wrote "God became man so that man might become God,"[32] and Irenaeus similarly noted, "The

---

30. Ibid., 16.
31. Ibid., 68.
32. Athanasius, *De Incarnatione*, 54, 3.

Part III: Towards a Radical Church

Word of God, our Lord Jesus Christ, who did, through his transcendent love, become what we are, that He might bring us to be even what He is Himself."[33] Bonhoeffer, whose own life and death epitomized that suffering love that makes us Christ-like, wrote, echoing Athanasius: "We must be assimilated to the form of Christ in its entirety, the form of Christ incarnate, crucified and glorified . . . He has become like a man, so that men should be like him."[34] The biblical basis for *theosis* is found in Gen 1:27, when we read about humans being made in the image of God, and particularly in St. Paul: "When we cry, 'Abba! Father!' it is that very Spirit bearing witness with our spirit that we are children of God, and if children, then heirs, heirs of God and joint heirs with Christ—if, in fact, we suffer with him so that we may also be glorified with him" (Rom 8:15–17).

Given that we live in an age where all sorts of religious and semi-religious (New Age) phenomena are *en vogue*, e.g., parapsychology, astrology, magic, and tarot cards, Sölle attempts to show the difference between "true" and "false" mysticism. Fundamentally, she asserts that true mysticism always includes ethical criteria.[35] These ethical criteria are universal because God is universal to humankind. Mysticism means communion with God. Any mysticism that does not address the importance of communion with God and an ethics of creation, the createdness of the human being and the world, but rather suffers from egomania, or, as in the case of Nazi "mysticism," from political-racist delusions, is not genuine mysticism. In Jewish mysticism, doing God's will, i.e., living according to God's commandments, is seen as mystical union, *unio mystica*, with God. That one's will can become identical with the divine will is an expression of this union.[36] To do God's will brings the human closer to God; true mysticism presupposes that it is possible to be of one will with God. The mythological delusions of the Nazis stood in radical opposition to this sense of the good and doing the good according to the divine will. In that way, Sölle rightly ascertains, it becomes misguided ideology whereby the leader of a group is

---

33. Irenaeus, *Adversus Haereses*, Book 5, Preface.
34. Bonhoeffer, *Cost of Discipleship*, 272.
35. Sölle, *Mystik und Widerstand*, 77–80, at 80.
36. Sölle, *Mystik und Widerstand*, 80.

A Theology of Liberation: Dorothee Sölle

worshipped like an idol. One would add that in the life and leadership of religious sects somewhat similar characteristics may arise.

In this context, Sölle quotes a verse from an English hymn to sum up her idea:

> Breathe on me, Breath of God
> Fill me with life anew,
> That I may love what thou dost love
> And do what thou wouldst do.

How then might the mystical be experienced today? Inspired by Matthew Fox, Sölle draws an outline for a possible mystical journey with the keywords: Amazement-Letting go-Resistance.[37]

Instead of starting with purification and the sense of the fall, of original sin, which has been the traditional point of departure, Sölle insists that one should start with a sense of the goodness and the original blessing of creation. In this way, she speaks about amazement and surprise. It is the *via positiva*. To be amazed again and again at the beauty of creation and at the processes of life-giving liberation, at happiness, but also at the darker sides of existence, threat, and pain—this constitutes the start of the mystical journey. Amazement, awe, and deep wonder about life are a way of praising God. And even with ever-increasing scientific knowledge, this being simply amazed at the "miracle" of existence must not cease. In short, life without wonder is not worth living, Sölle insists. Again, she quotes Herder who said that such responses in the human being to life in all its variety are prerequisite to creating something truly great. This then may lead to contemplation, meditation, rest, and prayer.[38]

Amazement, wonderment, and admiration are at the same time the beginning of a letting go. In being amazed, we let go and are liberated from our own fears. This is the *via negativa*, which can entail negation, *ascesis*, a letting go of one's desires. In a world rampant with consumerism and instant gratification, this may seem a rather unattractive option. Yet, Sölle maintains, we need purgation from our consumerist mentality and illnesses of addictions. Moreover, awareness of the ecological crisis on our planet is essential. Indeed, it is against

37. Ibid., 123–28.
38. Ibid., 125–26.

the threat of ecological catastrophe that we must think of our mystical journey today.[39] To live in God, to come into union with God, means to participate in creation. "To praise God and at the same time to be aware of the absence of God leads to a 'life-in-God,' which the tradition called 'the *via unitiva*,'" i.e., our co-creation and becoming one with the divine.

Finally, the third step on the mystical journey "leads to healing, which at the same time is resistance."[40] Healing and salvation means that people learn compassion and do justice as co-creators. Union is not individual self-realization, but works towards transformation of a death-oriented reality. This is manifested in the various forms of resistance, i.e., in liberation, in a world that works for peace and lets go, at least to some extent, of the need to accumulate possessions and have "success."

Sölle concludes by using the image of the rainbow, which, she feels, is "perhaps the most powerful symbol" of mystical union. The rainbow "is the sign that creation does not perish, but continues to live in seed and harvest, day and night, summer and winter, birth and death."[41]

Conclusion: Orthopraxis, Discipleship, and the Church

Dorothee Sölle was a theologian and thinker of her time, deeply involved with theological, political, societal and cultural issues. Most impressive is her concrete merging of her life with her work, i.e., her mystical spirituality and theology, her uncompromising stance for justice, peace, feminist issues and the integrity of creation, for a theology that must not remain comfortable theory but, as she says, must "end in praxis."[42] Sölle paid the price: in Germany she never had the privilege of being granted a—more than deserved!—chair in theology. On the other hand, her work, somewhat on the margin rather than in the center of the church or university, gave her the freedom to write on what mat-

---

39. Ibid., 127–28.
40. Ibid., 128.
41. Ibid., 128.
42. Mawick, "Gott will nicht allein sein." Referring to the political evensongs in which she was involved in Cologne, Sölle comments: "Irgendwann dämmerte es uns, dass wir uns nicht nur theoretisch mit theologischen Fragen beschäftigen durften, sondern dass diese Beschäftigung in eine Art Praxis einmünden muss."

tered most deeply to her. Her unceasing call for a faith that does justice and her political engagement have made her a "saint" in the eyes of some and a "red rag" for others.[43]

Sölle lived through a century that saw tremendous historical events and changes, the Second World War, the Hiroshima bomb, the breaking up of communism and of the Eastern block, hunger in the developing world, the invention of television and the beginning of the computer age, and growing globalization. In the light of these events it is heartening to see that there are theologians and thinkers like her who remain faithful to their radical vision of a more just and peaceful world, of a "green" globe, and who are not shy to propagate this time and again.

Naturally, questions remain and some themes, e.g., the "God is dead" theology, that were central to her in the past have been criticized and were consequently differently phrased by Sölle herself. Some of the concerns in her works, read nowadays, are not as pertinent as they were even two to three decades ago. Occasionally they even seem a little passé from our post-1989 perspective. The "right" and "left"—still clearly defined until the 1980s—no longer exist in such obvious fashion after the break up of the Eastern bloc. Demonstrations against atomic power plants, nuclear weapons, and the arms race have largely quietened down if not ceased altogether. Young adults today often seem more concerned with careers, image, computers, and the internet than with idealistic hopes, left-wing rebellion, and political demonstrations for a better world. Radical voices and prophetic speech have become faint against the accelerating speed and greed of neo-capitalism around the globe, even though the financial crash in 2008 will have made many people think again about norms and values in our lives. The virtual reality of cyberspace and consumerist gratification seem more alluring to many than fighting injustice, environmental exploitation, and the suffering of ethnic groups and asylum seekers, even if the latter concerns are addressed by some groups and individuals. However, closing our eyes in apathy against the immensity of the world's problems often seems the immediate option.

Yet, our age with its renewed turn towards religion—or what might be called "the religious" in the widest sense—from New Age esoteric trends to Buddhism and mysticism obviously cries out for something

---

43. Mawick, "Gott will nicht allein sein."

Part III: Towards a Radical Church

that ultimately has more substance and sustenance than rampant consumerism, and individualism. Hence Sölle's book on mysticism is topical. However, the term "mysticism," rather than the term "resistance," in the book's title will be likely to attract the contemporary uninitiated, non-political reader—especially given the fact that the search for the mystical and interest in religion today is frequently driven by an overemphasis on the affective and an accompanying anti-intellectualism. Sölle points out that mystical faith, and, more particularly, mystical Christianity, has little to do with a superficial, naïve, self-centred "feel-good" spirituality of the individual, but rather it means *Nachfolge*, i.e., discipleship and *orthopraxis*. Mysticism *is* resistance. It involves entering into the darkness of God, to experience Godforsakenness, the abyss; it means amazement, letting go, healing—a healing not just of the self but a healing of society, of the environment, perhaps, one may suggest, even of religion itself. Indeed, Sölle was pessimistic about the very survival of the religions in the light of consumerism and the domination of the market. In that sense, mysticism can be markedly countercultural.

It is not surprising that Sölle has sometimes been taken for a Catholic given her insistence on *orthopraxis*. In fact, as she sees it, the opposites of grace and good works quite simply do not hold: "Jesus fed the hungry and made the lame walk. Is that work or grace?" she asks. With such remarks she rightly tries to make her readers aware that traditional theological "boxed-in" truths or myths need to be deconstructed and re-thought.

To some Sölle appears unorthodox. For example, her idea that it is not just we who need God, but that God needs us, is most akin to the mystical writers. Traditionally, however, this idea would have been questionable in the light of the notion of God's omnipotence, the unmoved (male!) mover who reigns independently from above. Sölle's criticism of such notions of the divine is relevant and aligns her with other contemporary theologians.

Leaving aside the God of Aristotle and considering the life and death of Jesus Christ, who, after all, is the center of our faith, we remember the Christ who called, and indeed, *needed* his apostles and friends to propagate and live his message: "Christ has no other hands than ours, he is dependent on us," i.e., on our apostolic and diaconal work. "When there are no more Christians, Christ is dead."[44]

44. Cf. the third chapter "Der Stellvertreter" and the epilogue in *Stellvertretung*,

A Theology of Liberation: Dorothee Sölle

Sölle held that Jesus' omnipotence lies in the very fact that he did *not* condemn but, instead, *forgave* those who failed him, and gave his own life for them and the world. If we can speak at all of the *omnipotence* of the triune God, it is here, in God becoming the lowliest of all through overflowing, suffering love. This is what Sölle intends to emphasise in her advocacy of a Christology "from below."

From what has been said above, it follows that Sölle's vision of the church was a "modest" one, modest in the sense that she pleads for a "participatory," "mystical" Christianity (with reference to Rahner), a community of believers who search for mutuality, relationship, community.[45] She points out that she herself was "not deformed or neuroticized by the church."[46] Sölle distinguished between a church from "above" and "below," as one might put it, at the one end being the "powermonger Pope Innocent III," at the other the "*poverello* Francis."[47] One stands for the corruption and abuse of church power, the other for an authentic, credibly lived faith. While she is aware that her theology never sought to simply conform to the church, she notes, on the other hand, "it is a postmodern mistake to think that without traditions we are freer."[48] She refers to her friend, Daniel Berrigan, who likened the church to "an umbrella." It can protect us from the rain, even though at times "it opens too slowly and we get rained on."[49] Sölle also uses the metaphor of "tent," and she remarks: "Perhaps the church is not so much the crumbling edifice we see but more a tent for the wandering people of God."[50] The church must integrate the sacramental, the image, the sensuous, our bodily well-being, and we must discover and rediscover the saints and quasi-saints from whom we can still learn today. She points out that it is the authoritarian aspect of hierarchy that she—like many Protestants and Catholics alike—finds the most problematic aspect regarding the Catholic Church. In this context, Sölle also mentions a "new kind of religiosity" which has developed that transcends the dif-

---

111–70, 175–84. "Christus hat keine anderen Hände als unsere, er ist auf uns angewiesen. Wenn keine Christen mehr da sind, ist Christus tot" (180).

45. Cf. Boschki and Schuster, *Zur Umkehr fähig*, 72–85.
46. Sölle, *Against the Wind*, 90.
47. Ibid., 90.
48. Ibid., 91.
49. Ibid.
50. Ibid.

Part III: Towards a Radical Church

ferent denominations whereby Protestants and Catholics approach and reach out to one another. It is this kind of ecumenical church, a church of the people of God, that she has in mind. Sölle believed in a church that advocates liberation, basic communities, the equality of women and men in ministry and elsewhere, and that cares for the earth and all its living creatures. "I seek to find out how we can 'love God above all things.'" This is what fundamentally mattered to her.

Finally, considering her work as a whole, it is true to say that Sölle was not a specialist in ecumenical studies. Her work has not concentrated on solving intricate questions in contemporary ecumenical dialogue. Still, and perhaps all the more, Sölle was a deeply ecumenical theologian who *lived* ecumenically rather than talking about it in great detail. She critically and constructively appropriated Catholic strands into her theology that more "party-loyal" theologians and church members (Catholic or Protestant) might be afraid of, for the simple reason that they might "lose" something of their own ecclesial identity, security, and conviction. For Sölle, such narrow faith and ecclesiology obviously were anathema. Ultimately, one concludes, what seemed relevant to her was not so much whether ideas are "Protestant" or "Catholic" but whether they are conducive to the life of a committed, radical faith, church, and theology. Sölle apparently had no fear she would lose something of her Lutheran identity by integrating what those of other denominations positively (as she sees it) have to offer. In the First Letter of John we read that "there is no fear in love, but perfect love casts out fear" (1 John 4:18). One would suggest that Sölle took this to heart—in her life and in her theology.

7

A New Left Church? Terry Eagleton

Introduction

BORN IN SALFORD, ENGLAND, in 1943, Terence Francis Eagleton is recognized as one of the most influential literary theorists working today. A third-generation Irish Catholic immigrant in Britain, Eagleton grew up in a working-class environment with strong Republican leanings. Unsurprisingly, his working-class background contributed to a sense of inferiority. However, in his nascent academic career, he worried initially about his roots receding from him, "but then I became rather stoical about it. It was foolish to believe this was a divide that could be simply crossed. I had no illusion that I could turn the clock back... But instead what I tried to do was write on behalf of my father's people."[1]

Eagleton obtained his MA and PhD from Trinity College, Cambridge. He was a Fellow of Jesus College, Cambridge (1964–1969), a tutorial fellow at Wadham College, Oxford (1969–1989), and lecturer in critical theory at Linacre College (1989–92). Eagleton was appointed Thomas Warton Professor of English Literature at Oxford University (1992–2001), and John Edward Taylor Professor of Cultural Theory at Manchester University (2001–2008). At present, he holds a Visiting Professorship at the National University of Ireland, Galway, and at other universities, including Lancaster, Yale, and the University of Notre Dame.

---

1. Quoted by Wroe from Eagleton's memoir, *The Gatekeeper*, in a review article, "High Priest of lit crit."

His works—spanning subjects concerning literary theory, criticism, Marxism, colonialism, nationalism, and Ireland—are numerous, comprising not only academic publications, but also two plays, a novel, and a memoir.[2]

While Eagleton established himself as a literary theorist, he has been interested in, and has also critically engaged with Christian theology and the church, especially his own Catholic Church. What might be almost forgotten are his earliest writings from the 1960s, which concern connections between faith, theology/ecclesiology, politics, and literature. Hitherto Eagleton has rarely featured as a discussion partner among theologians. However, with his latest publications, this is now changing. His earliest writings, including amongst others *The New Left Church*,[3] as well as his recent *On Evil*[4] and *Reason, Faith and Revolution: Reflections on the God Debate*[5]—a sharp, witty, polemical response to Richard Dawkins' and Christopher Hitchens' militant atheist agenda—invite us to pay new attention to his theological writings and views on Christian faith. In fact, *Reason, Faith and Revolution*, written over forty years after *The New Left Church*, contains some echoes from his earliest works. In the following I will refer to both his early and most recent writings, as there exists an essential continuity in his line of thought, even if the issues and contexts have changed considerably.

In the 1960s, Eagleton found himself enthused by the liberalizing developments of the Second Vatican Council initiated by John XXIII. In Cambridge at the time, he was involved with a group of undergraduate students who, with the help of some priests, decided that a periodical dedicated to a "radical examination of the Roman Church and its ideas should be launched."[6] As it found resonance, the editors then ventured to bring this to a larger audience. Another group, the "December Group," which had already been founded a few years prior to *Slant* and met every December (hence the name) joined with the *Slant* members. The contributors were largely Catholic and produced *Catholics and the Left: "Slant Manifesto"* in 1966. Another publication,

2. See Wroe, "High Priest of Lit Crit." *Literary Theory: An Introduction* put Eagleton on the "world stage."
3. Eagleton, *New Left Church* (1966).
4. Eagleton, *On Evil* (2010).
5. Eagleton, *Reason, Faith and Revolution* (2009).
6. Middleton, "Introduction," *Slant Manifesto*, xvii.

From Culture to Revolution, arose from the Slant Symposium in 1967. It included young scholars who were to become leading thinkers in and outside the Catholic Church, including, amongst others, Raymond Williams, Fergus Kerr OP, and Charles Taylor.[7] In addition to *Slant*, Eagleton authored a monograph in 1966, *The New Left Church*, and, in 1968, he edited *Directions: Pointers for the Post-Conciliar Church* with contributions from several theologians and other authors, including Nicholas Lash and Rosemary Haughton.[8]

In the following I will, firstly, outline central themes and insights from Eagleton's above-mentioned writings on the church, faith, culture, and society. Secondly, in the concluding section, I will attempt to critically explore how some of these insights may be relevant to theological and ecclesiological discourse in our contemporary church, society, and culture.

Why Still Bother with Socialist Ideas?

The fundamental aim for members of *Slant* was to explore the idea that "Christian commitment at the moment carries with it an obligation to be socialist."[9] Being Christian should mean to be committed to a society where Christ is manifested to the highest possible degree. Change towards a better world would have to come about in "socialist terms." Of course, the *Realsozialismus*, as practiced in the Eastern bloc, was not envisaged or condoned by this group of idealistic young students, priests, and academics. In fact, the New Left arose in the aftermath of two events that occurred in close proximity in 1956: the Franco-British invasion of the Suez Canal and the suppression of the Hungarian Revolution by Soviet tanks. In a critical, reflective article on the emergence of the ("first") New Left, cultural theorist and sociologist Stuart Hall notes that "these two events . . . unmasked the underlying violence and aggression latent in the two systems that dominated political life at the time—Western imperialism and Stalinism."[10] Thus the New Left sought a "third political space somewhere between these two meta-

---

7. Eagleton and Wicker, *From Culture to Revolution*.
8. Eagleton, *Directions*.
9. Middleton, "Introduction," in *Slant Manifesto*, xvii.
10. Hall, "Life and Times of the First New Left."

Part III: Towards a Radical Church

phors. Its rise signified . . . the end of the imposed silences and political impasses of the Cold War, and the possibility of a breakthrough into a new socialist project."[11] The movement included educators and activists in Britain and in the U.S. who intended a series of reforms arising from the failures of Eastern bloc so-called Socialism, as well as from university protests and the Hippie movement later in the 1960s.[12]

In an interview in 2004, Eagleton remarked: "If you want the most trenchant account of Stalinism you have to go to Marxism, not liberalism . . . Stalinism wasn't, from our point of view, radical enough. Long before Tiananmen Square the mainstream Marxists were saying the Soviet system is a travesty. You can't build Communism in backward conditions. You need international support. You need a society with a liberal democracy. Marx always saw socialism in continuity with middle-class democracy."[13]

---

11. Ibid. "This 'third position' paralleled the political aspirations of many of the people who came together to form the early British New Left . . . The New Left represented the coming together of two related but different traditions —also of two political experiences or generations. One was the tradition I would call, for want of a better term, communist humanism, symbolized by the *New Reasoner* and its founders, John Saville and Edward and Dorothy Thompson. The second is perhaps best described as an independent socialist tradition, whose centre of gravity lay in the left student generation of the 1950s and which maintained some distance from 'party' affiliations. It was people from this layer who, in the disintegration of those orthodoxies in 1956, first produced *Universities and Left Review*."

12. Political theorist, Paul Blackledge, notes: "The birth of the New Left in 1956 marked an important turning point in post-war British history. For the first time since the Second World War a political space opened within which socialists could hope to make headway building a movement independent of both Labourism and Stalinism. Moreover, in struggling for this space, the activists of the New Left made the first steps towards rearticulating a democratic vision of socialism from below to which we remain indebted today. All contemporary anti-capitalists who insist in the face of the collapse of the Soviet Union that 'another world is possible' owe a debt to the New Left's attempt to unpick the authentic socialist tradition from Stalinism. We are also indebted to their challenge to the narrow horizons of contemporary British society: the post-war economic boom had brought relative prosperity in its train, but it did not overcome alienation, and the New Left recognised this fact and aimed to overcome it . . . Against the inhumanity of both Stalinism and Western capitalism, the New Left embraced the idea of 'socialist humanism', and while the ambiguities of this idea meant that for some it acted as the medium through which they bade their farewells to Marxism, at its most powerful it pointed beyond the morass of Stalinism towards Marx's humanist critique of capitalism." Blackledge, "New Left's Renewal," 112.

13. Eagleton quoted in D. Smith, "Cultural Theorists, Start Your Epitaphs."

A New Left Church? Terry Eagleton

Obviously, in today's radically changed world—after the fall of the Eastern bloc, 9/11, with global capitalism, and the World Wide Web—political, economic, and social issues in many regards have changed and differ from those with which Eagleton and his colleagues were occupied in the 1960s. Eagleton takes account of this in his *Reason, Faith, and Revolution*. Yet he also offers some pertinent comments on why one should be a Marxist even today:

> The radical answer to the question of whether modernity is a positive or negative phenomenon is an emphatic yes and no. One of the best reasons in my view for still being a Marxist, apart from the gratifying exasperation it sometimes occasions to others, is that no other doctrine . . . claims that the liberal Enlightenment . . . has been at one and the same time an enthralling advance in humanity and an insupportable nightmare.[14]

Similarly, Hall, in 2010, can still conclude that—despite the shortcomings, mistakes, and errors of the "first" New Left—the "third space" "it had defined" and sought to open still appears to him as "the only hope for the renewal of the democratic and socialist project in our new and bewildering times."[15]

Eagleton's writings in the 1960s, informed by a confluence of socialist/Marxist leanings and Christian faith, may still, then, have something to say to our present concerns of being Christian in a fragmented world—a world dominated by the reign of liberal global capitalism, a product ultimately of the Enlightenment, which has shown its deep failures and divisions, driving an ever greater wedge not only between rich and poor in the Northern and Southern hemispheres, but also within European and Non-European societies.

Sölle, in her memoir, similarly reflects on how socialist ideas—so radically betrayed by Stalinism and twentieth-century eastern European countries' rulers—might not simply be cast to the rubbish heap of failed state systems, but that the "principles and insights" embodied in socialist concepts ought to be critically re-evaluated. She concludes: "Does anyone seriously believe that we could live without hunger and thirst for justice?"[16] Those who happily exploit the economics of capitalism and see no problem in arranging themselves with its

---

14. Eagleton, *Reason, Faith, and Revolution*, 69–70.
15. Hall, "Life and Times of the First New Left."
16. Sölle, *Against the Wind*, 144, 149.

long-term ill effects seem unbothered indeed; yet there are others who seriously question such systems of gross inequality, and these voices are getting stronger. One only has to think of the many NGOs, such as Amnesty International, Greenpeace, and the numerous charity and international development organizations who give expression to this desire for greater economic and social justice and a commitment to ecological sustainability. Even though we no longer live in the 1960s and the power-blocs of East and West no longer exist, countless people worldwide are aware of the looming human-made ecological disaster and severe injustices in the world; and they try to make their voice heard, even in as small a gesture as signing Avaaz petitions on the web.

"The Roots of the Christian Crisis"

In *Catholics and the Left: "Slant Manifesto,"* in a chapter with the above heading, Eagleton outlines what he regards as three critical issues in Christian and social nineteenth-century thought. He begins by noting that no "single, adequate interpretative account" exists between the church and the industrial revolution. Such a reflection he deems necessary for a "renewal in Christian social thinking" as a first step towards gaining insights for a contemporary Christian radicalism."[17] He wrote this chapter with specific reference to British society and, while not explicitly mentioning it, to the mainline churches in Britain. (A slight problem here is the fact that almost throughout his ecclesiological writings, he simply speaks of "the church." From the context we can deduce that he mainly has the Catholic Church in mind, but also the mainline churches, including the Anglican Church, on several issues.)

Eagleton points out that the relationship between the church(es) and the working classes in Britain in the nineteenth century was marked by deep contradiction. The church urgently sought to make contact with the working class; yet the motives were "ambivalent." On the one hand, there was real concern for the spiritual and social welfare of the people; on the other hand, the church's attempts to approach the working classes were driven by its aim of institutional survival.[18] Self-interest through the recruiting of souls played a large role, and the more

---

17. Eagleton, "Roots of the Christian Crisis," *Catholics and the Left*, 57.
18. Ibid., 58.

it was fostered, the more "self-defeating," alienating, and ambiguous the results could be. In such a context, therefore, critical ecclesial self-reflection was largely impossible. Ministers were unable to develop a real perception of working-class people as their foremost objective was to view them in terms of being potential new members of the church. "[T]he contradiction lies in the fact that the church needed support to validate ideas, values, and attitudes which were in fact discriminatory against the very classes whose support it so desperately needed."[19] Thus working-class participation in church services was a way of "self-verification" rather than a re-defining of the church's self-understanding. Eagleton remarks how this church–working class relationship grew out of and reflected the whole reality of nineteenth-century capitalism, where "a similar exclusion-participation" of the workers prevailed.

While positive energy was expended into recruiting members, the church at the same time sought to resist any attack or criticism of itself. Eagleton notes how the church was, in fact, "a major ideological instrument" in a process of mystifying people "to interiorize capitalist morality, either by direct teaching, or by transposing specific attitudes into grandly cosmic formulae."[20] Members of the working class could be seen as "dirty, debauched criminals" *and* simultaneously as "immortal souls" needing salvation. In this way they were repressed, and active recruitment went hand in hand with a sense of suspicion and hostility.[21] Eagleton comments that this sense of "confusion of altruism with hostility" was deep-seated in Victorian sensibility, Dickens' novels being a prime exponent of this situation. Missionary zeal and ecclesiastical self-interest were inextricably linked, and while "some genuine self-criticism went on within the church," fundamental values and structures were left unexamined.[22]

A second significant failure in nineteenth-century Christian social thought, Eagleton argues, was the inability to translate "a radical consciousness into terms of actual, detailed institutional change and its hostility . . . to all idea[s] of programmes and institutions as significant elements in social thinking."[23] Eagleton refers to F. D. Maurice, who

19. Ibid., 60.
20. Ibid., 63.
21. Ibid., 64.
22. Ibid., 67–68.
23. Ibid., 69.

Part III: Towards a Radical Church

voiced that Christian socialism was "a moral crusade, a revolution in men's hearts." Thus Christian socialism focused on human relationships and morality but kept aloof from concrete social-political organizations and issues. "The basic contradiction in Christian socialism was that it attempted a radical critique of contemporary society in the context of an ultimate disbelief in social reality as an object worthy of absolute attention."[24] And this, Eagleton observes, was Christian socialism's fundamental paradox—its "cosmic sense" and "depth" was the "basic cause of its impotence."[25] In its ultimate emphasis of the religious dimension in socialism—i.e., the human being in relationship with the divine and its distrust of, and lack of interest in, institutions—it failed to grapple with the actual social situation. Eagleton notes that Christian socialism therefore was characterized by a "poetic humanitarianism" and a "vague ethic of goodness which was cultivated in a separate compartment of feeling, distinct from institutional concern."[26] In contrast, the Oxford Movement stressed the concrete cooperative church community "as an image of an ideal society." However, it did not survive in its ambitions.[27]

Eagleton comments that this discrepancy between the moral and institutional has continued into our own time, the church being still uncertain about its involvement in actual social and political situations.[28] He suggests that what is necessary thus is a translation of personal authenticity and radical consciousness into communal, institutional engagement.[29]

The "third major failure," as Eagleton sees it, lies in the fact that Christian social thought in its attack of industrial capitalism often tended to "attack from the wrong positions."[30] He argues how in the nineteenth century reactionary elements were "built into most anti-capitalist protest."[31] Thus progressive and reactionary elements intertwined, and this dilemma was particularly obvious in Christian thinking of that epoch:

24. Ibid., 70.
25. Ibid., 71.
26. Ibid., 73.
27. Ibid., 74.
28. Ibid., 74–75.
29. Cf. ibid., 69.
30. Ibid., 77.
31. Ibid., 77.

> The need to attack industrial capitalism from the basis of known, alternative experience of relationship could mean a retrogressive attachment to a remembered "organic" society; a sense of the disruptive individualism of bourgeois democracy could lead to a call for a society under strong authoritarian structures; the need for prototypical relationships and communities could entail a social application of paternal and family relationships which became in political terms reactionary . . .[32]

Eagleton argues that Christian political protest was especially vulnerable to such negative elements due to its "innate conservatism." Attitudes of "medievalism" and "authoritarianism" were deeply ingrained in Christian history, and recourse to such attitudes could result in a context of a perceived loss of "true order" and "organic relationship." Thus socialism would not entail a necessary change of consciousness and a turn towards more complex assessments of the political, cultural, and social situation. Instead, apparent radical attitudes emerged from a conservative allegiance to an ordered, organic, pre-industrial society. What this actually signified was a disengagement from current society and its problems. Referring specifically to the Catholic Church in the 1960s, Eagleton notes that the failures in the nineteenth century—the lack of commitment and mistrust towards institutions and programs—were mediated into our own period, i.e., an inability to think beyond traditional "paternalistic and family models" in the context of church and community, as well as a preoccupation with personal activity instead of venturing into "complex sociological thinking."[33]

While social and theological renewal took place in the twentieth-century British middle class, the "conservative tradition" among the Catholic working class, "deeply influenced by Irish attitudes," meant that a genuine "radical alternative" to the merely liberal renewal of the middle class has not emerged. Thus the Catholic situation was a reflection of the general political situation. Eagleton concludes by stating the obvious: if Christians wish to be truly authentic radicals, we need to learn from our past mistakes.[34]

---

32. Ibid., 78.
33. Ibid., 81.
34. Ibid., 82.

Part III: Towards a Radical Church

"The Revolution Betrayed"[35]

No doubt, we ought to learn from our past mistakes. However, when one looks at the history of the church, it seems that while some lessons have been learned, recurring problems, sins, and, in some cases, unspeakable crimes (e.g., clerical sexual abuse) have emerged. The hope for a church that is consistently reformed, purified, and becomes increasingly holy, remains a hope, an aspiration, but clearly not a reality in the here and now. In his second chapter in *Reason Faith and Revolution*, Eagleton remarks:

> Apart from the signal instance of Stalinism, it is hard to think of a historical movement that has more squalidly betrayed its own revolutionary origins. Christianity long ago shifted from the side of the poor and dispossessed to that of the rich and aggressive. The liberal Establishment really has little to fear from it and everything to gain. For the most part, it has become the creed of the suburban well-to-do, not the astonishing promise offered to the riffraff and undercover anti-colonial militants with whom Jesus himself hung out.[36]

No doubt, this description holds for many churches, in particular in Europe and North America. It seems we have indeed learned little and frequently do not practice the revolutionary actions and teachings of Christ. In Europe, the churches today are largely middle-class establishments, which, while often eloquently preaching about the poor and outcasts, are for the most part shaped and attended by educated citizens who have never known hunger, thirst, homelessness, and lack of access to education. Of course, in the developing countries this is often not the case, as the churches, missionaries, and church-aid organizations are largely concerned with work among those who suffer most. Yet, there too connections and collusion between financial elites, state military, and certain high-ranking church officials are not uncommon.

Often and only too willingly Christians have arranged themselves with the culture and politics of the day rather than taking a decided stance against injustices and totalitarian politics. Eagleton does not hold back in pointing out that churchgoing Christians have frequently

---

35. Heading of chapter 2 in *Reason, Faith, and Revolution*, 47.
36. Eagleton, *Reason, Faith, and Revolution*, 55.

conformed "to the powers of this world, Christianity has become the nauseating cant of lying politicians, corrupt bankers, and financial neocons, as well as an immensely profitable industry."[37] The massive crimes by (mainly Catholic) clergy, who violently and/or sexually abused children, women, and men over decades must be added to the particular horrors of the church's betrayal of Christ. Again and again churches have betrayed their own foundations, their own preaching and belief in the God of love: through crusades, witch hunts, burning, and excommunications of so-called heretics, mindless indoctrination, and brainwashing. The churches frequently kept silent when they should have protested; they have been complicit with state powers such as during the Second World War in the face of the Holocaust. The institutional churches have suppressed women (despicably to this day in various denominations, not only in the Catholic Church), and silenced loyal critics, i.e., those theologians who have not given up hope for a more Christ-like society, a more Christ-like open church of apostolic witness, which at times entails radical questioning of church teachings, and the ecclesial and societal status quo. As Eagleton comments, "the Christian church has tortured and disemboweled in the name of Jesus, gagging dissent and burning its critics alive. It has been oily, sanctimonious, brutally oppressive, and vilely bigoted."[38]

No century—in the relatively short history of Christianity, measured in terms of the history of humankind—has been without betrayals of Christ; small, personal ones on a daily basis in the life of individual church members, and colossal ones in terms of the wrongs committed by church institutions, often hand in hand with state systems, i.e., the political and economic leaders who might profess personal and collective allegiance to the church of Christ, but often act starkly contrary to God's commandment of love of neighbor and good stewardship of the earth. Certainly Eagleton is right when he notes that these acts of betrayal stand under "the judgment of the Gospel itself."[39]

---

37. Ibid., 56.
38. Ibid., 56.
39. Ibid., 68.

Part III: Towards a Radical Church

The New Left Church

In the face of this history, then, what is Eagleton's vision of the new left church? The book (of the same title) contains articles on church, literature, and politics, Eagleton's "implicit claim" being that for Christians these three strands always affect each other. Thus he hopes to persuade Christians that to be church "involves commitment to imaginative culture and the political left."[40] He points out that these two spheres, imaginative culture and the political left, have had a strong link. What the church, politics, and the arts have in common is the fact that each goes some way to describe what it means to be human.[41] He argues that these three spheres ultimately "come . . . to the same description."

> One nodal point where the strands are drawn together is in the idea of culture: here we have the term which mediates each concern into the other, deepening our understanding of the church through literary insight and translating this into commitment within society. Or, conversely, deepening our understanding of politics through Christian insight and doing this in terms of literature: all movement within the web comes to the same centre.[42]

Again he notes how Christians have often been slow to make this vital connection between the divine/spiritual realm *and* the call to human, political commitment. For example, he argues that if a Christian is moved by the Spirit in a literary masterwork, she is in fact coming into contact with the depth of existential reality. Our "deepest vital instinct[s]" are "measured against" actual structures, relationships, and society. His central aim is thus to show that what we say about church and culture are also critical political statements.[43]

To belong to the new left church for Eagleton means to realize that fundamentally Christian faith is "extreme and uncompromising in its love and tolerance."[44] There is no room for half measure; being committed to Christ is total and thus can be potentially tragic. Such a way of

---

40. Eagleton, *New Left Church*, vii.
41. Ibid., viii.
42. Ibid.
43. Ibid., x.
44. Ibid., 2.

life in its intensity seems, however, largely incompatible with our existence as members of society, as it demands a degree of wholeness and integrity that in a capitalist system and in a culture of mediocre conformity (often branded as "individuality" or individualism) may lead more likely to self-destruction and failure than to success—"failure" at least in the eyes of the world, as Jesus' death seemed a failure to many.

A life of intensity, Eagleton notes, moves one towards a "thirst for truth" and in this way makes a person dangerous and stand apart from society.[45] In this context he mentions Arthur Miller's *Death of a Salesman* and *All My Sons*, as well as Ibsen's *Brand*. "Miller and Ibsen point to the general dilemma: how is intensity to be fed creatively to society?"[46]

As Christians, we are faced with the dilemma of being commanded by Christ to living intensely without compromise and thus potentially suffering for our faith, while at the same time we are supposed to offer ideas on how humans should live together in a good society. The problem lies in the fact that despite solemn proclamations from the Sunday pulpit or the best intentions expressed in "presidential addresses," individuals as well as societies in their structures and everyday life have consistently betrayed the very values and beliefs they hold dearest.[47] Undeniably, the vast discrepancy between the ideal and everyday reality is incessantly brought home to us through the various media.

What Eagleton advocates, then, is a society where "the common life of work" is understood as sacramental. With reference to Rahner and Daniélou, he points out how even progressive theologians—while going some way to stress the importance of just structures—have failed to go so far as to say that the need to build a "just material community" can be viewed as being "fully attuned to the creative movement of salvation history." Eagleton wrote this in the 1960s before the development of liberation theology, which sought to grapple with this issue, i.e., by drawing the link between praxis-commitment to just societies in *this* world while acknowledging that our faith is founded on the God who will only be fully known in the *eschaton*. Hence "the Christian task is . . . to fuse the intensity of spontaneous living with the common detail of

---

45. Ibid., 4–5.
46. Ibid., 5.
47. Eagleton, *Reason, Faith, and Revolution*, 46.

Part III: Towards a Radical Church

social life."⁴⁸ In turning to socialism, Eagleton holds, we find the possibility to address that dual commitment, which ultimately springs from a concern for wholeness. In a new engagement with socialism—itself in need of healing due to gross aberrations in the past—we must rediscover the sense of its "human depth" *and* its "practical force."⁴⁹

According to Eagleton, the English socialist intellectual, writer, artist, and textile designer William Morris (1834–1896) was exemplary in how this goal might be envisaged. In the context of the age of industrialization, Morris, who was associated with the Pre-Raphaelites and the English Arts and Crafts Movements, affirmed that work has a value in itself as an important part of human existence, not simply as a means of making a livelihood. The work process should have dignity; it should be useful and pleasant without leading to anxiety and burnout. As Morris saw it, the "price to be paid for so making the world happy is Revolution: Socialism instead of *laissez-faire*."⁵⁰ Morris supposedly exclaimed: "With the arrogance of youth, I determined to do no less than to transform the world with Beauty. If I have succeeded in some small way, if only in one small corner of the world, amongst the men and women I love, then I shall count myself blessed, and blessed, and blessed. . ."⁵¹

When one considers the ugly architecture in former states under *Realsozialismus*, with their complete lack of aesthetic beauty or imagination, one realizes that such architecture is indeed worlds removed from what high-minded, if highly idealistic, social thinkers like Morris had in mind. The same, of course, applies to the process of work, i.e., the alienated and alienating work that millions of people are forced to endure on a daily basis for bare survival—a far cry from a just, life-

---

48. Eagleton, *New Left Church*, 16.

49. Ibid.

50. In his lecture *Art and Socialism*, January 23, 1884, Morris stated: "*It is right and necessary that all men should have work to do which shall be worth doing, and be of itself pleasant to do; and which should be done under such conditions as would make it neither over-wearisome nor over-anxious.* Turn that claim about as I may, think of it as long as I can, I cannot find that it is an exorbitant claim; yet again I say if Society [sic] would or could admit it, the face of the world would be changed; discontent and strife and dishonesty would be ended. To feel that we were doing work useful to others and pleasant to ourselves, and that such work and its due reward could not fail us! What serious harm could happen to us then?"

51. Morris quoted in Marsh, *William Morris and Red House*, 65.

giving material community for all. In this context, Eagleton opines that Marxist humanists and Christians can give the "most meaningful accounts of work"; for both, work is usually understood as a communal, collaborative enterprise that should be creative and have meaning.[52]

From a wider focus of what it means to live as a socialist and Christian in society, Eagleton goes on to address "relationships and functions within the church as part of a wider social reality."[53] He comments that possibilities of relationships within the church are essentially "*cultural* possibilities, supplied to us by our kind of society," whereby it is impossible to neatly separate elements of the "world" from elements of the "church," but to realize that they exist in a "complex field of experience" where such clear distinctions and labels of "church" and "world" do not hold. Here he unfolds what he calls the "new theology" which

> prohibits this kind of distinction in many ways . . . by seeing that Christianity is about the collapsing of the old tensions between sacred and secular, concerned ultimately with the abolition of cult and ritual and the whole paraphernalia of religion, moving towards that fully human community in Christ where religion will have become outdated; it does it also by recognizing that the major way in which the layman is part of the church is the way he is part of the world: through his work and action. What we need to grasp is that the power of the liturgy as a social force, one transforming society, depends on the values and relationships we bring to it as well as those we take from it . . . What we are in church depends on what we are in the world, as well as vice versa: if we do not have the language for human communication in society then we will be equally inarticulate when we come to use the language of the word of God. Equally, of course, we cannot have a fully real society without a real church; by a *real* society I mean one in touch with the reality of the world since Christ . . . and therefore a godly society. This does not of course mean a society where 51% of the population attend Sunday mass or anything of that kind, since it seems obvious that one could quite easily have a godly society which was actively hostile to religion—in fact that at times one of the marks of godliness would be precisely this hostility.[54]

---

52. Eagleton, *New Left Church*, 63–64.
53. Ibid., 86–87.
54. Ibid., 87–88.

Eagleton notes that before one can say something about the priest and the changing of the priest's role in society one must become aware of the current political structures in a society. Writing in the 1960s, he asserts that fundamentally society had passed through a "liberal-paternalist crisis." A significant part of the problem of this crisis was that people largely refused to become conscious of it. First, therefore, the nature and reality of that crisis must be identified, in order to get away from its "mystification" and concealment. Only then could one hope to arrive at the "actual truth" of the present "social condition."

What essentially had happened in Britain, according to Eagleton, was a century-long process of change from "the idea of authoritarianism as a model of human relationships, to the idea of democracy."[55] Significantly, he asserts that the understanding of the role of the priest was and is directly linked to this liberal-paternalist crisis. Thus our ideas about priesthood are "not only theological ideas, but part of a general pattern of change in our whole society" in which relationships, roles and values have been redefined.[56]

The central problem regarding liberal paternalism is that it was a process of mystification: capitalist structures remained essentially untouched while interpretations and explanations were and are offered that on the surface are coherent enough to "block critical insight." "The progress of capitalism . . . has been to concede a great deal to growing . . . demands for humane responsibility, but only to a point where it can keep its essential social and economic structures unaltered."[57]

The "ladder" is the image that best conveys the "ethos" of liberal paternalism.[58] While those who climb the ladder may also now include members of the working classes, those from comfortable middle-class homes still are far more likely to succeed in the capitalist system than are their worker fellow citizens. The more unquestioningly one aligns oneself with the system, the better one's chances to "do well." Those who prefer values such as solidarity, equal rights, and justice to the ladder may choose a more difficult path. However, as Eagleton wryly remarks, everyone makes their compromises.

55. Ibid., 91.
56. Ibid., 89.
57. Ibid., 92.
58. Ibid., 94.

A New Left Church? Terry Eagleton

In factories operating in the mould of "old capitalism," grossly underpaid workers hated their mean employers and their alienating work. Yet, Eagleton notes how in the "new" capitalism workers are made to feel involved and *seemingly* cherished by their firms as if they were part of a big happy family. These firms, however, can be the most callous ones in the end. For example, managers of large multi-nationals and of banks may provide attractive *boni* for their employees as long as they and the company are gaining massive profits, but, if necessary, will have little hesitation to move their operation into other countries to get even better gains through a cheaper work force. Thus factories should be run on "the basis of cooperative equality."[59] Decisions about work should be made in common in a proper democratic process, whereby people are their own managers and take control of their lives. Such experiments have been tried, and in some cases companies have been successfully run on those premises. Looking, however, at today's economic situation with ever-larger international companies dominating the market, Eagleton's words, written over 40 years ago, are wonderful and true but disturbingly far removed from the stark reality of the world's capitalist systems in the early twenty-first century.[60]

Eagleton rightly comments that for Christians "free selfhood" is an essential aim.[61] The freedom of a Christian is fundamental. Here he concurs with a certain monk from Wittenberg who affirmed this already half a millennium earlier! Paternalism is a mode of operation that Christians should reject. Not paternalism but love, friendship, and respect between all humans as equals before God ought to guide Christian life and community. It is Christ himself who made the point of calling his disciples—us—not subordinate servants but friends: "You are my friends if you do what I command you. I do not call you servants any longer, because the servant does not know what the master is doing; but I have called you friends, because I have made known to you everything that I have heard from my Father. You did not choose me but I chose you. And I appointed you to go and bear fruit . . . so that the Father will give you whatever you ask him in my name. I am giving you these commands so that you may love one another" (John 15:14–17).

59. Ibid., 98.
60. For an analysis of globalization and the church, see Mannion, "Driving the Haywain," 13–34.
61. Eagleton, *New Left Church*, 98.

Part III: Towards a Radical Church

One of the most relevant, uncompromising insights in Eagleton's *The New Left Church* is his perceptive examination of how paternalism operates in both society and the church. Here he refers specifically to the Catholic Church: "The problem, with church and society, is how to meet and satisfy demands from 'below' without relinquishing real power, without opening the floodgates to basic structural change."[62] Here he lays his finger on *the* issue that has been crucial since the Second Vatican Council. He points out how terms such as "lay participation" and "consultation" have guided the *modus operandi* in progressive post-Vatican II church circles. These, *apparently* progressive, notions, however, are essentially "*mystifying and self-justifying paternalist attitudes.*"[63] This observation points to the crux of the matter, and it is rare to find a Catholic thinker who has said this so frankly:

> "Consultation" is the familiar paternalist word: it suggests the General-de-Gaulle-technique of bending a kindly ear without any ultimate necessity to accept the opinions of those consulted; it suggests, more deeply, that the policy-making remains in traditional hands, but the policy-makers are now more willing to listen to constructive proposals from outside. This is also what "participation" can suggest: sharing in processes which remain ultimately the monopoly of others. . . . The whole of English catholicism [sic] has conspired to make the present situation one of paternalism.[64]

Eagleton comments how the (British) middle class, while today more educated and more engaged in free, liberal discourse, will, however, mostly stay within the boundaries of "liberal conformism." He asserts that any genuine *radical* thinking emerged from those who were either "born into the working class," or who have been "sympathetic to its political traditions."[65] In an interview with the German weekly newspaper *Die Zeit* in 2010, the French sociologist Luc Boltanski strikingly argues along similar lines. Asked what he would suggest about envisioning "projects" that would aim to oppose social-economic situations of "dependency and oppression," he notes that such projects really only emerge in revolutionary rebellion. The French Revolution and later the

62. Ibid., 101.
63. My emphasis.
64. Eagleton, *New Left Church*, 101–2.
65. Ibid., 103.

workers' movement have shown that anger and dismay are necessary to bring about new ideas, a view that finds its origin already in Schiller and Marx.[66]

Eagleton argues that fundamentally the changing ideas of the priest's role and of the understanding of the (Catholic) Church are akin to society's change from authoritarianism through liberal paternalism to "full democracy." While he acknowledges that much change has happened, it is not going far enough. What must be addressed first is the "structure of the parish."[67] Renewal of parish life is insufficient; what needs to be realized is the fact that the parish operates from the "wrong kind of structure." Parishes should not function as separate "welfare states" within society, but "work alongside and within the general social movement towards a good society."[68] Thus he emphasizes that work in the parish should be "within the social structures, not in duplicated structures" as this makes our ideas of what it is to be church "more flexible and spontaneous." Eagleton writes that the need for local community has often been taken as the grounds for keeping the parish system. However, while he concedes that it is important to continue to celebrate church services in local groups, it is essential to assert that "the only parish is ultimately the whole of society." In the final part, I will come back to this point, as his argument here is as attractive as it is controversial and idealistic—especially in view of today's multicultural and multi-religious societies—a fact that was not as pressing four decades ago when he wrote his book.

Eagleton becomes even more radical in reflecting on the parish as the organizational structure of the local church. He considers the parish an "inadequate progressive idea" and advocates a "common culture," whereby the idea of subsidiarity must be rejected, as it is a pre-industrial view of society. Rather we should seek "to create a society where any *random* group could celebrate the eucharist meaningfully because their sense of community" would not be grounded in specific geographical locations or common activities, but in one's "belonging to the same society."[69] This society, in which democracy is fully realized, would be a

---

66. Cf. von Randow's Interview with L. Boltanski, "Regeln sind nicht göttlich."
67. Eagleton, *New Left Church*, 105.
68. Ibid., 106.
69. Ibid., 108.

community of genuine "*common* responsibility," a community of "care," "guilt" and "consolation"; i.e., a holistic community where everyone contributes to the building of that society.[70] He is aware, however, that we are far from the realization of such a society, a society based on true democratic equality.

The priest then should not be a person set apart in a "caste" and operating in a paternalist fashion. S/he should not be a duplicate of psychologists or sociologists. Essentially the priest is the one who presides at the liturgical assembly, the one whose task it is to preach the word of God. However, he points out that while the priest has the authority to celebrate the liturgy, we may have to "return" to view the idea of the priest's function "as much less permanent and more intermittent," as the liturgy itself is intermittent. Wearing black, being celibate, and spending one's time in between services as a "social welfare officer" should not be required of the ordained. Rather—and here his stance is radical as he develops the idea of the worker-priest—we will not be rid of paternalism until clergy are

> ordinary workers with families who have this special function to preside over the liturgy in a church where the activities of teaching, welfare, and preaching are genuinely common, not the monopoly of a caste. The ideal is a self-teaching, self-caring church, as well as a self-teaching, self-caring society: teaching must be a continuous activity involving everyone, both as teacher and taught, a shared network of learning . . .[71]

Thus we ought to return to viewing the priest in a much more limited role, as a "man" (I suggest that today Eagleton would most likely say "man or woman"), who is "delegated for a special function." Thus the priests' function is "in a sense to eliminate themselves so that the church can operate."[72] Fully aware that this re-definition of the priestly role is a long-term issue—and again a highly idealistic one—steps should be taken now to start this process of democratization. As long as parishes form the local church, laity ought to elect their priests. Clergy must be responsible to the parish and the parish must have the right to dismiss priests. Unless the local churches return to the practice of electing their

---

70. Ibid., 108–9.
71. Ibid., 112.
72. Ibid., 113.

priests—as in the early church and in many Protestant churches—"no real democracy is possible."[73]

In this context he also makes some critical observations about the idea of "service" that has been propounded as "an ideal image of the relationship between priest and people and church and society."[74] The notion of service is, to some extent, another progressive theological idea, which, he notes, still falls into the mode of liberal paternalism: it appears to present an "acceptable description . . . of a situation which remains structurally unacceptable."[75] With reference to Raymond Williams' *Culture and Society*, Eagleton astutely observes how the "upper servants" in a given society may be perceived to "serve" the "lower servants," but that the lower servants may not necessarily feel at all that they belong to the community in any meaningful and real sense. Thus the idea of "service" actually mystifies as it masks the fact that the structures and the status quo go unchallenged and remain as they are. Any kind of true sense of service, therefore, namely the building of "a whole relationship" must not be confused with a service that simply ratifies the status quo.[76] No doubt, he is right when he comments that priests and, in particular, bishops are described as servants when in truth they, especially the hierarchy, still make all the rules in top-down fashion.

Eagleton further notes how the manner and act of communication are vital in this context. Do we use language in the church that is truly democratic, thereby communicating a genuine sense of equality and respect? Do we communicate this in our sermons, and do our sermons communicate what it means to build a true community? "What we are looking for in society is a kind of communication which will establish community between men [and women], as in the liturgy Christ is established at the focus of a number of converging human communications."[77] Hence, if we can truly grapple with theses issues, the move from liberal paternalism to "real community" might be possible.

73. Ibid., 114.
74. Ibid., 114–15.
75. Ibid., 115.
76. Ibid., 117.
77. Ibid., 118.

Part III: Towards a Radical Church

In a surprisingly frank confession of faith, Eagleton states that "since the resurrection, the meaning of community has been Christ."[78] Christ is at the "creative centre of all life." To live in and through Christ is the very meaning of what it is to be human and what it is to be community. Echoing Rahner (whether he read Rahner or not cannot be ascertained here) with his notion of the anonymous Christian, Eagleton comments that all humans share in the "Christ reality of the universe." Thus if we "build community" we "build Christ irrespective of the conscious belief and commitment of the builder."[79] If we fail to establish community we fail Christ. Unlike many of Eagleton's other radical views, such emphatic christological, Christ-centered statements would be shared by most conservative Christians. Christianity, then, is "the way" Christ and the Christian community are "present in the world."[80]

Eagleton relates his understanding of community in Christ to the Marxist meaning of reality and historical progression: if Christians do good, i.e., when they build community, they are in touch with reality in the "Marxist sense" of a "definitive, significant direction in history." Marxists, too, contribute to the progress of history by building "community within capitalism."[81] However, while such a view was still attractive in the 1960s, it seems rather out-of-date in today's postmodern world after the fall of the Eastern bloc and failure of *Realsozialismus*. In fact, the Enlightenment notion of history as ever progressive had already ceased with World War I.

Yet Eagleton is right when he refers to the historicity of Christianity, a notion that became urgent to theologians like Moltmann, Sölle, and Pannenberg in the aftermath of the Second World War and the Holocaust. Eagleton rightly observes that Christians have often tended to equate "the real" with an interiorized life of faith, "a concealed spiritual reality behind physical actuality."[82] In this sense his plea for action in the material reality of human history, i.e., the call to building community, remains an urgent task. An interior, privatized life of prayer, while important, is certainly not sufficient in building Christian

78. Ibid., 142.
79. Ibid., 143.
80. Ibid., 162.
81. Ibid., 143.
82. Ibid., 144.

community and a Christian society. Anyone who commits to fostering community in the reality of human existence lives in the spirit of Christ.[83] And so he asserts, again as Rahner would, that any person who acts in a humane fashion, anyone who is "most human," is "living the life of Christ."[84] "The Christian and the social radical are saying the same thing: we belong to ourselves insofar as we belong to each other."[85]

Eagleton notes that "real" could be replaced by "authentic." We are authentic if we are in touch with human reality; we live authentically if we are "in touch with Christ." Being most authentic means to do good spontaneously by being truly oneself.[86] Eagleton uses the image of the dance to convey the meaning of humans living in harmonious community. In the dance each member is fully her/himself while also interwoven with others. In dance both "physical selfhood" and community with others are fully realized. In such a community people can be their authentic selves, without compromising hypocrisy, having to keep silent, or, in extreme cases, having to die for their beliefs. Here Eagleton mentions how thinkers like Dickens, Mill, and Carlyle were critical of Victorian society not just as a "bad" society but as a "false" society. However, while Victorian society is long past, the greedy, materialist, and individualist yet conformist societies of today do little to promote an authentic, community-centered, Christ-like life either.

If people cannot be truly themselves, i.e., live authentically, they are alienated from themselves and others. This can lead to breakdown in communication, to withdrawal, the alienated self feeling increasingly outside the community, as he or she does not find him/herself heard and valued by the dominant group. It was Marx who examined social alienation at length, commenting on how in capitalism workers are alienated as the work does not belong to themselves.[87] Instead of being creative, spontaneous, imaginative, and taking responsibility and charge of their work, creativity and the imagination as well as a sense of ownership and self-worth are stultified. Thus the worker will become inauthentic as she loses any sense of seeing herself in her work and

83. Ibid.
84. Ibid., 145.
85. Ibid., 150.
86. Ibid., 146.
87. Ibid., 158.

Part III: Towards a Radical Church

its products. This creates severe loss of meaning, when survival (i.e., money) becomes the sole object of work. With reference to R. D. Laing, Eagleton observes that such a situation is ultimately schizophrenic, as the schizophrenic sees himself as "persecuted by reality itself."[88]

Eagleton then relates these insights to the idea of Christian community. The significance of Marx's and Laing's insights, he comments, lies in the fact that Christian community is essentially about "authentic living"; it is about how we build Christ in the world, how he is present among us. In Christ, we are reconciled to our true selves. In Him we live "with his life."[89] Similarly, in true socialism, as envisaged by Marx, people should "live out the real meaning of being human, find themselves truly reflected in their work, live with each others' lives."[90] Therefore instead of being reduced to objects, the task is to foster a society in which people are *subjects*, a society where one orders one's life with autonomy *and* responsibility towards one another in a community free of exploitation.[91] On the other hand, to fall away from Christ is to fall away from community and human meaning.

Eagleton asks how this can be achieved and points out that for Christians such a kind of society has its prototype in the liturgy. In the liturgy, everyone, with their own concerns and situation, is "reconciled in Christ." Christ is "the living unity which resides in the interior of each subjectivity, the whole community present simultaneously within each member of it, and fully available simultaneously to each member . . . [T]he basis of community is a reciprocity of subjects each interiorizing the subjective, free self of the other and being mutually interiorized."[92] Eagleton asserts that this is possible for Christians if they truly "live Christ's life . . . encountering Christ in the other."[93]

While one would like to agree with Eagleton, the question arises whether Christians *actually experience* the liturgy as the prototype of a Christian society. Are our *actual* weekly celebrations of liturgical worship and Eagleton's *idea* (*ideal*) of the liturgy as the prototype of a

---

88. Eagleton quoting R. D. Laing, *Divided Self*, 80, in Ibid., 154.
89. Eagleton, *New Left Church*, 163.
90. Ibid., 163.
91. Ibid., 165–66.
92. Ibid., 167.
93. Ibid.

Christian society and community congruent? I will return to this question in my conclusion.

To live authentically then is to live in community and therefore to live "the life of Christ."[94] All creation and all life spring from God in Christ, and "the church is the way he makes all his creation his own."[95] Eagleton notes that Christians have often failed to realize that Christianity is essentially "about community" and not about "judgement."[96] We know we are sinners, yet this must not lead us to self-condemnation, but be the basis on which we build community. In this sense it is essential also that each person in community must respect and love her/himself if s/he truly wants to love others. Otherwise "the real danger involved in entering sympathetically into all life" may risk a "loss of identity."[97] A healthy sense of self-identity is the ground for entering into relationship with others, and likewise it is in community where we find our true selves. It is crucial to achieve this balance.

Yet, being in community is demanding. Building community with fellow human beings who confess their Christian faith on Sundays and exploit their fellow human beings during the week is a serious challenge: "How are we to be inwardly sympathetic to men who drop A-bombs and operate policies which prevent millions of people all over the world from living real human lives?"[98] Yes, indeed!

Moreover, attending to *one's own* shortcomings in living the life of Christ is an equally serious challenge. To work for, with, and in the Christian community is as demanding as it is beautiful and it includes humility as well as the readiness to suffer for one's deepest beliefs. Thereby each member has to find the balance between sympathy with others and living authentically, a task that can entail significant pain and failure.

Eagleton closes his book by reasserting how the liturgy anticipates the ultimate community in Christ and how establishing a Christian society implies profound commitment. If we are not prepared to "dirty our hands," as one might put it, we will make the "stock liberal under-

---

94. Ibid., 169.
95. Ibid., 172.
96. Ibid.
97. Ibid., 174.
98. Ibid., 178.

estimation" of what is asked of us to build a Christian society.[99] We are not beginning "from scratch," but in working towards such a society we "*extend* what we believe already exists as a real fact in the liturgical community."[100] We are thus beginning "from the future, as it exists now in the liturgy, and make this live in the present."[101] And so he asserts that the "relation between world and liturgy is two-way, for it is through our ordinary insight into politics, literature, psychology, that we begin to understand the meaning of the liturgical community. If the church is to help create a common culture, it needs all the resources of our present culture—not as weapons at its disposal, but as ways of understanding the world, and therefore itself."[102] Finally, in order to achieve such a common culture, Eagleton proposes that as a start one might develop a "common language—to begin to build that linguistic community between church and world which has been absent for so long."[103] Such a common language may aid us in making "meanings intelligible to ourselves" and thus to others.[104]

Conclusion: Towards a Christian Society and a New Left Church?

In the final part of this chapter, I will critically discuss some of Eagleton's insights, especially in relation to the question of whether and how his views on being church in our age may have continued relevance today.

Critical Apologia of Faith

When one considers Eagleton's earliest and most recent writings on the themes of faith, church, and culture, one is immediately struck by how the context of his writing has changed. *The New Left Church* is a contribution to a wider, radical ecclesiology, written essentially with the aim of reflecting on the nature and purpose of the contemporary church and

99. Ibid., 179
100. Ibid.
101. Ibid.
102. Ibid., 179–80.
103. Ibid., 180.
104. Ibid.

its connection with society and culture. How to envisage a left church today, how to bring about a more Christian society characterized by genuine equality and cooperation between all members? These issues occupied Eagleton and his friends in a (mainly) British context, where the reality of the World Wide Web, globalization, global capitalism, and pluralistic multi-faith, multi-ethnic societies had not yet become center-stage. It was still the era of a more clear delineation between "left wing" and "right wing" politics, values, and parties. The map of Europe was markedly different, and the northern hemisphere was still split into the eastern and western blocs with two opposed economic systems.

The New Left Church was published two years preceding the student revolts in an atmosphere of emphatic leftist and idealistic convictions among young people who preferred to "make love, not war" and who still dreamt of a world in which true socialism might yet become a reality. In the 1960s, Western Europe also experienced rapid secularization and theologians like Rahner and Tillich found themselves having to reflect on the grounds of Christian faith and church before an increasingly secularized audience, or at least an audience whose faith life was retreating more and more into the private realm without church attendance.

The Yale lectures that make up *Reason, Faith, and Revolution: Reflections on the God Debate*, are written against the contemporary background of the reality of growing globalization, multi-media communications, world-wide capitalism, and pluralistic societies. The most obvious difference when compared with *The New Left Church* is that it is no longer the church, but the very *raison d'être* of Christian faith itself—in a critical response to the cheap atheist agenda of critics like Dawkins and Hitchens—that concerns Eagleton here. This book has been written in our context which is marked by a "return" to religion, including a heightened search for new spiritualities and new ways of faith praxis, as well as a growing secularism, on the one hand, and religious fundamentalism, on the other. Intercultural theology, interreligious dialogue, and, in particular, Christian-Islamic relations, were not yet on syllabi in the 1960s; in our century, however, these studies are obligatory if one wishes to engage with contemporary faith and culture. Eagleton's *Reason, Faith, and Revolution* refers to some of these issues in his discussion. His book is an impassioned yet entirely reasoned, sharp, and entertaining apologia of faith taking to task the militant atheism put forward by "Ditchkins." It is this, as he says, "cheap" atheism, based on downright ignorance, caricature, and prejudice that Eagleton attacks, while at the same time being acutely aware of the "squalid tale of bigotry, superstition, wishful thinking and oppressive ideology" that has been part of religion throughout history.[105] Thus it is as a believer *and* loyal critic of the church that he writes his critical defense of Christian faith, "taking issue" not only with ideological atheists but also with the "political left" who are in "dire need of good ideas."[106] Rightly he notes how the left for the most part has kept an "embarrassed silence" when it comes to learning from the Jewish-Christian Scriptures, which, as he emphasizes, have vital things to say about life, suffering, death, love, forgiveness, etc. Certainly, while being open to Buddhism and Judaism, thinkers on the political left have often shown strong aversion to Christian faith, in particular the institutional churches, and sometimes with good reason. As a Christian with a Marxist background, Eagleton hence calls the left to learn some lessons from religion. Significantly, he urges intellectuals et al. to engage with the "radical impulses" that can be gleaned from contemporary theology.[107]

In considering both works written forty-two years apart from each other, there is thus a sense of continuity in that Eagleton has essentially kept a Christian and Marxist perspective in his thought. Yet, unsurprisingly in the light of contemporary developments in religion and society, his concerns have shifted from more emphatic ecclesiological interests in a more defined (British/European) context to a concern with the role of Christian faith in the world against the agenda of an uninformed atheism, on the one hand, and the context of a renewed interest in religion, on the other.

Before I go on to reflect on some of the issues raised by Eagleton's prophetic voice, it should be said that, considering his writing on the church and on faith as a whole, a more thorough inclusion of past and present theological writings would have benefited his own ideas. While it is obvious that he is aware of thinkers like Aquinas, McCabe, Barth, and Tillich, a wider and more in-depth engagement with theologians would not only have strengthened his argument, but in doing so he

---

105. Eagleton, *Reason, Faith, and Revolution*, xi.
106. Ibid., xi–xii.
107. Ibid., 167.

A New Left Church? Terry Eagleton

might also have found some radical voices in the church's tradition to support his own vision. However, this is a small criticism and does not take away from his radical arguments, which at times read like a breath of fresh air!

Advocating Liberation Theology

In reflecting on the nature and purpose of the church today, one needs to look back. In spite of the church's often flagrant infidelity towards Christ in history up to our own day—in particular by many who have been involved in church leadership—the church as the people of God has existed and survived through its countless unsung heroes, those faithful who try to live to the best of their capacity according to the message of Christ.

Eagleton's incisive critique of the church's betrayal through the centuries of its radical and revolutionary roots is necessary and to the point. As demonstrated in the first part of this chapter, he does not hold back in speaking about the church's often abysmal unfaithfulness towards Christ and His teachings through history. It is in the light of Eagleton's awareness of Christianity's continuous failures that his reflection on the church and his defense of faith become all the more convincing and urgent. His comments have much in common with a theologian like Leonardo Boff, who, in his controversial book *Church: Charism and Power* (1981), presented a strident critique of his church. Writing about the "pathologies of Roman Catholicism," Boff notes:

> The absolutizing of a form of the Church's presence in society led to the oppression of the faithful . . . The drive for security was much stronger than that for truth and authenticity. Tensions were, and are, frequently suffocated through a repression that often violates the basic human rights . . . The rejection of Protestantism was a historical mistake not only because Luther was excommunicated but because any possibility of true criticism or questioning of the system in the name of the Gospel was also expelled. Catholicism became a total, reactionary, violent and repressive ideology.[108]

---

108. Boff, *Church*, 85–86.

Part III: Towards a Radical Church

Thirty years and countless revelations of church abuses later, including not only sex and violence abuses but also the suppression of loyal dissent of numerous theologians (including Boff) and clergy, Boff's comments are as topical as they were in the 1980s, possibly even more so. It does not come as a surprise, therefore, that Eagleton with his background in left politics and a highly critical outlook on his own church, has much in common with theologians like Boff. In fact, Eagleton refers to liberation theology in *Reason, Faith and Revolution*, and goes so far as to say, that "all authentic theology is liberation theology."[109]

While in recent years liberation theology has sometimes been considered a bit "passé," one needs to point out that as long as there are millions in our world who lack the basics of life, liberation theology is anything but obsolete, but remains an imperative. Speaking out for the under-privileged is what faith in Jesus Christ demands from Christians and theologians. And this not only applies to the economically poor but to all human beings who suffer discrimination and marginalization of any kind (race, women, children, people of same-sex sexual orientation, etc.), and it applies with particular urgency to our planet. Therefore the various liberation theologies that emerged from the 1970s onwards must continue to be developed and play a significant role in contemporary theology.

In a recently published volume, *Movement or Moment?*, an assessment of the theology of liberation forty years after Medellín, David Tombs concludes that while liberation theology's term "liberation" may seem outmoded in a world of neo-liberal economics, theology in developing countries need to "keep faith with and build upon" the political, epistemological, and methodological principles of liberation theology, especially as poverty in Latin America has not improved but worsened.[110]

In the light of a continuing awareness among theologians about the relevance of the various liberation theologies as they began to take hold in the two-thirds world over three decades ago, Eagleton's linking of socialism and Christian faith throughout *The New Left Church* and in his most recent writings make him an ideal conversation partner for,

---

109. Eagleton, *Reason, Faith, and Revolution*, 32.
110. Tombs, "Latin American Liberation Theology," 52–53.

A New Left Church? Terry Eagleton

and ally with, those theologians operating from a liberation-theological and socially engaged Christian perspective.

Rethinking Church Structures

In reflecting on the church as apostolic, ecumenical, and prophetically radical, as has been our concern, one wonders whether the vision of a "new left church," as envisaged by Eagleton et al. in the 1960s, still is an option for ecclesial self-understanding. Could such a church be the answer to deep ecclesiastical failures? Will the radical ideas for the change of church structures, as proposed by Eagleton, ever have the chance of realization?

PATERNALISM

One of the considerable strengths in *The New Left Church* is Eagleton's sharp analysis of the way paternalism has been central in capitalist societies and in church leadership. Here he takes issue, in particular, with the Catholic Church. Power in both society and church remains in the hands of a few and the "ladder" is the quintessential image of the structure of Western economies and of a hierarchical church. Vatican II was a major attempt to reform the Catholic Church. "Consultation" and "lay participation" became key concepts for a greater role of lay involvement in the church. But, as Eagleton rightly points out, these notions are in themselves paternalist. They veil the fact that church leaders, while involving the laity more than in the past, basically retain all the power in decision making, leadership, and design of ecclesial organization.

The church is not a democracy, John Paul II told Austrian bishops in 2002, and he added that truth cannot be decided upon from below. What an irony indeed that the church of Christ is founded on a person who emerged from "below," from "the people," and who died a violent death due to his challenging of political and religious power-holders. Strongly hierarchical structures in the Catholic Church with top-down decision-making leading to fear, repression, and conformism have in many ways remained unchanged. Countless theologians have lamented this fact, and to some Vatican II now seems an event of the past, which, even if it brought about significant changes, in some respects remained

Part III: Towards a Radical Church

aspirational. Over forty years ago, Eagleton wrote his book under the influence of the new hopes brought about by the second Vatican Council. However, many of those hopes have not been fulfilled, and in some cases developments have regressed rather than progressed.

A stark fact that underscores this lamentable state of affairs is that even forty years later, the Catholic Church, the Orthodox churches and various Lutheran, Anglican, and other churches still operate as the last bastions of women's oppression in their refusal of women's ordination, thus preventing women from obtaining leading positions in the church. This situation is so grossly offensive that in this day and age it is difficult to show patience towards those who are determined to keep the status quo in this matter. Almost twenty years ago, in 1992, George Tavard, a peritus at Vatican II, remarked on the "emancipation of women in modern society" and hence the "inescapable" fact of their "parallel emancipation" also within the church. He called for the ordination of women, as have other theologians, male and female.[111] Indeed, time for serious change is long overdue. However, this should not mean that women simply take on and accept ecclesial structures as they have existed through Christendom. Rather, it is for women and men to creatively and ecumenically *rethink together* the church in its institutional make up. While Eagleton does not express any of these sentiments in his early writings on the church—feminist theology only emerged in the 1970s and 80s—I have little doubt that such views would concur with his ecclesiological thought today.

PRIESTHOOD

Eagleton offers us some pertinent insights for a contemporary understanding of priesthood and the priest's role in church and society. His views here are quite radical and should be considered in ecumenical contexts and within particular churches. Eagleton holds that priests essentially ought to be delegated for a "special function," namely to preside at the congregation's liturgy. This is their primary function. The priest therefore should not be set apart as if in a special caste and working in a paternalist mode. In the future, one might envisage priests having a more limited role. Their priestly tasks may not exclude that they could

---

111. Tavard, *Church*, 169–70.

A New Left Church? Terry Eagleton

have other sources of work and income. And, like all other Christians, they should be free to marry. Priests ought to be elected by the community—as in the early church and in most Protestant churches—and not be appointed from above. Eagleton comments that, in a sense, priests should strive to "eliminate" themselves, so that a truly democratic church can emerge, with everyone being involved in ecclesial activities.

If we look at the structures of the Roman Catholic Church, we become aware that the organization of some Christian fellowships are much closer to those ideals proposed by Eagleton than a hierarchical church. Put very generally, one could say that the more hierarchical a church, the less Eagleton's ideas on priesthood and organization apply. Yet, would he feel at home in a Quaker fellowship or similar setting then? I sense not. However, his ideas are similar to some of such fellowships and communities, and especially to the base communities, as advocated by liberation theologians.

His views here are also remarkably akin to Boff's proposal of an alternative church structure—namely "charism as the organizing principle."[112] Boff takes up St. Paul's emphasis on charism as the "concrete function" that each person exercises in the Christian community. Here, then, we see a concrete link to how the church and its organization ought to be apostolic *and* radical—or radical in being apostolic, and apostolic in being radical, as one might put it—by embracing ideas that are congruent with both St. Paul's apostolic teachings *and* with the radical views that contemporary theologians and intellectuals like Boff and Eagleton propound. All members of the church must take part in shaping and sharing in the community alongside and in equality with the ordained.

THE PARISH: THE WHOLE OF SOCIETY?

Eagleton puts forward some radical views not only on how parishes should operate, but, more fundamentally, he critically challenges the "basic structure of the parish."[113] The problem is not that parishes are not alive, but that their structures are not right.

---

112. Boff, *Church*, 154–64, at 157.
113. Eagleton, *New Left Church*, 105.

He holds that it is "vital that Christian energies should not be directed towards creating a network of Christian welfare states called parishes within societies, but should work alongside and within the general social movement towards a good society," i.e., the church should not duplicate other social structures.[114] Such embeddedness of the church "within social structures" would make the idea of being church more "flexible" and "spontaneous." We must assert that "the only parish is ultimately the whole of society: it is here that our sense of community must be gathered and focused."[115]

The idea of subsidiarity, he emphasizes, "must be rejected," while it is important to foster a sense of community. Eucharistic services and worship "should be celebrated in the local cultural centres which we expect to be focal points of community."[116] The sense of community in this parish/society "will be mediated to us in different and secondary ways: through our work groups, through the local geographical community, and so on."[117] What matters is to operate from a "general sense of the whole community" which must be carried into and lived in the various groups within this community.[118] The ultimate aim is a "fully human community in Christ." This will be largely brought about by the lay person's work and action. In establishing this community in Christ, religion and all its paraphernalia, its cults and rituals will finally "become outdated."

Here one is reminded of one of Bonhoeffer's key ideas, i.e., a "religionless Christianity," which he developed in his letters from prison to Eberhard Bethge on April 30, 1944:

> What is bothering me incessantly is the question what Christianity really is, or indeed who Christ really is, for us today. The time when people could be told everything by means of words, whether theological or pious, is over, and so is the time of inwardness and conscience—and that means the time of religion in general. We are moving towards a completely religionless time; people as they are now simply cannot be religious any more. Even those who honestly describe themselves as "re-

---

114. Ibid., 106.
115. Ibid., 107.
116. Ibid., 107.
117. Ibid., 107.
118. Ibid., 108.

ligious" do not in the least act up to it, and so they presumably mean something quite different by "religious."[119]

It is obvious that Bonhoeffer argues from a more concretely historical perspective than Eagleton. Against his own early mid-twentieth-century context of Germany in the Second Word War, he talks about the decline of religion and growing secularization. Yet Eagleton and Bonhoeffer essentially concur in their Christocentric approach, their stress on Christian community, witness, and their view that Christian faith must be realized in the midst of everyday existence—i.e., a faith and obedience to God that demands commitment to do justice and to build community in *this* world.

Eagleton's ideas, then, from both our contemporary perspective as well as from the perspective of the history of the church in modernity, seems both highly attractive and highly idealistic. One might even suggest that it has an almost eschatological dimension in his expressed advocacy of the hope for a "fully human community" living as a "godly society." One would love to agree with his idea that ultimately the parish should be the whole of society, i.e., a society/parish of equals who take full responsibility for their lives and actions, whose work is meaningful and creative, and who help each other in all things; a society in which communities truly reach out to one another in hope and love, nourished by a life of faith, prayer and worship that is commonly shared by all in community. This is the ideal Christian society, the "godly society," the ideal "parish" and it has much in common with the earliest Christian community as described in Acts 2:43–47.

In the world of the third millennium, however, which includes a multitude of churches and Christian fellowships, in a world made up of societies divided by colossal economic injustice, ethnic tensions, gross inequalities in access to medical welfare, health insurances and education, such an idealistic view is hardly ever going to become a reality. If Eagleton could argue in such fashion forty years ago, we now seem even further removed from his ideas. Globalization and migration in Europe and elsewhere have led to increasingly pluralistic cultures and societies with multi-religious belonging. While people of non-Christian backgrounds might be attracted to, and agree with, the notion of love of neighbor, and other ethical notions pertinent to Christian faith, it is

---

119. Bonhoeffer, *Letters and Papers from Prison*, 152.

highly unlikely that they would be interested in building a society that understands itself as specifically Christian, confessing God as Trinity and adhering to other truths of Christian faith. Perhaps one might go so far as to say that societies that are able to integrate various religious groups in such a way that each will be able to live their faith in a mutually respectful manner and with a genuine reaching out to one's neighbor, this would already be a step in the direction that Eagleton proposed.

In parallel with Eagleton's focus on ecclesiology in his early writings and his latest where he concentrates on a defense of faith itself, we are now acutely aware that in our contemporary multi-faith and multi-ethnic societies we can no longer focus only on the churches and inner-Christian ecumenism but must engage in interreligious dialogue and intercultural theology. The very question of God and how to think of God comes to the fore here.[120] For many theologians today, such dialogue presents more attractive opportunities than an ecumenism limited to the Christian churches. Still, as long as there is disunity among Christian churches, Christians must continue to reflect on how to establish and maintain credible and life-giving church structures that help us to live according to Christ and his message of the kingdom of God as love and unity. Here, I think, Eagleton's stress on a radical notion of church where all must take responsibility and be involved through different charisms, and his idea of the priest or liturgical leader who may also work in other occupations, will continue to be of relevance in ecclesiological discourse. His ecclesiological ideas pose some real challenges, especially to his own Catholic Church with its pronounced hierarchy, its lack of transparency and its many scandals that have arisen from *systemic* problems in its institutions. Here, Eagleton's radical suggestions and ideas for real change remain as pertinent as ever.

A Christian Society?

THE LITURGY: PROTOTYPE OF A CHRISTIAN SOCIETY?

Social and cultural insights regarding art, communication, and the nature of community from *The New Left Church* gave impetus to Slant members in their reflections on the connections between liturgy and

---

120. See, for example, Hintersteiner, *Naming and Thinking God*.

culture, i.e., liturgy's political role. Liturgy is, of course, a public event where each congregation, each parish, becomes most visible and where believers meet, form community, establish friendships, and are nourished and sustained in their faith life. In particular, Eagleton mentions the liturgy as "a social force" that may be able to help transforming society, depending "on the values and relationships we bring to it as well as those we take from it." In the transformation of society and establishment of a common culture, he notes, we do not have to reinvent the wheel but to develop what in actual fact already exists in the liturgical community. Here he asserts that the relationship between liturgy and world is "two-way" as "ordinary insights" from politics, psychology, and literature help us to understand the meaning of the community who celebrates the liturgy. He goes so far as to say that ultimately the liturgy is the "prototype" of a truly Christian society made up of equals united and reconciled in Christ.

The question arising here is, of course, whether eucharistic services, liturgies, and other forms of worship are in fact experienced by the faithful as the "prototype of the Christian society." Naturally, it is impossible to make any precise statements here. How members of congregations worldwide experience and view worship in their churches depends on each denomination's and each community's social, economic, ethnic, and religious contexts, and, in particular, on the clergy's pastoral work in each parish. The variety of worship as celebrated in the different denominations is so large that one can only make some tentative comments. One suspects that, if asked, most church-going Christians would say that first and foremost community worship sustains the believers' faith and spiritual life and that it helps them in building community relationships and be supported, to a greater or lesser extent, by that community. Others may feel dissatisfied and frustrated with what is offered as liturgy in their local congregation: poor sermons, run-of-the-mill liturgies, lack of a sense of community where people may worship for years, yet do not know each other.

One imagines that there would be very few, even among educated middle-class congregations, who would have a sense of the liturgy as the "prototype of a Christian society" with the task of "transforming" society. An awareness of the liturgy as having an expressly social-political function, one imagines, will hardly be to the forefront among those sitting in the pews. In other words, Eagleton's concept of liturgy will

Part III: Towards a Radical Church

more likely than not be found among a few church intellectuals, notably trained theologians and pastors with a leaning towards "left wing" theologies. In that sense his idea, while pertinent and worth exploring further, is one essentially of aspiration and again a highly idealistic one. That is not to say that it is not relevant. On the contrary, if pastors are committed to encouraging social and political commitment among the faithful and in society, including the option for the poor, then this stance might well play a role and bear fruit at least in some local contexts if not in whole societies. As an aspiration, a high goal, as one might put it, his idea here should not be cast aside but further developed by theologians, committed lay people, and ministers.

CHRIST AT THE CENTER

Towards the end of *The New Left Church*, Eagleton emphatically speaks out not only for a church that builds community, but ultimately he advocates for the transformation of society towards a Christian society. Although he does not speak about Christ at any length, what he says is radical and implies what is required to build such a society, namely radical conversion to Christ. A Christian society and the Christian Church must live in the spirit of Jesus. "What is being a Christian to feel like in a world which demands uncompromising, revolutionary force and energy before it is converted to Christ?"[121] Thus a Christian society is one that reflects Christ, demanding each member's full commitment. Yet, as noted above, the realization of a Christian society seems to be far removed from our present context of global capitalism and multi-faith societies.

Still, however, radical commitment to Christ remains paramount for Christian witness in this world. And such commitment entails the recognition that in Christ all worldly values are turned around, that in him the outcasts, sinners, the marginalized, and sick, i.e., all those who do not belong to "the winners" in society find their hope, their reason to live, and their salvation. Christ came to redeem all humankind, but his life, death, and resurrection witnessed that he came especially to save the downtrodden through his death on the cross—a God who died a violent, political death as a "blasphemer" and challenger of the political

---

121. Eagleton, *New Left Church*, 178.

A New Left Church? Terry Eagleton

and religious status quo. As Eagleton notes, "[f]rom the viewpoint of Jewish tradition, a murdered messiah" was "an outrageous anomaly."[122]

Echoing Bonhoeffer as well as the social commitment of liberation theologians, Eagleton asserts that for Christians "the rift between public and private is collapsed in Christ: all creation is taken up into him, so that to be most inwardly myself is to be actively engaged in the world."[123] Eagleton's Christocentric approach, which does not only emphasize radical conversion to Christ for members of the church but in relation to the whole of society, should not be cynically belittled as a merely unrealizable dream of a left-wing intellectual. Thinkers like Sölle, Eagleton, and committed liberation theologians and pastors ought to have their voices heard and re-heard in an increasingly cynical world where individualism, materialism, and greed are sold as "virtues" by those who drive open-market capitalism. Christians must challenge apathy, selfishness, and instant gratification, and it is here that Eagleton, who speaks of Jesus' revolutionary siding with the "losers" and "riffraff," has much to contribute. As he points out, God is not "patriarch," "superego," or "accuser," "but lover, friend, fellow-accused, and counsel for the defense."[124]

Finally, a church that is radical in its apostolicity and apostolic in its radicality is in continuity with, and expounded by, Eagleton's impassioned plea for the church as a community of love and ultimately his call for a "Christian society." One would hope that his Christocentric, sometimes uncomfortable and provocative theological and ecclesiological views will be inspirational to theologians, ministers, artists, intellectuals, politicians, economic leaders, and the people of God into the future.

---

122. Eagleton, *Reason, Faith and Revolution*, 19.
123. Eagleton, *New Left Church*, 141.
124. Eagleton, *Reason, Faith and Revolution*, 20.

Conclusion: Towards an Apostolic, Ecumenical, Radical and Prophetic Church

IN THE PRECEDING CHAPTERS I have attempted to reflect on various themes that relate to an understanding of the church as apostolic, ecumenical, prophetic, and radical. In drawing the book to a conclusion, I will attempt to explore these attributes and their links a little further.

While the terms "ecumenical" and "radical" are not found in the creeds, "apostolic" has been a creedal mark of the church since early Christian times. Christians have believed and confessed their faith in the church as "one, holy, catholic, and apostolic." Apostolicity is central to the tradition, continuity, and mission of the church. The apostles were sent to proclaim the good news and preserve the church's unity and orthodoxy. These first Christian preachers were sent out by Christ himself (1 Cor 15:1–11; Gal 1:15–16). "Apostolic" in the creeds indicates that "the church is, according to Eph 2:20, 'built on the foundation of the apostles and prophets' whose essential task was the proclamation of the gospel (1 Cor 1:17; Acts 9:15). The church is apostolic because the gospel that she hears in faith and to which she gives witness is apostolic."[1] Those involved in *episcope* (oversight), i.e., deacons, presbyters and bishops, are entrusted in particular with the church's teaching remaining in the truth, including reconciliation, pastoral care, and the right administering of word and sacrament. Yet, as the Lutheran-Roman Catholic Commission asserts in its document *The Apostolicity of the Church* (2006): "No human authority is able to guarantee the truth of the gospel since its authenticity and its power to evoke faith is inherent to the gospel itself (its *extra nos*). On the other hand, however,

---

1. Lutheran-Roman Catholic Commission on Unity, *Apostolicity of the Church*, 2006, par. 75.

Conclusion

the faithfulness of the church requires certain forms of traditioning and a particular ecclesial ministry of proclamation, reconciliation and teaching in order to ensure the orderly transmission of the apostolic teachings. This leads to dynamic tension that has constituted challenges to the church from the very beginning."[2] It is this tension with which we have to live and grapple, and which in itself has frequently led to conflict within the church.

Foremost, apostolicity means the apostolicity of the *whole* church, the priesthood of all believers, i.e., each Christian sharing in the apostolic task of witnessing their faith in the world. In the final analysis, as Pannenberg has pointed out, "the apostolic" (*das Apostolische*) means not simply conservation of apostolic teaching but nothing less than the presentation of the finality of the truth of what happened in Jesus Christ, the future truth through which our incomplete world is brought to completion. Apostolicity is thus always concerned with the preservation and handing on of the truth of the Gospel in every generation, and this is not limited to the ordained but the fundamental task of each member of the church. Fundamentally, therefore, apostolicity has a past and future dimension. It demands responsibility as well as creativity and imagination among those entrusted with handing on the apostolic faith in every age. It requires a sense of recognition of the church's tradition *and* the wisdom to positively face and cope with change, to offer new perspectives, and, at times, to make decisions that will have lasting implications into the future. In this way apostolicity is radical: sincere commitment to the faith tradition *and* the need for openness to the new and for prophetic insight and action. It must always refer us back to "the roots" of our faith to the earliest Christian communities, and it demands ongoing reflection, commitment, and decision.

For example, how can we, as the *whole* church, the ordained and non-ordained, respond to contemporary issues in a manner that remains faithful to the truth of apostolic teaching, holiness, and oneness when, in fact, Christians are split into hundreds of different denominations and communities, with new churches emerging all the time, including a wide spectrum of beliefs and convictions?

Or, how can we speak of a church as catholic, holy, apostolic and one when that church propagates certain teachings that to many have

---

2. Ibid., par. 64.

Conclusion

long ceased to make sense and are disobeyed, with ensuing double standards, lies, and a repressive—exclusively male—hierarchy, whose abusive actions and/or silence in the face of unspeakable crimes of its ordained ministers have offended and alienated thousands of its own members, as well as those of other churches? These are just two ecclesial issues that pertain to apostolicity and that both call for the radical memory of the *truth of Christ*, i.e., his fundamental command of *love* of God and neighbor through the power of the Holy Spirit. Indeed, the apostolic task is a radical, ever-present one, which does not allow for complacency but for attending at all times to the *koinonia* and love that Jesus Christ desired for his disciples.

It seems we often fail to remember that throughout Christianity radical witness of, and apostolic commitment to, Christ has been demonstrated by countless martyrs, saints, and so-called "simple people of faith." Certainly, it is one thing to live the relatively comfortable life of a bishop in a European church at the beginning of the twenty-first century; it is quite another to be faced with the possibility of being killed for one's faith as a bishop in a South American country, as Oscar Romero was in El Salvador in 1980. In that way, ministers and bishops such as Romero have represented through their *life*—and not just through their words—authentic radical apostolicity. Such a *Christ-like existence* is ultimately more convincing of any notion of apostolicity than any well-intended words can ever convey.[3] It is through such exemplary lives that the Christian community, the local churches, and individual members may be inspired to live the Gospel in their own respective contexts. This is the apostolic mission to which each member and, in particular, each minister and bishop is called, the instruments of that mission being word and sacrament,[4] radical witness, community building, and pastoral care.

In this way, too, we also may overcome, at least to some extent, the traditional Protestant-Catholic polarizations of the ecclesiology of the cross and an ecclesiology of glory. The church on earth is *simul iusta et peccatrix*: "only through the sufferings and the cross of Jesus is the Christian community, local, regional, and universal, called to share in

---

3. Cf. also O'Mahony, *Do We still Need St Paul?*, 15.
4. Avis, *Reshaping Ecumenical Theology*, 137–38.

the resurrection of Christ."[5] Cross and glory, suffering and redemption, are fundamentally linked in the life of each church and in each of the faithful.

Eagleton, Sölle, Bonhoeffer, and other (liberation) theologians remind us that discipleship is costly. If Christians are God's messengers, if they are to be involved in the *missio dei*, then the cross, i.e., uncompromising love, must be at the center of the life of all those belonging to the church. In this way the church is sacrament and eschatological: Christ's love is embodied in each member, and through her or his witness the believer points to the life in God and shares in God's life and mission.

The Second Letter of Peter reads:

> His divine power has given us everything needed for life and godliness, through the knowledge of him who called us by his own glory and goodness. Thus he has given us, through these things, his precious and very great promises, so that through them you may escape from the corruption that is in the world . . . and may become participants in the divine nature. For this very reason, you must make every effort to support your faith with goodness, and goodness with knowledge, and knowledge with self-control, and self-control with endurance, and endurance with godliness, and godliness with mutual affection, and mutual affection with love. For if these things are yours and are increasing among you, they keep you from being ineffective and unfruitful in the knowledge of our Lord Jesus Christ. (2 Pet 1:3–8)

This passage is noteworthy; it tells the Christian community what is necessary for an apostolic life: godliness to the point of *theosis*, a faith that is shaped by goodness, knowledge, affection, love, and endurance. Ultimately the church, i.e., everyone sharing in its mission, is to be conformed to, and empowered by, God's will, sharing in the nature of the triune God, who in Godself is relationship, and as tri-unity has inspired the ecumenical quest for over a century.[6]

In this context, Nicholas Healy's observations on the church and on engaging in ecclesiology are insightful. In the above citation from 2 Peter, there is a clear emphasis on how Christians ought to *relate* and

---

5. Tavard, *Church*, 202.
6. Cf. Collins' and Powell's "Afterword: The Gift of Mission," in Collins, Mannion, Powell, Wilson, *Christian Community Now*, 188–96, at 193.

Conclusion

act. The church, i.e., each member of Christ, is asked to act through love and goodness. Healy notes that the concrete church must be viewed "more in terms of agency . . . than of being. Its identity is constituted by action."[7] While effective witness and discipleship depend entirely on the Holy Spirit, apostolic work is human work. In essence, the apostolic task includes helping Christians to "become better disciples." This may be brought about by teaching, conducting worship, pastoral work, and exercising loyal and constructive criticism of the church, when necessary. Healy therefore advocates ecclesiology as a *practical-prophetic* discipline rather than as a speculative-systematic one.[8] Instead of applying ecclesiological methods that seek to develop "blueprints" or normative models of church "with abstract and idealistic approaches," he notes that ecclesiology's central function is "to help the church respond as best it can to its context by reflecting theologically and critically upon its concrete identity."[9] Healy rightly notes that ecclesiology has focused on descriptions of the church's essential and theoretical identity rather than on its concrete and historical identity.[10] Reflecting on the church in this way (concrete, historical), he argues, must also include insights from other disciplines. Significantly, however, Healy points out that the "concrete church" does not only mean the church as institution or as a system of beliefs, but rather as a *"distinctive way of life*, made possible by the gracious action of the Holy Spirit."[11] No doubt, Healy's argument is relevant in an age of church crises, atheist agendas, religious fundamentalism, and interreligious dialogue. Through a "theo-dramatic" approach (an appropriation of Balthasar's theory) and in conversation with contemporary pluralist and inclusivist ecclesiologies, he proposes his practical-prophetic ecclesiology.

Further, Mary McClintock Fulkerson observes—in the context of her concern as a theologian with racial discrimination and marginalization—that it is not enough "being nice in church" as we might content ourselves with "focusing on faith as primarily an intentional, belief-centred human activity" rather than constructing it in such a way

---

7. Healy, *Church, World and the Christian Life*, 5.
8. Ibid., 21.
9. Ibid., 22.
10. Ibid., 3.
11. Ibid., 4. My emphasis.

"so as to allow for the role of bodies, the visceral, and fear/anxiety in our practices for 'including' the marginalized."[12] In this way, she suggests our theologies may remain "too 'cognitive' and thus 'too nice' to matter."[13]

In some of my own discussion, I have endeavoured to take a similar concrete approach, trying to analyze some issues relating to the actual reality and challenge of living our—always inadequate—Christian faith and ecumenical witness, i.e., of being church, an *ecclesia semper reformanda*. Healy's argument is inspirational and timely, as he, like liberation theologians (and others, e.g., Bonhoeffer and Moltmann) takes specific account of the fact that theology/ecclesiology always arises in social, political, and cultural contexts. The raw material for theological/ecclesiological reflection is found in the very life of Christian communities, as well as in society and culture, even if it cannot be reduced to that. In turn, then, this raw data must be related to the biblical sources and doctrines of the church, in order to develop further systematic and pastoral-theological insights.[14]

The church conceived as prophetic, radical, apostolic, and ecumenical is an attempt to stress the relation between the memory of Jesus the Christ and the early apostles, and the church of the present and of the future. In his *Ecclesiology for a Global Church*, Richard Gaillardetz—with reference to Johann Baptist Metz, Gustavo Gutierrez, and Bruce Morrill—elaborates on "apostolicity as eschatological memory." Fundamentally, this memory includes the "dangerous memories of Jesus."[15] Gaillardetz, referring also to Zizioulas, notes how in both the Protestant and Catholic Churches, apostolicity has focused primarily on historical memory. However, in Eastern Orthodox Christianity, there is an additional emphasis on the eschatological dimension: the twelve apostles do not simply symbolize the "reconstitution of the twelve tribes of Israel" but they "serve as the realization of God's kingdom in the eschaton, the full gathering or convocation of God's people."[16] Thus memory takes place here too, but it is memory also

12. McClintock Fulkerson, "Being Nice," 169.
13. Ibid.
14. Cf. Collins' excellent article, "Ecclesiology," 135–56, at 136.
15. Gaillardetz, *Ecclesiology for a Global Church*, 229–34. Metz, *Glaube in Geschichte*, esp. § 5, 10, 11. See also Morrill, *Anamnesis as Dangerous Memory*.
16. Gaillardetz, *Ecclesiology for a Global Church*, 230.

of the church's future, its fullness in the *eschaton* made present now. The apostolic church, the people of God, is thought of and "becomes a sign of the eschatological future of humanity."[17] Zizioulas notes that the synthesis of the historical and eschatological is most fully experienced in the eucharist.[18] According to Gaillardetz, this is a "fruitful" perspective, yet it is "limited" in that it presupposes a "sacramentally realized eschatology"—i.e., the eucharist as "manifesting our eschatological future" in the present celebration of the eucharist, which does not take account of "a more apocalyptic eschatology."[19] An emphasis on the apocalyptic allows for an eschatology that serves as a "challenge to history, a caesura that interrupts the customary way of viewing history and demands nothing less than historical transformation."[20]

Gaillardetz summarizes Metz's ideas for whom the dangerous memory of Jesus' death and resurrection constitutes the essence of the Gospel. It is dangerous as it includes Jesus' radical siding with the marginalised and poor, his political death, God's "vindication" through resurrecting Christ from the dead, and Jesus' preaching about the kingdom of God, which not only challenged his contemporaries, but also involves remembering "a future consummation of the kingdom," the promise of liberation of all the oppressed.[21] Metz writes: "What is meant . . . is that dangerous memory that threatens the present and calls it into question because it remembers a future that is still outstanding."[22]

Christians are called then not only to remember the past but also the future and are thereby encouraged to create new visions of a radically different world. Such memory crucially involves a *subversive* dimension and hence challenges the status quo. It does not only refer us to the eschatological future but to the future of *this* world. Dangerous memory demands living in "radical discipleship," in radical imitation of Christ. It thus anticipates in the here and not yet our commitment as co-workers to the coming of God's kingdom. This is an eschatological and concrete memory of freedom—freedom from any type of idolatry

17. Ibid.
18. Zizioulas, *Being as Communion*, 187.
19. Gaillardetz, *Ecclesiology for a Global Church*, 230.
20. Ibid.
21 Ibid., 231.
22. Metz, *Faith in History and Society*, 200, cited in Gaillardetz, *Ecclesiology for a Global Church*, 231.

and from any absolutizing of any political or worldly order. In Latin America, in the context of appalling socio-economic injustice, this memory has facilitated the process of conscientization among those living in base communities and in turn has informed liberation theologians in their work. According to Gutierrez, such dangerous memory of faith in Christ is "*denunciation*," i.e., a denouncing of anything dehumanizing, and "*annunciation*," the love of God that unites us with one another, calls us to action, and brings us into communion with God.[23]

Christian existence, historical and eschatological memory, therefore always has a *countercultural* dimension. If Christian life does not present a constant and significant challenge to the political, social, and economic systems of power of this world, our faith in Christ seems indeed of little worth. One cannot stress enough this countercultural element: the necessity to *protest* in the face of gross injustice and of institutional sin, the need to always consider the life and death of Christ as the first and central reference point for Christian discipleship. If Christian teaching, preaching, and action do not contain a *subversive* and *prophetic* element, Jesus' call for the liberation of the oppressed and of the suffering has fallen on deaf ears in those whose task it is to proclaim the good news. However, time and again we, Christ's followers, out of compromise, complacency, or fear, fail in this call to radical discipleship. Christian existence then ideally is an existence in continuous countercultural awareness, and this fundamentally means, as Gaillardetz remarks, a kind of "worldly disorientation." "In some ways it is this experience of disorientation in the world, the realization that all is not as it should be, that confirms that an ecclesial memory does preserve an authentic, alternative way of existence."[24]

While such awareness of the countercultural, of worldly disorientation, in Christian existence has been reflected upon, and advocated by, a number of theologians, there are those from other walks of life—notably writers, musicians, artists, and cultural commentators—who offer specific insights and perspectives in this regard and who have often been ignored among theologians.

---

23. See Gaillardetz quoting Gutierrez, ibid., 232.
24. Ibid., 233.

Conclusion

"Has theology become more perfect because theologians have become more prosaic?"[25] Rahner once asked and added that theology could only be regarded as complete if it includes all the arts as an integral part of itself; the arts ought to be nothing less than an intrinsic moment of theology. Similarly, Metz notes how theology became objectivist in the separation of theological system and religious experience, doxography and biography, dogmatics and mysticism.[26] Thus Metz observes that theology must always remember its rootedness in narrative and in biography. Not only is our primary theological source, i.e., the Bible, a book of poetry and story, but also the writings of theologians in the early church, of medieval mystics, as well as those of many contemporary (especially liberation, feminist, etc.) theologians remind us how theology is biographically and contextually informed. Hence theology involves "authentic subjectivity" (Lonergan) and imagination as well as system, objectivity, and precision in its discourse.

In the last three decades the recognition of this separation and, in turn, the desire for a more inclusive way of doing theology has been addressed, among others, by theologians involved in the interdisciplinary encounter of theology and the arts, a field of unprecedented growth. While I have worked in this area in depth elsewhere,[27] I would like to briefly note, in our context of envisioning the church as apostolic, ecumenical, prophetic, and radical, that the integration of the arts—literature, visual art, music, film, theater, etc.—can offer significant perspectives to ecclesiology in particular and systematic theology at large. It is probably not by chance that both Sölle and Eagleton with their radical, prophetic theological voices are scholars of literature and have expressed themselves not only through scholarly discourse but also through poetry and/or novels. To speak with the eighteenth-century poet Friedrich Gottlob Klopstock, there are things that cannot be expressed in any other way than through the poetic, the visual, or the musical. Similarly, Paul Tillich commented towards the end of his life, he had always learnt more from art than from theology. Certainly, the rich variety of human expression can enhance as well as challenge our understanding of our faith and of the church, i.e., the people of

---

25. Rahner, "Priest and Poet," 316.
26. Cf. Metz, *Glaube in Geschichte*, 195.
27. Thiessen, *Theology and Modern Irish Art* and *Theological Aesthetics*.

Conclusion

God and body of Christ through the centuries. It is here also that theology, by some regarded as an irrelevant pursuit, can reach out into the various groupings of society, the arts and the media, and in turn be informed by those strata.

Among ecclesiologists and other systematic theologians, this integration of the arts as "an integral moment" (Rahner) is still open for exploration. Here I very briefly want to reflect on two examples (each of which, of course, demands much greater in-depth perusal): 1. Caravaggio's innovative realism in depicting saints and holy figures—rendering them as *real people* with dirty nails, wrinkles, and torn clothes—points us to the *reality* of life in the early church and the church through the ages. In so doing Caravaggio makes the point that the disciples, apostles, and saints *were* fully human, often coming from the "lower strata" of society. Such a rendition is akin to Eagleton's concern with a "left" church built on Christ, the Son of Man born in a stable who came to liberate and save the oppressed and wretched, as well as to theologians like Gutierrez, Sölle, Boff, Healy, and Gaillardetz with their emphasis on a prophetic, practical, liberating ecclesiology "from below," advocating the preferential option for the poor. 2. Picasso's *Guernica* is one of the most iconic pictures of protest against war ever painted. Tillich called it the greatest "Protestant" painting. Picasso, brought up in Catholic Spain and a self-declared atheist, did not advocate that art be used as propaganda. The work includes a figure lying on the ground with outstretched arms, reminding us of the crucifixion, as well as a woman crying over her dead baby, reminding us of images of the Madonna and Child. Encapsulating his outrage at the atrocity committed in Guernica, this painting, Picasso commented, was, however, meant as propaganda, i.e., as an urgent call for peace by showing its polar opposite.

It is here, through the power of the imagination, visual expression, empathy, understanding, and artistic skill, that images like those by Caravaggio, Picasso, and countless others (as well as works of writers, composers, film makers, et al.) can present us with—sometimes surprising—direct or indirect insights into what it means to be the people of God—i.e., following the Christ who sided with the marginalized, who challenged the political and religious leaders of his day, and asked his disciples to live in peace and communion.

Conclusion

In short, I suggest that ecclesiological discourse can be seriously enhanced as well as challenged by engaging with and exploring the vast resources of visual art, literature, music, etc., past and present. Here, one should point out that theologians from different continents and countries might engage not merely with the leading artists of the world (who are often North American or European) but with the art produced in their own countries, i.e., in their own social, religious, political, and cultural contexts.[28]

In this context we are also reminded of Dostoyevsky's famous words that beauty will save the world. Neither cheap grace nor cheap beauty will give us clues about the kingdom of God and about the demands that faith and discipleship entail. As beauty belongs with truth and goodness, true faith and discipleship correspond to Jesus' call for truly witnessing the divine love in this world, a love that will be known fully only in the *eschaton*. If God revealed Godself most gloriously on the cross, the people of God, the church as the body of Christ, is most beautiful when discipleship is brought about in living Jesus' first and foremost command: to love God and one's neighbor as oneself, even to the point of being prepared to suffer for one's faith, supporting and standing with one's neighbor in need, and opposing any kind of injustice and evil. In so doing we may encounter, in the here and now, glimpses of the immeasurable beauty that is the kingdom of God. Here in the truest sense, we take up the challenge of being a church that is genuine in its apostolicity, radical in its witness, imaginative in its prophecy, and ecumenical in its realized *koinonia* of love.

---

28. For example, the poet and priest Ernesto Cardenal in Nicaragua who founded a basic Christian community that later became an artists' colony and his initiating *The Gospel of Solentiname*; or Paul Tillich who wrote on German Expressionism.

Bibliography

Augsburg Confession. Translated by F. Bente and W. H. T. Dau. In: *Triglot Concordia: The Symbolical Books of the Evangelical Lutheran Church.* St. Louis: Concordia, 1921. Online: http://www.iclnet.org/pub/resources/text/wittenberg/concord/web/augs-007.html and http://www.iclnet.org/pub/resources/text/wittenberg/concord/web/augs-008.html.

Augustin, George, SAC. "Ökumene als geistlicher Prozess." In *Kirche in ökumenischer Perspektive*, edited by P. Walter, K. Krämer, and G. Augustin, 522–50. Freiburg: Herder, 2003.

Avis, Paul. *Reshaping Ecumenical Theology: The Church Made Whole.* New York: Continuum, 2010.

Baptism, Eucharist and Ministry. Faith and Order Paper No. 111. Geneva: World Council of Churches, 1982.

Beinert, Wolfgang. "Die Apostolizität der Kirche als Kategorie der Theologie—Joseph Ratzinger zum 50. Geburtstag." *Theologie und Philosophie* 52:2 (1977) 161–81.

Betz, Otto. "Apostle." In *The Oxford Companion to the Bible*, edited by Bruce M. Metzger and Michael Coogan, 41. New York: Oxford University Press, 1993.

Birmelé, André. *Kirchengemeinschaft, Ökumenische Fortschritte und methodologische Konsequenzen.* Translated by Uwe Hecht. Münster: LIT, 2003.

———. "Zur Ekklesiologie der Leuenberger Kirchengemeinschaft." In *Kirche in ökumenischer Perspektive*, edited by P. Walter, K. Krämer, and G. Augustin, 46–61. Freiburg: Herder, 2003.

Blackledge, Paul. "The New Left's Renewal of Marxism." *International Socialism* 112 (2006). Online: http://www.isj.org.uk/?id=251.

Blaikie, N. W. H. "Comment." *Journal for the Scientific Study of Religion* 15:1 (1976) 79–86.

Blum, Georg Günter. "Apostel, Apostolat, Apostolizität II. Alte Kirche." In *Theologische Realenzyklopädie*, edited by Gerhard Krause and Karl Müller, 3:445–66. Berlin: Walter de Gruyter, 1978.

Bobrinskoy, Boris. "The Theological Basis of Common Prayer for Unity." *One in Christ* 3:3 (1967) 274–90.

Boff, Leonardo. *Church: Charism and Power: Liberation Theology and the Institutional Church.* Translated by John W. Diercksmeier. London: SCM, 1985.

Bonhoeffer, Dietrich. *The Cost of Discipleship.* Translated by Reginald Fuller. London: SCM, 1959.

Bibliography

———. *Letters and Papers from Prison*. Edited by Eberhard Bethge. Translated by Reginald Fuller. London: SCM, 1967.
The Book of Concord: The Confessions of the Evangelical Lutheran Church. 2nd ed. Edited by Robert Kolb, Timothy J. Wengert, and James Schaffer. Minneapolis: Fortress, 2001.
Boschki, Reinhold, and Ekkehard Schuster. *Zur Umkehr fähig. Mit Dorothee Sölle im Gespräch*. Mainz: Matthias-Grünewald, 1999.
Braaten, Carl E., and Robert W. Jenson, editors. *In One Body through the Cross: The Princeton Proposal for Christian Unity*. Grand Rapids: Eerdmans, 2003.
Burghardt, Walter J. "Apostolic Succession: Notes on the Early Patristic Era." In *Lutherans and Catholics in Dialogue IV, Eucharist and Ministry*, 173–77. Published by USA National Committee of the Lutheran World Federation and the Bishops' Committee for Ecumenical and Interreligious Affairs, 1970.
Burkhard, John J. *Apostolicity Then and Now: An Ecumenical Church in a Postmodern World*. Collegeville, MS: Liturgical, 2004.
Carlin, David R. "The Denomination Called Catholic." *First Things* 77 (1997) 18–21.
Charta Oecumenica: A Text, a Process, and a Dream of the Churches in Europe. Edited by Viorel Ionita and Sarah Numico. Geneva: WCC, 2003.
Cimino, Richard, editor. "The Evangelical Catholics: Seeking Tradition and Unity in a Pluralistic Church." In *Lutherans Today, American Lutheran Identity in the 21st Century*, edited by R. Cimino, 81–101. Grand Rapids: Eerdmans, 2003.
———. *Lutherans Today, American Lutheran Identity in the 21st Century*. Grand Rapids: Eerdmans, 2003.
Collins, Paul. "Ecclesiology: Context and Community." In *Christian Community Now, Ecclesiological Investigations*, edited by Paul Collins, Gerard Mannion, Gareth Powell, and Kenneth Wilson, Ecclesiological Investigations Series, 2:135–56. New York: Continuum, 2008.
Collins, Paul, and Gareth Powell. "Afterword: The Gift of Mission". In *Christian Community Now, Ecclesiological Investigations*, edited by Paul Collins, Gerard Mannion, Gareth Powell, Kenneth Wilson, Ecclesiological Investigations Series, 2:188–96. New York: Continuum, 2008.
Congar, Yves M.-J., OP. "The Theology of Prayer for Unity." Translated by Dom John Bolger, OSB. *One in Christ* 3:3 (1967) 262–73.
Curtis, Geoffrey. *Paul Couturier and Unity in Christ*. London: SCM, 1964.
Cyprian. "On the Unity of the Church." In *The Treatises of Cyprian*. Ante Nicene Fathers, vol. 5. Translated by Robert Ernest Wallis. No pages. Online: http://en.wikisource.org/wiki/Ante_Nicene_Fathers/Volume_V/Cyprian/The_Treatises_of_Cyprian/On_the_Unity_of_the_Church.
Eagleton, Terry. *Directions: Pointers for the Post-Conciliar Church*. London: Sheed & Ward, 1968.
———. *The New Left Church*. London and Melbourne: Sheed & Ward, 1966.
———. *On Evil*. New Haven: Yale University Press, 2010.
———. *Reason, Faith, and Revolution: Reflections on the God Debate*. New Haven: Yale University Press, 2009.
———. "The Roots of the Christian Crisis." In *Catholics and the Left: "Slant Manifesto,"* Adrian Cunningham, Terry Eagleton, Laurence Bright, OP, Neil Middleton, Martin Redfern, and Brian Wicker. 57–82. London: Sheed & Ward, 1966.

Bibliography

Eagleton, Terry, and Brian Wicker, editors. *From Culture to Revolution, The Slant Symposium 1967.* London: Sheed & Ward, 1968.
Eichele, Erich. "Reflections on the Universal Week of Prayer for Unity." *One in Christ* 3:3 (1967) 291–303.
van Elderen, Marlin. *Introducing the World Council of Churches.* Geneva: WCC, 1990.
Ensign-George, Barry. "Denomination as Ecclesial Category: Sketching an Assessment." In *Denomination, Assessing an Ecclesial Category,* edited by Barry Ensign-George and Paul Collins, 1–21. New York: Continuum, 2011.
Evangelische Kirche Deutschland (EKD): *Response to Communio Sanctorum – Communio Sanctorum: Die Kirche als Gemeinschaft der Heiligen.* 2000. Online: www.ekd.de.
Fey, Harold E., editor. *The Ecumenical Advance, A History of the Ecumenical Movement,* vol. 2, 1948–1968. London: SPCK, 1970.
Gaillardetz, Richard R. *Ecclesiology for a Global Church, A People Called and Sent,* Theology in Global Perspective Series. Edited by Peter C. Phan. Maryknoll, NY: Orbis, 2008.
Ganiel, Gladys. *21st Century Faith – Results of the Survey of Clergy, Ministers and Faith Leaders. 21st Century Faith – Results of the Survey of Laypeople in the Republic of Ireland & Northern Ireland.* Dublin: Irish School of Ecumenics/Trinity College, 2009. Online: http://www.ecumenics.ie/research/visioning-21st-century-ecumenism.
Goertz, Harald. *Dialog und Rezeption, Die Rezeption evangelisch-lutherisch/römisch-katholischer Dialogdokumente in der VELKD und der römisch-katholischen Kirche.* Hannover: Lutherisches Verlagshaus, 2002.
Granquist, Mark. "Word Alone and the Future of Lutheran Denominationalism." In *Lutherans Today, American Lutheran Identity in the 21st Century,* edited by R. Cimino, 62–80. Grand Rapids: Eerdmans, 2003.
Hahn, Udo. *Das kleine 1×1 der Ökumene, Das Wichtigste über den Dialog der Kirchen.* Neukirchen-Vluyn: Neukirchener Verlagshaus, 2003.
Haight, Roger. *Christian Community in History,* vol. 2: *Comparative Ecclesiology.* New York: Continuum, 2005.
Hall, Stuart. "Life and Times of the First New Left." *New Left Review* 61 (2010). Online: http://www.newleftreview.org/?page=article&view=2826.
Hall, Stuart G. "The Early Idea of the Church." In *The First Christian Theologians, An Introduction to Theology in the Early Church,* edited by G. R. Evans, 41–57. Oxford: Blackwell, 2004.
Hanson, Mark S., "The Future of Denominations: Asking Uppercase Questions." *Word & World* 25:1 (2005) 7–14.
Healy, Nicholas. *Church, World and the Christian Life: Practical-Prophetic Ecclesiology.* Cambridge: Cambridge University Press, 2000.
Heller, Dagmar. "Gebetswoche für die Einheit der Christen." In *Taschenlexikon Ökumene,* edited by Harald Uhl et al., 110–11. Franfurt: Otto Lembeck, 2003.
———. "Seele der ökumenischen Bewegung, Zur Geschichte und Bedeutung der Gebetswoche für die Einheit der Christen." In *Ökumene lohnt sich,* Beiheft zur Ökumenischen Rundschau 68, edited by Hans Vorster, 312–20. Frankfurt: Otto Lembeck, 1998.
Hilberath, Bernd Jochen, Ivana Noble, and Peter De Mey, editors. *Ökumene des Lebens als Herausforderung der wissenschaftlichen Theologie,* Tagungsbericht der

Bibliography

14. Wissenschaftlichen Konsultation der Societas Oecumenica / *Ecumenism of Life as a Challenge for Academic Theology*, Proceedings of the 14th Academic Consultation of the Societas Oecumenica, Beiheft zur Ökumenischen Rundschau, 82. Frankfurt: Otto Lembeck, 2008.

Hintersteiner, Norbert, editor. *Naming and Thinking God in Europe Today—Theology in Global Dialogue*. Amsterdam: Rodopi, 2007.

Holeton, David R. "'Religion without Denomination? The Significance of Denominations for Church and Society': Some Reactions." *Communio Viatorum* 44 (2002) 38–44.

Ickert, Scott S. "Adiaphora, Ius Divinum, and Ministry: A Lutheran Perspective." In *The Church as Koinonia of Salvation: Its Structures and Ministries*, edited by Randall Lee and Jeffrey Gros, FSC, 209–25. Agreed Statement of the Tenth Round of the Lutheran-Roman Catholic Dialogue with Background Papers. Evangelical Lutheran Church of America/United States Conference of Catholic Bishops, 2004, first printing 2005.

———. "Recent Lutheran Reflections on Universal Ministry." In *The Church as Koinonia of Salvation: Its Structures and Ministries*, edited by Randall Lee and Jeffrey Gros, FSC, 247–66. Agreed Statement of the Tenth Round of the Lutheran-Roman Catholic Dialogue with Background Papers. Evangelical Lutheran Church of America/United States Conference of Catholic Bishops, 2004, first printing 2005.

Ignatius. *Letter to the Smyrnaeans*. Translated by J. B. Lightfoot, 1891. Online: www.earlychristianwritings.com/text/ignatius-smyrnaeans lightfoot.html.

Irenaeus. *Adversus Haereses/Against Heresies*. Translated by Alexander Roberts and William Rambaut. Edited by Alexander Roberts, James Donaldson, and A. Cleveland Coxe. *Ante Nicene Fathers*, vol. 1. Buffalo, NY: Christian Literature, 1885. No pages. Online: www.newadvent.org/fathers/0103426.htm.

Jervell, Jacob. *Luke and the People of God*. Minneapolis: Augsburg, 1972.

John Paul II (Karol Wojtyla). *Ut Unum Sint: On Commitment to Ecumenism* (May 25, 1995). Online: www.vatican.va/holy_father/john _paul.../hf_jp-ii_enc_25051995_ut-unum-sint_en.htm.

Jüngel, Eberhard. "Credere in ecclesiam: Eine ökumenische Besinnung." In *Kirche in ökumenischer Perspektive*, edited by P. Walter, K. Krämer, and G. Augustin, 15–32. Freiburg: Herder, 2003.

Kasper, Walter. "Es gibt keine Alternative zur Ökumene." In *Sich regen bringt Segen*, edited by Norbert Sommer, 40–53. Berlin: Wichern, 2003.

———. *That They May All Be One*. New York: Continuum, 2004.

(Ressmeyer) Klein, Christa. "Lutherans, Merger and the Loss of History." *The Christian Century*, January 2–9, 1985, 18–20.

———. "Denominational History as Public History: The Lutheran Case." In *Reimagining Denominationalism, Interpretive Essays*, edited by Robert Bruce Mullin and Russell E. Richey, 307–17. Oxford: Oxford University Press, 1994.

von Kloeden, Gesine. *Evangelische Katholizität, Philip Schaffs Beitrag zur Ökumene - Eine reformierte Perspektive*. Studien zur systematischen Theologie und Ethik, E. Lessing, P. Neuner, D. Ritschl, vol. 12. Münster: Lit, 1998.

Kock, Manfred. "Das Papstamt aus evangelischer Perspektive." Lecture, 4 September 2001, Karl Rahner Akademie, Cologne. Online: www.ekd.de/vortraege/kock/6213.html.

Bibliography

Lennan, Richard. "Ecclesiology and Ecumenism." In *The Cambridge Companion to Karl Rahner*, edited by Declan Marmion and Mary E. Hines, 128–43. Cambridge: Cambridge University Press, 2005.

Lindbeck, George A. "The Lutheran Understanding of the Ministry: Catholic and Reformed." *Theological Studies* 30:4 (1969) 588–612.

Long, Charles H. "The Question of Denominational Histories in the United States: Dead End or Creative Beginning." In *Reimagining Denominationalism, Interpretive Essays*, edited by Robert Bruce Mullin and Russell E. Richey, 99–105. New York and Oxford: Oxford University Press, 1994.

Lumen Gentium (*Dogmatic Constitution on the Church*). Online: http://www.vatican.va/archive/hist_councils/ii_vatican_council/documents/vat-ii_const_19641121_lumen-gentium_en.html.

Luther, Martin. *The Large Catechism* ("The Apostles' Creed", art. 3). Translated by F. Bente and W. H. T. Dau. In *Triglot Concordia: The Symbolical Books of the Evangelical Lutheran Church*. St. Louis: Concordia, 1921. Online: http://www.iclnet.org/pub/resources/text/wittenberg/luther/catechism/cat-10.txt.

Lutheran-Roman Catholic Commission. *The Apostolicity of the Church*. 2006. Online: http://www.prounione.urbe.it/dia-int/l-rc/doc/e_l-rc_ap-02.html.

———. *The Church and Justification*. Geneva: Lutheran World Federation, 1994.

———. *Facing Unity. Models, Forms and Phases of Catholic-Lutheran Church Fellowship*. Geneva: Lutheran World Federation, 1985.

———. *The Ministry in the Church*. Geneva: Lutheran World Federation, 1982.

Mannion, Gerard. "Driving the Haywain: Where Stands the Church 'Catholic' Today?" In *Ecumenical Theology: Unity, Diversity and Otherness in a Fragmented World*, edited by Gesa Thiessen, 13–34. London: Continuum, 2009.

Marsh, Jan. *William Morris and Red House*. London: National Trust, 2005.

Mawick, Reinhard. "Gott will nicht allein sein." *Deutsches Allgemeines Sonntagsblatt*, September 24, 1999.

Meissen Common Statement. 1988. Online: http://www.unileipzig.de/~prtheol/Queens/declaration.htm.

McClintock Fulkerson, Mary. "'Being Nice in Church': Rituals of Propriety and the Sin of Oblivion." In *Church and Religious "Other,"* edited by Gerard Mannion, 168–81. New York: Continuum, 2008.

Metz, Johann Baptist. *Faith in History and Society: Towards a Practical Fundamental Theology*. New York: Crossroad, 1980.

de Mey, Peter. "A Call to Conversion: An Analysis of The Princeton Proposal for Christian Unity (2003)." *Ecumenical Trends* 34:4 (2005) 1–10.

Meyer, Harding. "Apostolic Continuity, Apostolic Succession and Ministry from a Reformation Perspective." *Louvain Studies* 21:2 (1996) 169–82.

Middleton, Neil. "Introduction." In *Catholics and the Left: "Slant Manifesto,"* Adrian Cunningham, Terry Eagleton, Laurence Bright OP, Neil Middleton, Martin Redfern, and Brian Wicker, vii. London: Sheed & Ward, 1966.

Morrill, Bruce T. *Anamnesis as Dangerous Memory: Political and Liturgical Theology in Dialogue*. Collegeville: Liturgical, 2000.

Morris, William. "Art and Socialism." Lecture, January 23, 1884. Online: http://www.marxists.org/archive/morris/works/1884/as/as.htm.

Mullin, Robert Bruce, and Russell E. Richey, editors. *Reimagining Denominationalism: Interpretive Essays*. New York: Oxford University Press, 1994.

Bibliography

Nicholl, Todd. "The Lutheran Venture and the American Experiment." *Word and World* 12:2 (1992) 154–64.

Noll, Mark A. "American Lutherans Yesterday and Today." In *Lutherans Today, American Lutheran Identity in the 21st Century*, 3–25. Grand Rapids: Eerdmans, 2003.

———. "The Lutheran Difference." *First Things*, February 20, 2002, 31–40.

O'Gara, Margaret. "Apostolicity in Ecumenical Dialogue." *Midstream* 37:2 (1998) 175–212.

———. *The Ecumenical Gift Exchange*. Collegeville: Liturgical, 1998.

———. "A Roman Catholic Perspective on Ius Divinum." In *The Church as Koinonia of Salvation: Its Structures and Ministries*, edited by Randall Lee and Jeffrey Gros, FSC, 226–46. Agreed Statement of the Tenth Round of the Lutheran-Roman Catholic Dialogue with Background Papers. Evangelical Lutheran Church of America/United States Conference of Catholic Bishops, 2004, first printing 2005.

O'Mahony, Kieran J., OSA. *Do We Still Need St Paul? A Contemporary Reading of the Apostle*. Dublin: Veritas, 2009.

Origen. *Commentary on the Gospel of Matthew*, Book 12. Translated by John Patrick. Edited by Allan Menzies. Ante Nicene Fathers 9. Buffalo, NY: Christian Literature, 1896. Revised and edited for New Advent by Kevin Knight. Online: http://www.newadvent.org/fathers/101612.htm.

Pannenberg, Wolfhart. "The Significance of Eschatology for the Understanding of the Apostolicity and Catholicity of the Church." *One in Christ* 6:3 (1970) 410–29.

Pastor aeternus. Abridged from Vatican Council I, Dogmatic Constitution Pastor aeternus on the Church of Christ. July 18, 1870. Online: www.ewtn.com/faith/teachings/papae1.htm.

Pelikan, Jaroslav. "American Lutheranism: Denomination or Confession?" *The Christian Century*, December 25, 1963, 1608–10.

Pesch, Otto Hermann. "Hermeneutik des Ämterwandels? Kleine Ausarbeitung einer Frage." In *Kirche in ökumenischer Perspektive*, edited by P. Walter, K. Krämer, and G. Augustin, 417–38. Freiburg: Herder, 2003.

Porvoo Common Statement. Online: http://www.porvoochurches.org/whatis/resources-0201-english.php.

"Prayer for Unity, The Report of the Consultation on 'The Future of the Week of Prayer for Christian Unity.'" Geneva, October 16–20, 1966. *One in Christ*, 3:3 (1967) 251–61.

Rahner, Karl. "Ist Kircheneinigung dogmatisch möglich?" *Karl Rahner Sämtliche Werke*, vol. 27 *Einheit in Vielfalt*, edited by Karl Rahner Stiftung unter Leitung von K. Lehmann, J. B. Metz, K.-H. Neufeld, A. Raffelt, H. Vorgrimler, 119–34. Freiburg: Herder, 2002.

———. "Die eine Kirche und die vielen Kirchen." *Karl Rahner Sämtliche Werke* 27, 93–104.

———. "Priest and Poet." In *Theological Investigations*, 3:294–317. London: Darton, Longman & Todd, 1967.

Von Randow, Gero. "Regeln sind nicht göttlich." Interview with Luc Boltanski, *Die Zeit*, May 6, 2010.

Ratzinger, Joseph / Benedict XVI. Cited in Vatican City, May 10, 2006 (Zenit.org). Translation Copyright 2006, Libreria Editrice Vaticana.

Richey, Russell. "Denominationalism." In *Dictionary of the Ecumenical Movement*, edited by Nicholas Lossky et al., 294–96. Geneva: WCC, 2002.

Bibliography

Roelvink, Henrik, OFM. "The Apostolic Succession in the Porvoo Statement." *One in Christ* 30:4 (1994) 344–54.
Roloff, Jürgen. "Apostel, Apostolat, Apostolizität." *Theologische Realenzyklopädie*, edited by Gerhard Krause and Karl Müller, 3:430–45. Berlin: Walter de Gruyter, 1978.
Root, Michael. "Once More on the Unity We Seek: Testing Ecumenical Models." In *The Unity We Have & the Unity We Seek*, edited by Jeremy Morris and Nicholas Sagovsky, 167–77. New York: Continuum, 2003.
Smith, Dinitia. "Cultural Theorists, Start Your Epitaphs." *The New York Times*, January 3, 2004. Online: http://www.wehaitians.com/cultural%20theorists%20start%20your%20epitaphs.html.
Sölle, Dorothee. *Gegenwind*. Munich: Piper, 1999 (1995). English translation: *Against the Wind*. Minneapolis: Fortress, 1999.
———. *Gott denken, Einführung in die Theologie*. Munich: dtv, 1997.
———. *Im Hause des Menschenfressers, Texte zum Frieden*. Reinbeck: Rowohlt, 1981.
———. *Mystik und Widerstand: Du stilles Geschrei*. Hamburg: Hoffmann & Campe, 1997. English translation: *The Silent Cry: Mysticism and Resistance*. Minneapolis: Fortress, 2001.
———. *Stellvertretung. Ein Kapitel Theologie nach dem "Tode Gottes"*. Stuttgart: Kreuz Verlag, 1965. English translation: *Christ the Representative: An Essay in Theology after the Death of God*. Minneapolis: Fortress, 1967.
Tanner, Mary. "The Anglican Position on Apostolic Continuity and Apostolic Succession in the Porvoo Statement." *Louvain Studies* 21:2 (1996) 114–25.
Tanner, Norman P., editor. *Decrees of the Ecumenical Councils*. 2 vols. Washington, DC: Georgetown University Press, 1990.
Tavard, George H. *The Church, Community of Salvation: An Ecumenical Ecclesiology*. Collegeville: Liturgical Press, 1992.
Tertullian. *De Praescriptione Haereticorum*. Translated by Peter Holmes. *Ante Nicene Fathers*, vol. 3. Online: www.earlychristianwritings.com/text/tertullian11.html.
Thiessen, Gesa, editor. *Ecumenical Theology: Unity, Diversity and Otherness in a Fragmented World*. New York: Continuum, 2009.
———, editor. *Theological Aesthetics: A Reader*. Grand Rapids: Eerdmans, 2004.
———. *Theology and Modern Irish Art*. Dublin: Columba, 1999.
Tjørhom, Ola. "Apostolic Continuity and Apostolic Succession in the Porvoo Common Statement: A Challenge to the Nordic Lutheran Churches." *Louvain Studies* 21:2 (1996) 126–37.
Tombs, David. "Latin American Liberation Theology: Moment, Movement, Legacy." In *Movement or Moment? Assessing Liberation Theology Forty Years after Medellín*, edited by Patrick Claffey and Joe Egan, Studies in Theology, Society and Culture Series, 1:29–53. Oxford and Bern: Peter Lang, 2009.
Tygart, C. E. "On the Inadequacies of the Utilization of the Concept of 'Denomination' in the Explanation of the Position of Clergy on Social Issues." *Journal for the Scientific Study of Religion* 15:1 (1976) 87–90.
The Unity of Christians: The Vision of Paul Couturier. Special edition of *The Messenger of the Catholic League*, 280, no author named. Oxford: The Catholic League, 2003.
Vereinigte Evangelische Lutherische Kirche Deutschlands. Online: http://www.velkd.de.
Villain, Maurice, S.M. *L'Abbé Paul Couturier, apôtre de l'unité chrétienne: Souvenirs et documents*. Collection Eglise Vivante. Tournai: Casterman, 1957.

Bibliography

———. *Introduction à L'oecuménisme*. Collection Eglise Vivante. Tournai: Casterman, 1958. English translation: *Unity: a history and some reflections*. London: Harvill, 1963.

Vogt, Karl Heinz. "Evangelische Allianz." *Taschenlexikon Ökumene*, edited by Harald Uhl et al., 90–91. Frankfurt: Otto Lembeck, 2003.

Warner Bowden, Henry. "The Death and Rebirth of Denominational History." In *Reimagining Denominationalism: Interpretive Essays*, edited by Robert Bruce Mullin, and Russell E. Richey, 17–30. Oxford: Oxford University Press, 1994.

Wengert, Timothy J. *Harvesting Martin Luther's Reflections on Theology, Ethics, and the Church*, edited by Paul Rorem. Grand Rapids: Eerdmans, 2004.

Wenz, Gunther. "Das kirchliche Amt—evangelisch." *Stimmen der Zeit* 6 (2003) 376–85.

Wroe, Nicholas. "High Priest of lit crit." *The Guardian*, February 2, 2002. Online: http://www.guardian.co.uk/books/2002/feb/02/academicexperts.highereducation.

Wuthnow, Robert. *Christianity in the Twenty-first Century, Reflections on the Challenges Ahead*. New York: Oxford University Press, 1993.

———. *The Restructuring of American Religion*. Princeton, NJ: Princeton University Press, 1988.

Zizioulas, John. *Being as Communion: Studies in Personhood and the Church*. Crestwood, NY: St. Vladimir's Seminary Press, 1985.

Index

Altizer, T., 114
Amos, 112
Anglican, Anglicans, xiii, 19, 30, 33–34, 38–39, 42, 44, 51–57, 72–76, 78, 90–92, 99, 132, 158
apostle(s), xii, 3–13, 15–17, 23–24, 29, 49, 51, 54, 77, 93, 109, 124, 166, 171, 175
Apostolicity, apostolic, xi, xii, xiv, 3–64, 68, 70, 74, 86, 88–89, 93, 124, 136, 157, 159, 165, 166–76
    Apostolic succession, 7, 9–11, 13–14, 17, 21, 24, 26, 28–29, 35–38, 48–51, 56
Aristotle, 124
arts, 138, 140, 174–75
    architecture, 140
    art, artist(s), 140, 162, 165, 173–76
    dance, 149
    English Arts and Craft Movement, 140
    film, 174–75
    literature, literary, xiv, 109–10, 112, 127–28, 138, 152, 163, 174, 176
    music, musician(s), composers, 173–76
    poetry, 112, 118, 174
    Pre-Raphaelites, 140
    theatre, 174
    visual art, 174, 176
Athanasius, 119n32, 120
atheism, atheistic, xiv, 113, 128, 153–54, 170, 175
Augustin, G., 97n30

Augustine, 16, 21, 50
authenticity, authentic(ally), 4, 7, 36–37, 52, 84, 89, 109, 125, 130n12, 134–35, 149–51, 155–56, 166, 168, 173–74
authority, 3–4, 8, 10–13, 17, 25, 27n13, 36n19, 41, 48, 54–56, 146, 166
Avis, P., 39n24, 168n4

Bach, J. S., 84
Bachmann, I., 118
Balthasar, H. U. von, 170
baptism, 30–32, 71
Baptism, Eucharist, Ministry/BEM, 30, 33, 41, 57, 92
Barth, K. 82, 154
beauty, 121, 140, 176
Beinert, W., 50
Berger, P., 84
Berrigan, D., 125
Bethge, E., 160
Betz, O., 3n1, 4n6, 6n17, 7n20
Birmelé, A., 43n5, 45
Blum, G. G., 10–16
Bobrinskoy, B., 92n12, 94n21, 95, 98, 100
Boff, L., 155–56, 159, 175
Boltanski, L., 144
Bonaventure, 110
Bonhoeffer, D., 84, 109, 120, 160–61, 165, 169, 171
Boschki, R., 113n11, 114nn13–14, 125n45
Bowden, H., 81

Index

Braaten, C. E., 99n36
Buber, M., 118–19
Buren, P. van, 114
Burkhard, J. J., 4, 6, 8–9, 11–14, 19, 22, 35–37, 43, 49, 57, 63

Calvin, J., 46, 60, 75
Capitalism, 85, 112, 123, 130n12, 131, 133–35, 142–43, 148–49, 153, 164–65
Caravaggio, M., 175
Cardenal, E., 176
Carlin, D., 72
Carlyle, T., 149
Catholics, Catholic Church, catholic, catholicity, xiii–xiv, 3, 5, 9, 11–12, 16, 19–20, 22–29, 32–33, 35–39, 41–47, 49, 51–64, 68–70, 72–88, 90–94, 98–99, 101, 103–4, 113, 124–29, 132, 135, 137, 144–45, 155, 157–59, 162, 166–68, 171–75; *see also* Roman Catholic(s)
charism, charismatic, 6–7, 12, 16, 43, 50, 79, 155, 159, 162
Christendom, 49, 70, 73n15, 90, 158
Christian, Christians, xii–xiv, 3–4, 8, 11, 13, 15–17, 28–29, 36, 42–43, 45, 47, 48, 50, 52, 54, 58, 61, 67, 69–70, 72, 74–75, 79, 85, 87–99, 102, 104, 109–15, 117–19, 124, 128–29, 131–39, 141, 143, 148–73, 176n28
  Christian society, xiv, 149–53, 161–65
Christianity, 124, 136–37, 148, 160, 168
Christocentric, 161
Christology, christological, 7n21, 20, 22, 30, 34, 48, 50, 70, 117, 125, 148; *see also* Jesus Christ
church
  abuse(s), xi, 52, 125, 136, 156
  apostolic. *See* apostolicity, apostolic
  authoritarian(ism), 16, 125, 135, 145; *see also* authority

church (*continued*)
  bishop(s), 9–18, 21, 24–25, 27–29, 32–38, 47, 49–54, 57, 64, 99, 111, 147, 166, 168
  body of Christ, xii, 22, 31–32, 42, 50, 85–87, 175, 176
  (Christian) community, xii, 3, 6, 7, 9, 12, 14, 18, 21, 23n9, 24n9, 26n12, 35, 45, 49, 50, 57, 73, 76, 94–96, 102–3, 115, 118, 125, 134–35, 139, 141, 143, 145–46, 148, 150–52, 159–65, 168–69, 176
  clergy, 16, 27n13, 53, 101n41, 103, 137, 146, 156, 163; *see also* priest, minister(s), bishop(s)
  confession, confessional, 31, 39n24, 40, 46, 62, 70–75, 77–85, 98
  congregation(s), 8, 11, 21, 26n12, 27, 32, 38, 68, 70–71, 73–74, 76–77, 90, 102, 158, 163
  countercultural, xii, 124, 173
  deacon(s), 8–10, 11n39, 25, 34, 38, 47, 51, 53, 166
  ecclesia semper reformanda, 171
  episcopacy, episcopal, episcopate, *episcope, episcopoi*, 10–12, 14, 16–18, 21–22, 24–25, 27, 29, 31, 33–39, 44, 47–49, 51–53, 56, 62, 111, 166
  hierarchy, 47, 70, 125, 147, 162, 168
  holy, holiness, 16, 23n8, 30, 32, 34, 38, 41, 59, 70–71, 74, 86, 88, 136, 166–67
  institution, institutional, xi, 8, 9, 15, 22, 24, 26–27, 30–31, 36, 71, 86, 97, 114, 118, 132–35, 137, 154, 158, 162, 170, 173
  koinonia, 20–23, 25–27, 29, 31, 43, 51, 56, 99, 168, 176
  leader(s), leadership, 5–6, 9, 12, 35, 45, 49–50, 52–53, 56, 61–62, 64, 79, 84, 92, 99, 102–3, 155, 157
  liturgy, liturgical, 58, 68, 74, 80, 100, 104, 110, 141, 146–47, 150–52, 158, 162–63; *see also* eucharist, holy communion, service(s), worship

church (*continued*)
- local/universal, 9, 11–12, 16, 21–23, 27n12, 37, 44, 46, 54, 56, 62, 67, 73–74, 76, 87, 93, 96, 98, 145–46, 168
- marks of the church, xi, xiii–xiv, 3, 40
- minister(s), xii, 10, 27n13, 27, 29, 31–32, 36, 39, 53, 69, 100, 109, 133, 164–65, 168
- ministry, xii, 10, 20–21, 22nn4–5, 24, 27n13, 28–38, 41, 44, 49–53, 55–57, 85, 87, 92, 100, 126, 167
- ministry, ordained, 21, 22n4, 24, 27n13, 31, 33, 35, 51
- office(s), episcopal office, xii, 4, 8, 10–11, 13, 15, 17–18, 25, 27, 31–32, 34–39, 49n15, 51, 54–55, 57, 61, 64
- one, oneness, 13n50, 14, 23n8, 27, 37–38, 41–42, 46, 48–49, 70–71, 74, 86–87, 90, 98, 166–67; *see also* unity
- ordination, 12, 14, 17, 20–21, 32, 35–36, 38, 51–53, 57–58, 80, 158
- oversight, 20–21, 28, 31–32, 34–35, 38, 42, 44, 51, 166; *see also* episcope
- people of God, xii–xiii, 26, 31–32, 43, 50, 60, 62–63, 94, 101, 125–26, 155, 165, 172, 175–76
- papacy, 28, 44, 51–55, 58; *see also* pope
- parish(es), 26n12, 27n12, 33, 89–90, 101–3, 145–46, 159–61, 163
- pastor(s), pastoral, 25, 27, 31, 34–35, 37–38, 41–42, 51, 53–54, 76, 92, 102, 109, 163, 164–66, 168, 170–71
- paternalism, paternalist, paternalistic, 135, 142–46, 157–58
- power, xi, 9–10, 15, 24, 27, 52, 54, 70, 113–14, 125, 155, 157
- presbyter(s), presbyteral, 9–12, 17–18, 27, 34, 36, 50–52, 166

church (*continued*)
- priest(s), priesthood, priestly, 24, 27n13, 34, 36, 38, 47, 51–52, 54, 57, 87, 92, 100, 102, 128–29, 142, 145–47, 151–59, 162, 167
- priesthood of all believers, 52, 87, 167
- prophetic, prophecy, xi, xiv, 88, 112, 166–76
- radical, xi–xiv, 39, 68, 88, 110–76
- reactionary, 134, 155
- subversive, 172–73
- tradition(s), xii, 7, 11n43, 12–14, 16, 20, 24, 27–28, 31, 35, 36n19, 46, 48, 52–53, 61, 69, 71, 75, 77–78, 81–82, 85, 98, 101, 118–19, 122, 125, 155, 166–67

Cimino, R., 75n18, 79nn28–29, 83n41, 85n53
Clement I, 9–10
Clement of Alexandria, 9, 15, 17, 23, 50
Collins, P., 169n6, 171n14
communion(s), church communion, 9, 13, 22–23, 25–26, 29, 33–35, 38, 46, 56, 69, 73; *see also* Holy Communion
Congar, Y., 93n18, 96
Couturier, P., 92–93, 96
creativity, creative, 14, 63, 139, 141, 148–49, 158, 161, 167
creed(s), 9, 23n8, 31, 48, 74, 77, 80, 136, 166
Cross, xiv, 85, 99, 116–18, 164, 168–69, 176; *see also* Jesus Christ
culture, cultural(ly), multicultural, intercultural, 8, 16, 62, 69, 76–77, 84–87, 117, 122, 124, 127, 129, 135–36, 138–39, 141, 145, 152, 153, 160–63, 171, 176; *see also* church, countercultural
Curtis, G., 91n8, 92nn11, 13, 96n15
Cyprian of Carthage, 9, 14, 16

Dawkins, R., "Ditchkins," 128, 153–54
denomination(al), denominations, xii–xiii, 8, 20, 28, 30, 34, 42, 44–47, 49, 56, 58, 61, 63, 67–91, 99–100, 102, 126, 137, 163, 167

187

Index

Dickens, C., 133, 149
discipleship, disciple(s), 5, 89, 94–96, 117, 122, 124, 143, 168–70, 172–73, 175–76
divinization, *theosis*, 119–20
docetism, 117
Dostoyevsky, F., 176
Driel, E. C. van, 78n27

Eagleton, T., xiv, 127–65, 169, 174–75
ecclesiology, ecclesiological, xi, xiii–xiv, 13, 22–23, 25–27, 29, 37, 40–63, 70–71, 77, 78n26, 80, 97, 126, 128–129, 132, 152, 154, 158, 162, 165, 168–71, 174–76
ecumenical, xi–xiv, 4, 7, 9, 13, 17, 19–21, 23, 25, 27, 29, 31, 33, 35–37, 39, 40–47, 49–51, 53, 55–64, 67–70, 72, 74–78, 80–82, 84–88, 89–90, 92–105, 113, 126, 157–58, 166–76
    ecumenical dialogue(s), xi–xiii, 17, 33, 36, 40–41, 43–45, 58–62, 126
ecumenism, xiii, 30, 41–42, 45, 56, 58–61, 78, 85, 87, 89–105, 162
Eichele, E., 96
Elderen, M. van, 92n10
Engels, F., 112
Enlightenment (the), 67, 70–71, 76, 131, 148
Ensign-George, B., 73–75, 86
eschatological, *eschaton*, 5–7, 34, 87, 117, 139, 161, 169, 171–73, 176
D'Escoto, M., 116
evangelical, 14, 27n13, 75, 90
experience, 30, 37, 77, 97, 112, 116, 118–19, 130n12, 135, 141, 163, 173–74
faith, xiv, 15–17, 28, 61, 88, 97n31, 110, 114, 128, 131, 138, 151, 153–54, 156, 161–62, 171
faithful, (the), 13, 23, 50, 61, 101–3, 155, 163–64, 169; *see also* lay, laity
fellowship, 20, 21n4, 23n8, 39, 47, 57, 68, 70, 74–75, 87, 102, 159, 161

Fey, H. E., 93n20
Flanagan, B. P., 78n27
Fox, M., 121
Francis, St., 118, 125
Freedom, xiii–xiv, 28, 36, 39, 44, 48, 50, 52–53, 63, 80, 87–88, 101, 118, 122, 143, 172
Friedrich Wilhem III, 80
Fundamentalism, 79, 97n31, 99, 153, 170

Gaillardetz, R., xiv, 171–73, 175
Gandhi, M. K., 118
globalization, global, 69, 109, 123, 131, 143n60, 153, 161, 164
Gnosticism, gnostic, 9, 11, 15, 17
God, xii–xiv, 4–15, 22–26, 28, 30–32, 34–36, 43, 48, 50, 60, 62–64, 70–71, 73n15, 83, 86–88, 93–96, 101, 110–17, 119–26, 128, 137, 139, 141, 143, 146, 151, 153, 155, 161–62, 164–65, 168–69, 171–73, 175–76
    Trinity, trinitarian, 5, 20, 22–23, 31, 34, 48, 94, 102, 162
Goertz, H., 41n1
Granquist, M., 79
Gutierrez, G., 171, 173, 175

Hahn, U., 41
Haight, R., 45–47
Hall, S., 129, 131
Hall, S. G., 8–16
Hamilton, W., 114
Hammarskjöld, D., 118
Hanson, M., 86–87
Haughton, R., 129
Healy, N., xiv, 169–71, 175
Helder Camara, Dom, 118
Heller, D., 90n4, 91nn6, 8, 93n19, 100n39, 101n42
Herder, J. G., 119, 121
Hermas, 11
Hintersteiner, N., 162
Hippolytus, 9, 14, 17, 23, 50
Hitchens, C., "Ditchkins," 128, 153–54

Index

Holy Communion, 32, 68, 100, 104
    eucharist, 11n39, 30–34, 41, 56, 58, 61–62, 68, 80, 92, 98, 100–101, 104, 145, 160, 163, 172
    Eucharistic hospitality, 32–33, 58, 68, 101
    Intercommunion, 58, 80, 101
Holy Spirit, 5–6, 22–23, 25, 29, 31, 36, 49–50, 79, 95, 97, 101, 168, 170
Hudson, W., 84
Hus, J., 59

Ibsen, H., 139
Ickert, S., 27n13, 55, 57n25
Ignatius of Antioch, 9, 11, 49
imagination, 85n50, 105, 140, 149, 167, 174–75
Irenaeus, 9, 11–14, 17, 49–50, 119, 120n33
Isaiah, 112

Jenson, W., 99n36
Jerome, 27, 52
Jervell, J., 8, 49
Jesus/Christ, xii–xiv, 3–12, 14–17, 22–25, 27–28, 31, 35, 36n19, 42, 47–49, 51, 54, 61, 67, 69, 71, 73n15, 77, 80, 85–92, 94–99, 105, 111–12, 114, 116–18, 120, 124–25, 127, 129, 136–39, 141, 143, 147–51, 155–57, 160, 162–65, 167–73, 175–76
    Resurrection, 5, 6, 10, 114, 116–18, 148, 164, 169, 172
John, St., 89, 91, 93–95, 143
John, of the Cross, 118
Joint Declaration, 21n4, 25n10, 29, 43–44, 56, 59, 99
Jüngel, E., 50
justice, injustice, xiv, 88, 109–10, 112–13, 117, 122–23, 131–32, 136, 142, 161,173, 176

Kasper, W., 42, 93n16, 97, 103–4
Kerr, F., 129
Kierkegaard, S., 84

Kingdom of God, xii, xiv, 10, 30, 110, 112, 162, 172, 176
Klein (Ressmeyer), C., 78–79, 81–82, 84
Kloeden, G. von, 75
Klopstock, F. G., 174

Laing, R. D., 150
Lash, N., 129
Lawrence, D. H., 118
lay, lay person, lay people, 15, 54, 101, 116, 141, 144, 157, 160, 164
left, (the), left church, xiv, 74, 78–79, 110, 112–13, 123, 127–33, 135, 137–41, 143–45, 147, 149–57, 159, 161–65, 175
Lennan, R., 60
Lewis, C. S., 118
liberation theology, liberation theologian(s), liberation theological, xiv, 62, 112–13, 115, 117–18, 139, 155–57, 159, 165, 169, 171, 173
Lindbeck, G., 51
Lombard, Peter, 27n13
Long, C. H., 75n19, 76n21
love, God of love, xiv, 11n39, 48, 88, 94–96, 109, 113–14, 116–17, 119–21, 125–26, 137–38, 140, 143, 151, 153–54, 161–62, 165, 168–70, 173, 176
Luke, St., 4–8
Luther, M., 16, 28, 30, 46, 52–53, 59–60, 70, 75, 77, 83, 85, 88, 116, 155
Lutheran(s), xiii–xiv, 17, 19–20, 22–31, 33–34, 36, 38–39, 41–42, 44–45, 51–59, 67–88, 99, 103, 113, 126, 158, 166
    (Evangelical) Lutheran Church(es), Evangelische Kirche/EKD, xiii, 20, 25, 27nn12–13, 29–30, 33–34, 39, 44, 52, 55–56, 59, 67–87, 103, 111
    ELCA, 27n12, 74, 78n26, 79n28, 84–86

189

Index

Lutheran(s) (*continued*)
    Lutheran World Federation (LWF), 29, 69–70
Luther King, M., 109, 116
Mannion, G., 45n10, 143n60, 169n6
marginalization, marginalized, 117, 156, 164, 170–71, 175
Marsh, J., 140
Marx, Marxism, marxist, 112, 128, 130–31, 141, 145, 148–50, 154
Mary, 99
Maurice, F. D., 133
Mawick, R., 110n1, 122n42, 123n43
McCabe, H., 154
McClintock Fulkerson, M., 170
Meissen (agreement), xiii, 30–31, 33–34, 38, 55
Melanchthon, P., 28, 84
Methodists, 84
Metz, J. B., 171–72, 174
Mey, P. de, 43n6, 99
Meyer, H., 39
Michalon, P., 93
Middleton, N., 128n6, 129n9
Mill, J. S., 149
Miller, A., 139
mission, missionary, church's mission, 5–7, 29, 31, 33–35, 38, 42, 50, 77, 85–86, 92, 109, 133, 136, 166, 168
Moltmann, J., 114, 148, 171
Morrill, B., 171
Morris, W., 140
Mullin, R. B., 75n20
mysticism, mystic, 15, 109, 111–13, 117–25, 174

Nhat Hanh, T., 118
Nicholl, T., 82, 84–85
Nietzsche, F., 114
Noll, M., 82–85, 87

O'Gara, M., 19, 21, 23, 27, 57, 64
O'Mahony, K., 168n3
Origen, 9, 15, 17, 23, 50
Orthodox (Church), 57, 67, 72–73, 81, 87, 91, 94, 99, 104, 119, 158, 171

orthopraxis, 122, 124
Oxford Movement, 90
Pannenberg, W., 5, 148, 167
Paul, St., pauline, 3–7, 12, 24n10, 43, 48, 71, 91, 118, 120, 159
peace, peaceful, xiii, 28, 72, 110–11, 113, 122–23, 175
Pelikan J., 81–83
people of God. *See* church
Pentecostal Church(es), 47, 72–73, 87
Pesch, O. H., 18, 44–45, 59
Peter, St., petrine, 4–5, 9, 12n47, 15–16, 46n13, 53–54, 58, 91, 118
Phillips de Lille, A., 90
Picasso, P., 175
piety, xii, 112
pietism, pietist, 79, 81–82
pneumatological, xiii, 6, 14–17, 20, 22, 48, 50; *see also* Holy Spirit
political(ly), politics, xii, xiv, 16, 62, 79, 84–85, 97n31, 109–13, 118, 120, 122–24, 128–31, 134–38, 142, 144, 152–54, 156–57, 163–65, 171–73, 175–76
Pontifical Council for Promoting Christian Unity, 94, 97, 104
pope, 9, 14, 28, 53–55, 57–58, 60, 91
    Popes, Benedict XV, 91; Benedict XVI / Ratzinger, J., 49; Innocent III, 125; John XXIII, 128; John Paul II, 41, 53, 57–58, 98n35, 99, 157; Leo XIII, 91; Pius IX, 91; Pius X, 91
Porvoo (*Common Statement*), xiii, 17, 19, 29–30, 33–35, 38–39, 43–44, 51–52, 55, 57, 87
Powell, G., 169n6
Presbyterian(s), 78, 84
Protestant(s), Protestantism, 23n7, 47, 52, 54, 57–60, 67, 72, 74–75, 80, 82–84, 92, 94, 98, 103–4, 110–11, 115, 119, 125–26, 147, 155, 159, 168, 171, 175
Pugin, A. W., 90

Quaker, 159

Index

Rahner, K., xiii, 46, 55n22, 60–64, 125, 139, 148–49, 153, 174–75
Reformation, 26n11, 28, 31, 36, 46, 55n22, 56, 59, 67, 75, 102
Reformed Church(es), 31, 68, 75, 80
revolution(ary), 112, 129, 132, 134, 136, 140, 144, 155, 164–65
rich and poor, divide between, xii, 129, 131
Richey, R. E., 75n20, 76n22, 81n33
Roelvink, H., 37
Roloff, J., 4–7
Roman Catholic(s), xiii–xiv, 19–20, 22–25, 36, 38–39, 41, 44, 46–47, 51, 55–56, 67, 78, 90–92, 98–99, 101–11, 159, 166
Romero, O., 109, 168
Root, M., 56
Runcie, R., 30

sacrament(s), sacramental(ly), sacramentality, 12, 20, 23–27, 35, 37–38, 41, 56, 58, 71, 78n26, 125, 139, 166, 168–69, 172
Sagovsky, N., 56
Sauter, M., 76
Schaff, P., 75n18
Schiller, F., 145
Schuster, E., 113n11, 114nn13–14, 125n45
Scripture(s), 4, 8–9, 14, 20, 31, 48, 154
Second Vatican Council/Vatican II, 14, 22–23, 25, 44, 49, 93, 98, 100, 128, 144, 157–58
service(s), 21, 24, 31, 37–38, 41–42, 68, 74, 98, 100, 102–4, 110, 133, 145–47, 160, 163; *see also* church, Eucharist, Holy Communion, liturgy, worship
sin, xi, 24, 61, 98, 121, 136, 173
social, society, xii, xiv, 16, 62, 74, 76, 83–84, 88, 91, 102, 112, 117–18, 124, 129–35, 137–42, 144–47, 149–55, 157–65, 171, 173, 175–76
godly society, 141, 161

Socialism, socialist, 112, 130, 134–35, 140, 150, 153, 156
Christian socialism, 134
Realsozialismus, 129, 140, 148
Söderblom, N., 92
solidarity, 113, 142
Sölle, D., xiv, 109–26, 131, 148, 165, 169, 174, 175
Steffensky, F., 111

Tanner, M., 39, 56
Tanner, N., 9
Tavard, G. H., 158, 169n5
Taylor, C., 129
teaching(s), xiii, 5, 9–10, 12–14, 16–17, 20, 23–25, 28, 35, 41, 47, 49, 51–53, 58, 60, 62, 78, 80, 83–84, 93, 104, 110, 133, 136–37, 146, 155, 159, 166–67, 170 173
Tertullian, 9, 13, 17
Thiessen, G., 78n27, 174n27
Thomas Aquinas, 27n13
Tillich, P., 153–54, 174–75, 176n28
Tombs, D., 156
transcendence, transcendent, 30, 34, 115, 120
Troeltsch, Troeltschian, E., 76, 82
truth(s), 5, 12–15, 17, 20, 22, 25, 47, 64, 95, 97, 124, 139, 142, 147, 155, 157, 162, 166–68, 176

unity, Christian unity, xii–xiv, 3, 9, 11, 13n50, 14–18, 20–23, 27–29, 31–42, 44, 46, 49, 51–64, 67–68, 70–72, 74, 76–78, 80–104, 109, 150, 162, 166, 169

Villain, M., 92
Vogt, K. H., 90n2

Walther, C. F. W., 83
Wattson, L. T., 91
Wattson, P. J. F., 91
Wengert, T., 71n8
White, L., 91
Williams, R., 129, 147

Index

Wilson, K., 169n6
witness, xii, 6, 20, 23, 31, 34, 35n19, 37, 52, 88–89, 94, 96, 109, 120, 137, 161, 164, 166–71, 176; *see also* disciple, discipleship
women, 7, 96, 110, 126, 137, 140, 147, 156, 158
    women's ordination, 57–58, 80, 158
worship, 31–32, 35, 42, 76, 78n26, 80, 86, 102, 104, 150, 160–61, 163, 170, *see also* church, eucharist, holy communion, liturgy, service(s)
World Council of Churches (WCC), 56, 91–94, 101, 103–4
Wroe, N., 127n1, 128n2
Wuthnow, R., 76n24, 79n28

Zizioulas, J., 171–72

www.ingramcontent.com/pod-product-compliance
Lightning Source LLC
Chambersburg PA
CBHW031427150426
43191CB00006B/431